25

SEASONS AT DEEPDALE

THE COMPLETE RECORD

1977-78 TO 2001-02

David Powter

British Library Cataloguing in Publication Data
A catalogue record for this book is available from the British Library

ISBN 1-86223-070-6

Copyright © 2002, SOCCER BOOKS LIMITED (01472 696226)
72 St. Peter's Avenue, Cleethorpes, N.E. Lincolnshire, DN35 8HU, England

Web site   http://www.soccer-books.co.uk
e-mail   info@soccer-books.co.uk

The Publishers, and the Football Clubs itemised are unable to accept liability for any loss, damage or injury caused by error or inaccuracy in the information published in this guide.

Printed by Bookcraft

CONTENTS

PRESTON NORTH END
25 SEASONS 1977-78 TO 2001-02

PRESTON NORTH END FC CLUB RECORD

Year Formed: 1881

Turned Professional: 1885

Ground: Deepdale, Sir Tom Finney Way, Preston, PR1 6RU

Telephone: 01772 902020

Capacity: 22,226

Record Attendance: 42,684 vs Arsenal (1937-38)

Pitch Measurements: 110 x 77 yards

Colours: White shirts, navy blue shorts, white stockings.

Nickname: The Lilywhites

League History: 1888 – Football League founder members • 1901-04 – Division 2 • 1904-12 – Division 1 • 1912-13 – Division 2 • 1913-14 – Division 1 • 1914-15 – Division 2 1919-25 – Division 1 • 1925-34 – Division 2 • 1934-49 – Division 1 • 1949-51 – Division 2 1951-61 – Division 1 • 1961-70 – Division 2 • 1970-71 – Division 3 • 1971-74 – Division 2 1974-78 – Division 3 • 1978-81 – Division 2 • 1981-85 – Division 3 • 1985-87 – Division 4 • 1987-92 – Division 3 • 1992-93 – Division 2 • 1993-96 – Division 3 • 1996-2000 – Division 2 • 2000– Division 1

Record League Victory: 10-0 vs Stoke City (1889-90)

Record League Defeat: 0-7 vs Blackpool (1947-48)

Most League Points (2 for a win): 61 in the Third Division (1970-71)

Most League Points (3 for a win): 95 in the Second Division (1999-2000)

Most League Goals: 100 in the Second Division (1927-28) and First Division (1957-58)

Highest League Scorer (in aggregate): 187 goals – Tom Finney (1946-60)

Highest League Scorer (in a season): 37 goals – Ted Harper (1932-33)

Most Goals in a game: 7 goals – Jimmy Ross vs Stoke (1888-89)

Most League appearances: 447 – Alan Kelly (1961-73)

Longest Sequence of League Wins: 14 (from 25/12/1950 to 27/3/1951)

Longest Sequence of League Defeats: 8 (from 1/10/1983 to 5/11/1983 and also from 22/9/1984 to 27/10/1984)

Longest Sequence of Unbeaten League Games: 23 (from 8/9/1888 to 14/9/1889)

Longest Sequence of League Games without a Win: 15 (14/4/1923 to 20/10/1923)

Most Capped Player: 76 – Tom Finney (for England)

Record Transfer Fee Received: £4 million (plus) from Manchester City for Jonathan Macken (March 2002)

Record Transfer Fee Paid: £1.5 million to Manchester United for David Healy (December 2000)

MAJOR HONOURS (4 TROPHIES)

Football League Champions Twice: 1888-89 and 1889-90

F.A. Cup Winners Twice: 1888-89 and 1937-38

OTHER HONOURS

Football League Second Division Champions on 4 occasions: 1903-04, 1912-13, 1950-51 and 1999-2000 (third-flight)

Football League Third Division Champions Twice: 1970-71 & 1995-96 (fourth-flight)

PRESTON NORTH END FC CLUB RECORD DURING THE 25 SEASONS 1977-78 TO 2001-02

Highest League Victory: 6-0 vs Chesterfield (1988-89), vs Mansfield Town (1995-96) and also vs Stockport County (2001-02)

Highest League Defeat: 0-6 vs Northampton Town (1985-86) and vs Wolverhampton Wanderers (1988-89)

Most League Points (2 for a win): 61 in the Third Division (1970-71)

Most League Points (3 for a win): 95 in the Second Division (1999-2000)

Most League Goals Scored: 79 goals (1988-89) & (1993-94)

Most League Goals Conceded: 100 goals (1985-86)

Highest League Scorer (in aggregate): 96 goals – Alex Bruce

Highest League Scorer (in a season): 29 goals – Andy Saville (1995-96)

Most Goals in a game: 4 – Alex Bruce vs Colchester United (1977-78)

Number of League Hat-tricks: 16 (includes 4 goals in a game once)

Leading Scorer over most Seasons: Alex Bruce (on 4 occasions)

Most League appearances: 363 – Lee Cartwright

Number of Ever-Present Players throughout a Season: 15

Most Seasons Ever-Present: 3 – Roy Tunks

Highest Average Home League Attendance: 14,883 (2001-02)

Highest Home League Crowd: 21,014 vs Manchester City (2001-02)

Lowest Home League Crowd: 2,007 vs Scunthorpe United (1985-86)

Longest Sequence of League Wins: 5 (from 22/3/1985 to 4/4/1985, from 24/1/1987 to 25/2/1987, from 21/8/1993 to 11/9/1993, from 26/12/1998 to 23/1/1999 and also from 12/11/1999 to 18/12/1999)

Longest Sequence of League Defeats: 8 (from 1/10/1983 to 5/11/1983 and also from 22/9/1984 to 27/10/1984)

Longest Sequence of Unbeaten League Games: 20 (from 19/8/1995 to 1/1/1997)

Longest Sequence of League Games without a Win: 11 (20/12/1997 to 24/2/1998)

Most Capped Player: 6 – Paul McGhee (Republic of Ireland)

Record Transfer Fee Received: £4 million (plus) from Manchester City for Jonathan Macken (March 2002)

Record Transfer Fee Paid: £1.5 million from Manchester United for David Healy (December 2000)

Major Honours: None

Other Honours: Second Division Champions (1999-2000) and Third Division Champions (1995-96)

INTRODUCTION

In the summer of 1977 Preston North End supporters were quietly confident that their side would do well in the following season. The club's highly-rated coach, Nobby Stiles, had just been promoted to manager (to replace the retiring Harry Catterick) and the team seemed to be progressing well. In fact, since slipping into the Third Division (for the second time in five seasons) in 1973-74, the Lilywhites had finished ninth (under Bobby Charlton), eighth and sixth, respectively. Catterick's side only missed promotion by five points in 1976-77.

However, the fans were disappointed that two of the squad's better young players – Mark Lawrenson and Gary Williams – had been sold to Brighton & Hove Albion during the summer of 1977. Moving in the opposite direction (together with some much needed cash) were Graham Cross and Harry Wilson. The two former Seagulls joined a fairly useful squad at Deepdale. Roy Tunks was proving to be a reliable keeper and Mick Baxter was shaping up well at centre-half. With right-back John McMahon, midfielder Gordon Coleman, former Manchester United youngster Francis Burns and a strike-force of Mike Elwiss and Alex Bruce, Stiles had the framework of a side to work around.

Preston had been on the slide since Tom Finney's retirement and were relegated from the First Division in 1961. But there was a strong belief that 1977-78 was going to be the start of a new beginning.

1977-78

Preston took a few weeks to gel under Nobby Stiles, and drew five of their first eight fixtures. However, the arrival of Sean Haslegrave from Nottingham Forest strengthened the midfield and they gradually moved into promotion contention. From the end of October onwards North End never slipped lower than eighth and during an eight match unbeaten run in the New Year actually topped the Third Division table.

Although their form dipped slightly during the run-in, the Lilywhites proved just good enough to hold down a promotion position. They finished third, five points behind the champions Wrexham. Having only scrambled a draw at home to Shrewsbury Town in the last fixture of the season, Preston were made to sweat for two days to discover whether they had secured promotion. If Peterborough United (who lost their penultimate match) collected maximum points from their re-arranged trip to the champions, then they and not North End would have filled the last promotion spot. Happily, Wrexham took their task seriously and held Peterborough to a goalless draw, allowing Preston to go up courtesy of their better goal difference.

Stiles had the luxury of a settled side in 1977-78, with 11 men featuring in at least 30 matches. Consistent keeper Roy Tunks (who picked the ball out of his net only 38 times) and striker Mike Elwiss (transferred to Crystal Palace in the following summer) were ever-present. In addition, leading scorer Alex Bruce (with 27 goals), defender Mick Baxter and midfielder Gordon Coleman only missed one match each. The other significant members of the squad were John McMahon, Danny Cameron, Graham Cross (in his first campaign after his switch from Brighton & Hove Albion), Francis Burns, Stephen Doyle, and Haslegrave.

FACTFILE 1977-78

Manager: Nobby Stiles

LEAGUE STATISTICS

Final position: 3rd place in Division Three

Games played: 46   **Points:** 56
Biggest Victory: 4-0 vs Bury (H), vs Colchester United (H) and also vs Lincoln City (H)
Biggest Defeat: 1-3 vs Carlisle United (A) and vs Wrexham (H)
Leading Goalscorer: Alex Bruce (27 goals)
Ever-Presents: Mike Elwiss and Roy Tunks
Four Goal Hero: Bruce
Other Hat-Trick Heroes: None
Average Home Attendance: 8,799
Highest Home Crowd: 16,078 vs Shrewsbury Town
Lowest Home Crowd: 5,319 vs Cambridge United

CUPS

F.A. Cup: Round 2
League Cup: Round 2

1978-79

The Lilywhites made a very promising start on their return to the Second Division. After drawing at Cardiff, Stiles' side destroyed pre-season promotion favourites Blackburn Rovers 4-1 in a full blooded local derby at Deepdale. Unfortunately, however, Preston dramatically lost their way and went eleven matches without winning to slide into the bottom two. The arrival of Brian Taylor (from Plymouth Argyle) and Don O'Riordan (from Derby County) helped bolster the defence and the side became a lot more resilient. Losing only four of their last 29 fixtures, Preston gradually clamoured up the table to finish in a very respectable seventh place. A club record 18 matches ended as a draw in 1978-79.

Alex Bruce was again the leading scorer (with 21 goals), while Michael Robinson (promoted from the reserves) chipped in with 13 goals in what proved to be his only full campaign at Deepdale. The strong striker was sold to Manchester City, the following summer, for a club record fee of £756,000. One man who made his 424th and last League appearance for Preston during the 1978-79 campaign was Alan Spavin. The midfielder had been the last member of the 1964 F.A. Cup Final side still playing the club. Arriving at Deepdale, towards the end of 1978-79, were striker Steve Elliott (from Nottingham Forest) and midfielder Graham Bell (from Oldham Athletic).

Deepdale tasted a little F.A. Cup glory in 1978-79 when First Division Derby County were defeated 3-0 in the third round, a brace by Bruce and another by Francis Burns inflicted the damage. It was Southampton, another top-flight side, who ended North End's interest in the competition in the next round.

FACTFILE 1978-79

Manager: Nobby Stiles

LEAGUE STATISTICS

Final position: 7th place in Division Two
Games played: 42 **Points:** 42
Biggest Victory: 6-1 vs Charlton Athletic (H)
Biggest Defeat: 1-5 vs Brighton & Hove Albion (A)
Leading Goalscorer: Alex Bruce (21 goals)
Ever-Present: Roy Tunks
Hat-Trick Heroes: None
Average Home Attendance: 12,117
Highest Home Crowd: 17,820 vs Wrexham
Lowest Home Crowd: 8,500 vs Charlton Athletic

CUPS

F.A. Cup: Round 4
League Cup: Round 2

1979-80

Preston spent the majority of 1979-80 in the top half of the table; but a lack of consistency prevented them making a serious push for promotion. A mammoth 19 matches were drawn (thus exceeding the record set 12 months previously) and they ended the season in tenth place. Steve Elliott (one of two ever-presents along with Roy Tunks) headed the list of scorers (with 16 goals). Mike Elwiss made a brief return to the side, on loan, and scored both goals in the 2-1 win at Leicester on his 'debut'.

Deepdale staged another F.A. Cup tie against First Division opposition in 1979-80; but Ipswich Town proved difficult opponents and returned to Suffolk as 3-0 winners.

FACTFILE 1979-80

Manager: Nobby Stiles

LEAGUE STATISTICS

Final position: 10th place in Division Two
Games played: 42 **Points:** 43
Biggest Victory: 3-0 vs Charlton Athletic (A) and also vs Shrewsbury Town (H)
Biggest Defeat: 0-3 vs QPR (H)
Leading Goalscorer: Steve Elliott (16 goals)
Ever-Presents: Steve Elliott and Roy Tunks
Hat-Trick Heroes: None
Average Home Attendance: 9,751
Highest Home Crowd: 13,069 vs Chelsea
Lowest Home Crowd: 7,407 vs Notts County

CUPS

F.A. Cup: Round 3
League Cup: Round 2

1980-81

Nobby Stiles' four year reign at Deepdale came to an end in the summer of 1981 after the club slipped back to the Third Division in 20th place (on goal difference). The Lilywhites won only 11 League games all term, including three of the last six games – one of which was the final rearranged fixture at Derby. Cardiff City's goalless draw (against champions West Ham United) on the same day proved just enough to send North End down.

An inability to find the net was the major problem in 1980-81, with Alex Bruce top scoring with 13 out of an inadequate tally of 41. The side never functioned fluently as a unit and, despite his best efforts, Stiles was unable to stop the rot. Among the men who played their last games for Preston in 1980-81 were Mick Baxter, Sean Haslegrave, Danny Cameron, Francis Burns and injury-jinxed youngster Ricky Thomson. In addition, Roy Tunks moved on to Wigan Athletic, but it was not the last Deepdale would see of him. One memorable debut during the season was made by goalie Peter Litchfield, who was outstanding in keeping Chelsea at bay to help his side win by the only goal.

There was no joy in the F.A. Cup in 1980-81 as Bristol Rovers (who later finished bottom of the Second Division) edged a seven goal thriller at Deepdale, in the third round. There was more satisfaction in the League Cup, though, with First Division WBA needing three games to shake off dogged North End in the fourth round.

FACTFILE 1980-81

Manager: Nobby Stiles

LEAGUE STATISTICS

Final position: 20th place in Division Two
Games played: 42 **Points:** 36
Biggest Victory: 3-0 vs Orient (H)
Biggest Defeat: 0-5 vs West Ham United (H)
Leading Goalscorer: Alex Bruce (13 goals)
Ever-Present: Mick Baxter
Hat-Trick Heroes: None
Average Home Attendance: 7,631
Highest Home Crowd: 18,970 vs Swansea City
Lowest Home Crowd: 4,748 vs Wrexham

CUPS

F.A. Cup: Round 3
League Cup: Round 4

1981-82

The man appointed to take over from Nobby Stiles was Tommy Docherty, who had been one of the club's best players in the 1950s. However, the Doc's return to Deepdale was to be a brief one. He was sacked in early December after leading Preston to just three victories in 17 League games.

Things had gone wrong from the start with a 2-1 defeat at Millwall, followed by a 4-0 reverse at Swindon in the next away game. Docherty brought in a clutch of new players to add to his summer signing Jonathan Clark (from Derby County). Experienced centre-half Tommy Booth and young midfielder Gary Buckley joined from Manchester City. Barry Dunn arrived from Sunderland, while John Kelly signed from Tranmere Rovers.

Results failed to improve and the fans started to lose patience with Docherty. The fans voted with their feet and some gates fell below the 5,000 mark. There was to be little Cup joy either. Leicester City were beaten 1-0 in the first leg of the second round of the League Cup; but gained revenge by winning the return leg 4-0. Preston conceded four more goals in the F.A. Cup, with Chesterfield defeating them 4-1 in the first round. After another League defeat (at Oxford) the board were bold enough to admit the error of their ways and sacked Docherty. Coach Alan Kelly took over on a caretaker basis, and after another home game was lost to Brentford, Gordon Lee was appointed as the new manager.

The ex-Everton boss immediately brought in goalkeeper Martin Hodge on loan and Preston's form took a turn for the better. Lee's side drew at Chesterfield and then won three matches on the trot. North End were rock bottom of the turn of the year, but they gradually climbed the table to finish in 14th place. Lee's side avoided relegation by eight points and could even afford to lose their final two fixtures of the campaign. The defence had become much more solid, the midfield was working twice as hard and, up front, both Alex Bruce and Steve Elliott were netting on a regular basis.

FACTFILE 1981-82

Managers: Tommy Docherty and Gordon Lee

LEAGUE STATISTICS

Final position: 14th place in Division Three
Games played: 46   **Points:** 61
Biggest Victory: 3-0 vs Walsall (A) and also vs Plymouth Argyle (A)
Biggest Defeat: 0-4 vs Swindon Town (A)
Leading Goalscorer: Alex Bruce (18 goals)
Ever-Presents: Alex Bruce and Don O'Riordan
Hat-Trick Heroes: None
Average Home Attendance: 5,496
Highest Home Crowd: 7,802 vs Carlisle United
Lowest Home Crowd: 4,162 vs Brentford

CUPS

F.A. Cup: Round 1
League Cup: Round 2

1982-83

The optimism generated during the second half of the previous season seemed well placed when 1982-83 kicked off with victory over Millwall. Steve Elliott netted all three goals in his side's 3-2 win to become only the third North End player to net a hat-trick in the first match of the season. However, the next four League fixtures were all lost causing a loss of both confidence and form.

Ironically, Preston's start to 1982-83 mirrored that of twelve months earlier under the hapless Tommy Docherty, with only three victories coming in the first 17 games. However, Lee weathered the storm and relegation was avoided, in 16th place. A purple patch of nine wins during the final 13 fixtures ensured that safety was achieved by five points. Elliott was the top scorer (with 19 goals), while Alex Bruce netted seven times to take his Preston total to 157 goals (from 363 League games) before moving to Wigan Athletic.

The Lilywhites enjoyed some success in the F.A. Cup, with wins over Shepshed Charterhouse and Blackpool setting up a third round meeting with Leeds United at Elland Road. The Yorkshire side were comfortable winners, though, leaving Preston to concentrate on digging their way out of the relegation zone.

FACTFILE 1982-83

Manager: Gordon Lee

LEAGUE STATISTICS

Final position: 16th place in Division Three
Games played: 46   **Points:** 58
Biggest Victory: 4-1 vs Wigan Athletic (H) and also Doncaster Rovers (H)
Biggest Defeat: 1-5 vs Exeter City (A)
Leading Goalscorer: Steve Elliott (19 goals)
Ever-Presents: None
Hat-Trick Hero: Steve Elliott
Average Home Attendance: 4,941
Highest Home Crowd: 7,565 vs Wigan Athletic
Lowest Home Crowd: 3,363 vs Wrexham

CUPS

F.A. Cup: Round 3
League Cup: Round 2

1983-84

Preston made another dreadful start in 1983-84. Only one of the first 15 fixtures was won, with a club record poor run of eight successive defeats pushing them into the relegation mire. In addition, they tumbled out of the League Cup (at home to Sheffield Wednesday) and the F.A. Cup (at Scunthorpe United) in the space of 12 days in November. So, it came as no surprise when Gordon Lee was sacked the following month. Club coach and former goalkeeping hero Alan Kelly was appointed in a caretaker capacity again. The switch had a positive effect on the players and the next two matches were won convincingly. Port Vale were defeated 4-0, then Kelly's side travelled to Scunthorpe and this time beat their F.A. Cup conquerors 5-1.

With the knowledge that the club was badly in the red, Kelly (having been appointed manager on a permanent basis) knew that if relegation was to be avoided it would have to be achieved with the existing squad. The team continued to struggle, but enough points were accumulated along the way to ensure the drop was staved off by ten points (with a 16th place finish). Peter Litchfield was magnificent between the posts in 1983-84, while John Kelly, Peter Houghton (one of Lee's last signings) and Steve Elliott all contributed on a consistent basis at the other end of the pitch. Elliott was sold to Luton Town, after scoring 70 League goals (in 208 appearances) for Preston, in the summer of 1984.

FACTFILE 1983-84

Managers: Gordon Lee and Alan Kelly

LEAGUE STATISTICS

Final position: 16th place in Division Three
Games played: 46   **Points:** 56
Biggest Victory: 5-1 vs Scunthorpe United (A)
Biggest Defeat: 1-4 vs Brentford (A)
Leading Goalscorer: Steve Elliott (16 goals)
Ever-Presents: None
Hat-Trick Hero: Steve Elliott
Average Home Attendance: 4,571
Highest Home Crowd: 8,745 vs Burnley
Lowest Home Crowd: 3,144 vs Orient

CUPS

F.A. Cup: Round 1
League Cup: Round 3

1984-85

The campaign started on an optimistic note with four of the first five League matches ending in victory. The good feeling around the club soon disintegrated, though, as Alan Kelly's side plummeted into relegation trouble by losing eight successive matches to equal the club record set in 1983-84. During this barren spell the Lilywhites lost an amazing match at Plymouth despite leading 3-1 and 4-3. The Pilgrims eventually won 6-4 after both Jonathan Clark and Tommy Booth had received their marching orders. During this appalling spell Preston also crashed out of the League Cup to Norwich City, 6-1 in the second round return leg (after the home leg ended 3-3).

A small revival followed and it appeared that Kelly's squad might dig their way out of trouble. However, they were brought crashing back to earth again in the F.A. Cup by Non-League Telford United. The Alliance side travelled north to Deepdale and were more effective than their Third Division opponents in every department. The scoreline was 4-1, but the damage to the team's morale was even more significant. After spending 27 years at the club in various capacities, Kelly handed in his resignation.

Player-coach Booth took over on a caretaker basis and was later handed the job on a permanent basis. Brian Kidd was appointed as his assistant. Booth was given a 'Mission Impossible' – to save the Football League's initial champions from tumbling into the Fourth Division for the very first time. It was a close run thing. Preston finished in 23rd place, but only one point behind Swansea City, who stayed up in 20th position. Preston's relegation was confirmed when they lost 5-2 at home to Wigan Athletic in the penultimate fixture. That was the twelfth occasion (across all competitions) during the campaign that they had conceded four goals or more. In the League, alone, the team conceded exactly 100 goals!

FACTFILE 1984-85

Managers: Alan Kelly and Tommy Booth

LEAGUE STATISTICS

Final position: 23rd place in Division Three

Games played: 46   **Points:** 46

Biggest Victory: 3-0 vs Cambridge United (A)

Biggest Defeat: 0-4 vs Bolton Wanderers (H) and also vs Gillingham (A)

Leading Goalscorer: John Kelly (7 goals)

Ever-Presents: None

Hat-Trick Heroes: None

Average Home Attendance: 3,749

Highest Home Crowd: 5,478 vs Bolton Wanderers

Lowest Home Crowd: 2,653 vs Cambridge United

CUPS

F.A. Cup: Round 2

League Cup: Round 2

1985-86

Many fans considered 1984-85 to be Preston's worst ever campaign. Yet, within 12 months, this opinion had to be revised! Without a shadow of a doubt the lowest point in the club's history came in 1985-86.

The campaign got off to a mixed start, with two wins over Blackpool in the League Cup compensating for a League start of just one point from three games. Hopes were positively zooming when Torquay United were defeated 4-0 at Deepdale; however, three days later, Tommy Booth's travelled to Northampton and collected a 6-0 spanking. As it turned out the side's best win of the campaign was immediately followed by its worst defeat.

Two victories at the end of September raised the spirits, but the full extent of the side's problems were highlighted when Chester City defeated them 6-3 at Deepdale. There was to be no joy in the F.A. Cup either as Third Division Walsall thumped them 7-3 in the first round. Booth acknowledged his failure by resigning. His assistant Brian Kidd took the reins, but by now Preston were completely off the track. A disastrous 11 match winless run saw them spiralling towards the very bottom of the table. Kidd brought in some new players, but no-one seemed able to turnaround the team's fortunes. The former Manchester United striker resigned in mid-March, with Preston languishing at the bottom of the League.

Jonathan Clark took over on a caretaker basis and the side immediately won five games on the trot. However, only two points were gained from the last five fixtures and, for the very first time, Preston North End had to re-apply for re-election (having finished in 23rd place). This campaign was the last in which the bottom four clubs were forced to go cap-in-hand as automatic promotion/relegation was sanctioned to operate from 1986-87 onwards. Only one Non-League club, Enfield, the Alliance champions, challenged Preston, Exeter City, Torquay United and Cambridge United. The outcome of the vote was as follows:

Exeter City	64
Preston North End	62.5
Cambridge United	61
Torquay United	61
Enfield	7.5

North End had kept its status as a League club, but the board vowed that it would learn by its mistakes.

FACTFILE 1985-86

Managers: Tommy Booth and Brian Kidd

LEAGUE STATISTICS

Final position: 23rd place in Division Four
Games played: 46   **Points**: 43
Biggest Victory: 4-0 vs Torquay United (H)
Biggest Defeat: 0-6 vs Northampton Town (A)
Leading Goalscorer: John Thomas (17 goals)
Ever-Presents: None
Hat-Trick Heroes: None
Average Home Attendance: 3,502
Highest Home Crowd: 5,585 vs Burnley
Lowest Home Crowd: 2,007 vs Scunthorpe United

CUPS

F.A. Cup: Round 1
League Cup: Round 2

1986-87

It was all change at Deepdale during the summer of 1986. A new manager, John McGrath, was appointed and the pitch was re-laid with a synthetic surface. The board had taken the latter gamble in an attempt to bring in much-needed extra revenue into the club.

Preston started the campaign positively and went on to string together several good runs, both in terms of performances and results. McGrath's side never slipped lower than seventh and, at the end of January, climbed into second spot. The Lilywhites could not remove Northampton Town from top spot, but were more than content to regain their Third Division status as the runners-up. Promotion was secured at the end of April, with four fixtures still outstanding.

For the second successive campaign John Thomas was the leading scorer (with 21 goals) as Preston lost only eight times and collected a club record 90 points. Gary Brazil netted 17 times to be the second top scorer, while the other key members of McGrath's squad were the ever-present Alex Jones, Sam Allardyce, Bob Atkins, Michael Bennett, Oshor Williams, Gary Swann, Ron Hildersley and player-coach Les Chapman (who achieved the rare career feat of making appearances on the grounds of all '92' clubs when he played at Swansea in the January). Goalkeeping duties were shared by David Brown and Alan Kelly (the 18 year-old son of the club's former manager). Towards the end of the season, Deepdale was treated to a little magic with the arrival of veteran striker Frank Worthington.

Preston enjoyed their best F.A. Cup run for many seasons in 1986-87 with Bury, Chorley and Middlesbrough being defeated before they were tipped out in the fourth round, at St James' Park, by First Division Newcastle United.

The lethal Thomas had attracted the attention of Bolton Wanderers and he moved to Burnden Park in the summer of 1987.

FACTFILE 1986-87

Manager: John McGrath

LEAGUE STATISTICS

Final position: 2nd place in Division Four
Games played: 46   **Points:** 90
Biggest Victory: 4-1 vs Burnley (A)

Biggest Defeat: 0-4 vs Scunthorpe United (A)
Leading Goalscorer: John Thomas (21 goals)
Ever-Present: Alex Jones
Hat-Trick Hero: John Thomas
Average Home Attendance: 8,079
Highest Home Crowd: 16,456 vs Northampton Town
Lowest Home Crowd: 4,362 vs Swansea City

CUPS

F.A.Cup: Round 4
League Cup: Round 2

1987-88

After the promotion winning campaign, 1987-88 turned out to be a great anti-climax. In fact an immediate return to the Fourth Division looked a distinct possibility early in the campaign with a clutch of new players struggling to bed in and the first three home fixtures all lost. However, John McGrath brought in two more new men – Tony Ellis and Brian Mooney – and these two inexperienced players (with only 17 League appearances between them) helped to kick-start the team's season.

Results gradually improved, but it was a long hard struggle and they were still as low as 20th in the table in mid-January. Preston eventually finished 16th, six points above the relegation line.

Ironically, North End's performances were often better than the general level of the results in 1987-88. Ellis and Gary Brazil had linked well together up front, while promising youngster Nigel Jemson excited the fans before moving to Nottingham Forest (for £150,000). In midfield Mooney and Gary Swann produced some quality displays, while Bob Atkins and Sam Allardyce were consistent at the back.

Although they crashed out at the first hurdle in each of the major cup competitions, North End enjoyed a decent run in the Freight-Rover Trophy in 1987-88. They progressed comfortably to the Area quarter-final stage and then defeated Mansfield Town (avenging their F.A. Cup defeat in the process). McGrath's side then won 2-0 at Hartlepool to set up a two-legged 'North' Final with Fourth Division Burnley. The Lilywhites looked favourites to make their first appearance at Wembley for 24 years when the first leg at Turf Moor ended goalless. A season's best gate of 17,592 packed into Deepdale for the return encounter, but the home contingent went home disappointed after the Clarets won 3-1 in extra-time.

FACTFILE 1987-88

Manager: John McGrath

LEAGUE STATISTICS

Final position: 16th place in Division Three
Games played: 46   **Points:** 58
Biggest Victory: 3-0 vs York City (H) and also vs Brighton & Hove Albion (H)
Biggest Defeat: 0-4 vs Bury (A) and also vs Gillingham (A)
Leading Goalscorer: Gary Brazil (14 goals)
Ever-Present: Gary Swann (including one substitute appearance)
Hat-Trick Heroes: None
Average Home Attendance: 6,194
Highest Home Crowd: 11,155 vs Blackpool
Lowest Home Crowd: 4,192 vs Fulham

CUPS

F.A. Cup: Round 1
League Cup: Round 1

1988-89

North End made a mediocre start to 1988-89, but six victories in eight games propelled them up to third in early November. They were not quite strong enough to gain automatic promotion, though, with their limitations never better exposed than in consecutive defeats at the end of November. They lost an F.A. Cup replay 3-0 at Fourth Division Tranmere and then were thrashed 6-0 at Molineux by fellow promotion hopefuls Wolverhampton Wanderers (who ended up as champions).

A spell of four wins from 15 fixtures suggested John McGrath's side were on course for a mid-table finish, but they ended the campaign with a flourish to grab a play-off berth in sixth place. Tony Ellis was the top scorer with 19 goals.

He netted a brace in the 6-0 demolition of Chesterfield, scored another two in the 3-1 win at Gillingham the following game and was also on target in the next two matches (which also ended in victories). Preston netted 17 times in this 15 day goal blitz, which was many supporters' favourite segment of the season.

The play-offs proved disappointing. Paired with Port Vale (who finished third) at the semi-final stage, Preston opened the scoring at Deepdale through Nigel Jemson (who had returned on loan), but were pegged back to a 1-1 draw. Vale won the second leg 3-1 and went on to win promotion by beating Bristol Rovers in a two-legged final.

Gary Brazil and Osher Williams left Deepdale in 1988-89, while Mark Patterson impressed greatly in his first season at the club (after signing from Blackburn Rovers) and contributed 15 League goals. Jemson was not the only old boy to return to Deepdale in 1988-89 as Roy Tunks re-joined from Hartlepool United and took over from David Brown between the posts. On a much sadder note, one of Tunks' former team-mates, Mick Baxter, died in the January aged just 32. The club's community officer died at Deepdale shortly after he had been working with some children.

FACTFILE 1988-89

Manager: John McGrath

LEAGUE STATISTICS

Final position: 6th place in Division Three
Games played: 46   **Points:** 72
Biggest Victory: 6-0 vs Chesterfield (H)
Biggest Defeat: 0-6 vs Wolverhampton Wanderers (A)
Leading Goalscorer: Tony Ellis (19 goals)
Ever-Presents: None
Hat-Trick Hero: Gary Brazil
Average Home Attendance: 7,737
Highest Home Crowd: 14,126 vs Wolverhampton Wanderers
Lowest Home Crowd: 4,963 vs Cardiff City

CUPS

F.A.Cup: Round 1
League Cup: Round 2

1989-90

Preston made an appalling start to 1989-90, drawing one and losing the other six of their first seven League and League Cup matches. A mammoth 22 goals were conceded in the process, with none of the three goalies used keeping the score down to less than three goals. The first success when it came was a comprehensive one though – a 5-0 drubbing of Chester City, with Brian Mooney bagging a hat-trick and Steve Harper scoring the other two goals. Three of the next four fixtures were also won and the Lilywhites seemed set for brighter times.

There were few smiling faces in Preston on the night of Saturday 9th December after news filtered back that the team had been defeated in the second round of the F.A. Cup at Northern Premier League Whitley Bay. The arrival of Mike Flynn helped strengthen the defence, but North End went through another bad patch of four successive defeats (at the end of January and into February). It was the final straw for McGrath who resigned leaving his assistant Les Chapman in temporary charge. The caretaker manager got off to the worst possible start when the visit to Reading resulted in a 6-0 hammering. However, the return of former fans' favourite John Thomas gave the side a lift and the next match (against Cardiff City) was won 4-0, with Graham Shaw netting a hat-trick. Meanwhile Tony Ellis was sold to Stoke City for £250,000.

Chapman earned his manager's contract by steering the side out of relegation trouble. Preston only just managed it, though, and their safety was not confirmed until the last day of the season. Chapman's side lost their last fixture 2-0 at Shrewsbury Town, but fortunately Fulham and Cardiff City, the two teams directly below them, lost too. The Welsh side filled the fourth relegation slot and the Lilywhites finished 19th, safe by a matter of only two points.

The leading scorer in 1989-90 was 11-goal midfielder Warren Joyce, while Brian Mooney, Harper and the ever-present Gary Swann all contributed significantly during the fight for survival. Bob Atkins played his 200th and last League appearance for the club during the campaign.

FACTFILE 1989-90

Managers: John McGrath and Les Chapman

LEAGUE STATISTICS

Final position: 19th place in Division Three

Games played: 46   **Points**: 52
Biggest Victory: 5-0 vs Chester City (H)
Biggest Defeat: 0-6 vs Reading (A)
Leading Goalscorer: Warren Joyce (11 goals)
Ever-Present: Gary Swann
Hat-Trick Heroes: Steve Harper and Brian Mooney
Average Home Attendance: 6,313
Highest Home Crowd: 9,135 vs Bolton Wanderers
Lowest Home Crowd: 4,480 vs Leyton Orient

CUPS

F.A. Cup: Round 2
League Cup: Round 1

1990-91

Preston had a new goalkeeper (Simon Farnworth) and a new right-back (Steve Senior), but once again they made a shaky start. Only one of the first six League and League Cup matches were won as Les Chapman's side conceded 18 goals. However, four of the next six League fixtures ended in victory and things stayed on an even keel for the rest of the season. Senior, Mike Flynn and 'Player of the Season' Jeff Wrightson excelled at the back, while Ian Bogie gave the midfield some polish. Goals were in short supply with Graham Shaw's tally of ten making him the top scorer. North End eventually finished in 17th place, with four more points than 12 months before.

There were first round exits in the League Cup and the F.A. Cup, but Preston did enjoy a long run in the Leyland DAF Cup in 1990-91. They thrashed Burnley 6-1 in their Area semi-final, but dreams of Wembley were dashed by Tranmere Rovers in the Northern Final. Rovers romped to a 4-0 victory at Prenton Park and the Lilywhites could only claw back one goal in the return at Deepdale.

Fifteen men made their Preston debuts in 1990-91, including impressive youngsters Lee Ashcroft and Lee Cartwright. However, the Deepdale faithful were less happy about the sales of their two favourite ball players Brian Mooney and Bogie.

FACTFILE 1990-91

Manager: Les Chapman

LEAGUE STATISTICS

Final position: 17th place in Division Three
Games played: 46   **Points:** 56
Biggest Victory: 5-1 vs Crewe Alexandra (H)
Biggest Defeat: 0-4 vs Tranmere Rovers (H) and also vs Exeter City (A)
Leading Goalscorer: Graham Shaw (10 goals)
Ever-Presents: None
Hat-Trick Heroes: None
Average Home Attendance: 5,214
Highest Home Crowd: 9,844 vs Bolton Wanderers
Lowest Home Crowd: 3,245 vs Mansfield Town

CUPS

F.A.Cup: Round 1
League Cup: Round 1

1991-92

The early season form was mixed, with five successive draws making it difficult for Preston to climb out of the bottom half of the table. January proved to a disastrous month. All four League fixtures were lost, Sheffield Wednesday knocked them out of the F.A. Cup and Hull City ended their hopes in the Autoglass Trophy.

Graham Shaw was again the main marksman (with 14 goals) as North End finished 17th again. The two Lees, Ashcroft and Cartwright, were again impressive, while Mike Flynn, Jeff Wrightson (in his last season at Deepdale) and, new signing, Colin Greenall produced solid displays at the back.

FACTFILE 1991-92

Manager: Les Chapman

LEAGUE STATISTICS

Final position: 17th place in Division Three
Games played: 46   **Points:** 57

Biggest Victory: 3-0 vs Wigan Athletic (H)

Biggest Defeat: 1-4 vs Hartlepool United (H) and also vs Exeter City (A)

Leading Goalscorer: Graham Shaw (14 goals)

Ever-Present: Graham Shaw (including one substitute appearance)

Hat-Trick Heroes: None

Average Home Attendance: 4,722

Highest Home Crowd: 7,738 vs Birmingham City

Lowest Home Crowd: 2,932 vs Hull City

CUPS

F.A. Cup: Round 3

League Cup: Round 1

1992-93

Preston became members of the Second Division at the start of 1992-93; but it was only a cosmetic change, following the breakaway of clubs to form the F.A. Premier League. Hampered by a string of injuries, Les Chapman was forced to give debuts to seven new players during the opening four League fixtures. One familiar face returning to the squad was Tony Ellis who had re-signed from Stoke City (for £140,000). Results were mixed with the side twice hitting four goals to win games (against Chester City and at Hull), but conversely they also conceded four twice in defeats (at Stoke in the League Cup and at Bradford).

The news, on 29th September, that the likeable Chapman had been sacked came as a shock to the bulk of the Deepdale faithful. Sam Allardyce was placed in caretaker charge and the results continued to be mixed. Victories at Blackpool (with Ellis hitting a hat-trick) and, at home to Reading and Wigan Athletic, were balanced by four League defeats and a 5-4 reverse at Deepdale against Bradford City in an F.A. Cup replay.

The Preston board had set their sights on John Beck (the boss of First Division Cambridge United) becoming their next manager. Eventually, on 7th December, Beck (and his assistant Gary Peters) took over from Allardyce. The new boss quickly made wholesale changes, but only one of the first five games of his reign did not end in defeat.

New arrival Mickey Norbury dovetailed well with Ellis and Mike Flynn again performed solidly (before moving to Stockport in March). However, the same could not be said for most of Flynn's fellow defenders. Only seven matches were won between Christmas and mid-April, but Beck's side still looked set to avoid relegation. And they would have, too, but for an appalling run of five successive defeats to end the campaign.

North End lost 4-1 at home to Leyton Orient and then lost at both Stoke and Swansea. Survival was still possible, though, especially when they were leading already relegated Mansfield Town 1-0 at Deepdale. However, then Norbury missed a penalty and the Stags went on to net five times to win 5-1. Preston were left needing to beat Bolton Wanderers by a healthy margin, in the last match of the season, to stand any chance of staying up. However, a 1-0 defeat sent the travelling convoy home north in tears. Those five defeats had stranded the Lilywhites in 21st place – three points behind 'safe' Hull City.

Preston were the Second Division's ninth highest scorers (with 65 goals – 22 of which were netted by top scorer Ellis) – but still found themselves back in the basement, after an interval of six years.

FACTFILE 1992-93

Managers: Les Chapman and John Beck

LEAGUE STATISTICS

Final position: 21st place in Division Two
Games played: 46   **Points**: 47
Biggest Victory: 3-0 vs Wigan Athletic (H)
Biggest Defeat: 1-4 vs Hartlepool United (H) and also vs Exeter City (A)
Leading Goalscorer: Tony Ellis (22 goals)
Ever-Presents: None
Hat-Trick Heroes: None
Average Home Attendance: 5,689
Highest Home Crowd: 10,403 vs Blackpool
Lowest Home Crowd: 3,329 vs Reading

CUPS

F.A. Cup: Round 1
League Cup: Round 1

1993-94

For a refreshing change, Preston made a bright start to the season – winning 11 of their opening 16 League fixtures to head the table at the end of November. Yet, they suffered a major loss of momentum, winning just once in their next 11 outings. They missed out on automatic promotion place by six points, in fifth place. However, elevation was still a possibility via the play-off route.

North End's opponents in the two-legged semi-final were Torquay United (who had finished sixth, below the Lilywhites only on goal difference), managed by Deepdale old-boy Don O'Riordan. It was the Gulls who looked favourites to reach Wembley after winning the first leg 2-0.

Whatever happened in the return leg it was to be Deepdale's last match on the soon to be torn up plastic pitch. Nearly 11,500 fans turned up for a really nerve tingling game. Tony Ellis headed an early goal to put the pressure on the Devon side, but Deepdale was soon silenced when Greg Goodridge restored Torquay's two goal advantage. Things swung back Preston's way following two incidents in the ten minutes before half-time. The visitors had defender Darren Moore dismissed for punching Paul Raynor. Then, a minute before the interval, North End's constant pressure paid off when David Moyes headed in. Another header by Stuart Hicks levelled the aggregate scores early in the second half. No more goals were scored before the end of 90 minutes and so extra-time was required before Preston found the net with yet another header, this time from Raynor. For the first time in 30 years, Preston North End supporters could saviour a trip to Wembley Stadium.

The Final was a super game; but the Football League's original Champions ended up being defeated 4-2 by its newest recruits – Wycombe Wanderers. John Beck's side belied their long-ball reputation to play some attractive football and scored two classy first half goals. Ian Bryson's outrageous bicycle-kick was immediately equalised, but a majestic header by Raynor restored the Lancastrian lead. Sadly, it all went wrong in the last 45 minutes of the season. In fairness, Martin O'Neill's Wanderers were scintillating in the second half and deserved their success. Wycombe netted three more times to consign the Lilywhites to a longer stay in the basement.

Ellis netted 26 times to be the Third Division's leading scorer in 1993-94. And although Preston failed to get out of the Fourth Division, Ellis did during the summer of 1994 when he joined Blackpool for a £165,000 fee. All-told, in his two spells at Deepdale, the striker hit 75 goals during 158 League appearances – a scoring rate of virtually one every other game.

Preston enjoyed some F.A. Cup success in 1993-94, defeating Mansfield Town, Shrewsbury Town and Bournemouth to reach the third round. However, very disappointingly, they slid out of the competition 1-0 at Non-League Kidderminster Harriers.

FACTFILE 1993-94

Manager: John Beck

LEAGUE STATISTICS

Final position: 5th place in Division Three
Games played: 42   **Points:** 67
Biggest Victory: 6-1 vs Shrewsbury Town (H)
Biggest Defeat: 0-3 vs Carlisle United (H)
Leading Goalscorer: Tony Ellis (26 goals)
Ever-Presents: None
Hat-Trick Heroes: Mike Conroy and Tony Ellis
Average Home Attendance: 7,377
Highest Home Crowd: 12,790 vs Chester City
Lowest Home Crowd: 4,941 vs Shrewsbury Town

CUPS

F.A. Cup: Round 4
League Cup: Round 1

1994-95

After eight seasons of being plastic, the Deepdale pitch was restored to grass in time for the fifth League match of the season, in early September, when Lincoln City were the visitors. The Red Imps were defeated 4-0 and another good season looked likely. However, John Beck's side hit a very bad patch later that same month. In fact seven successive League defeats completely took the wind out of their sails. With his beloved 'long ball' approach attracting increasing criticism, Beck resigned rather than change his tactics. His assistant Gary Peters stepped up to take the reins and began with four successive victories to turn things around.

The Lilywhites gradually moved into play-off contention and met that target by again finishing fifth. However, there was not to be another Wembley day out as North End found Bury (who had finished fourth) too good for them over the two legs of the semi-final. The Shakers netted the only goal of the Deepdale clash, in the first half, and then netted the return leg's only goal in the second half.

Preston badly missed Tony Ellis' goals during 1994-95, when the top scorer was Mike Conroy (with just ten goals). Ian Bryson excelled in midfield, while at the back David Moyes and full-back Andy Fensome were both impressive. In early March a 19 year-old East Londoner was signed on loan from Manchester United. His name was David Beckham!

Beckham's first taste of League football was the home game against Doncaster Rovers on 6th March. While his future Manchester United team-mates were trouncing Ipswich Town 9-0 at Old Trafford, David helped the Lilywhites draw 2-2 by scoring their second goal directly from a corner. He scored in his next game, too, a splendid free-kick in the 3-2 victory over Fulham. Preston remained unbeaten during Beckham's five match stay. Soon after his return to Old Trafford Alex Ferguson gave him his Premiership debut and he became a first-team regular in 1995-96.

FACTFILE 1994-95

Managers: John Beck and Gary Peters

LEAGUE STATISTICS

Final position: 5th place in Division Three
Games played: 42   **Points:** 67
Biggest Victory: 5-0 vs Bury (H)
Biggest Defeat: 1-3 vs Darlington (H), vs Hartlepool Utd. (A) and vs Colchester Utd. (A)
Leading Goalscorer: Mike Conroy (10 goals)
Ever-Present: Andy Fensome
Hat-Trick Heroes: None
Average Home Attendance: 8,469
Highest Home Crowd: 11,867 vs Carlisle United
Lowest Home Crowd: 6,377 vs Colchester United

F.A.Cup: Round 2
League Cup: Round 1

1995-96

With extra funds made available, Gary Peters brought in strikers Andy Saville and Steve Wilkinson during the summer of 1995. While the arrival of Russ Wilcox and Dean Barrick, early in the season, gave the defence extra steel. Although the opening fixture (at home to Lincoln City) was lost, Peters' side signalled their intentions to take the championship with a 21 match unbeaten run. Torquay United were defeated 4-0 on their own pitch, the same score by which Leyton Orient came unstuck at Deepdale, when Saville found the net three times. In between Mansfield Town had also been thrashed 6-0 (with both Saville and Wilkinson registering hat-tricks) and, on New Year's Day, Cardiff City were beaten 5-0.

The second League defeat of the season did not come until 6th January, at Barnet. Although the Bees later did the 'double' over them, Preston now had their sights set on the long-term leaders Gillingham. They edged past the Gills during March and sealed promotion with a 2-0 victory at Leyton Orient on 20th April. The Championship was clinched a week later with another 2-0 success, this time at Hartlepool. North End finished as champions, with 87 points, four more than runners-up Gillingham. They lost just six League games in 1995-96 – only two of which were away from home (at Underhill and at the Abbey Stadium).

Preston netted 78 times to be the Division's highest scoring outfit. Saville was the Division's joint top scorer (with 29 goals), while Wilkinson and midfielder Simon Davey each contributed ten valuable goals. However, what made 1995-96 such a successful campaign was the terrific way that the players worked together as a unit, playing a very attractive brand of football. The other key members of the Championship winning squad were goalkeeper John Vaughan, skipper Ian Bryson, David Moyes, Wilcox, Barrick, Lee Cartwright and Ryan Kidd.

The had been an important change off the pitch, too, during 1995-96. The antique West Stand had been demolished the previous summer and replaced by the superb 8,000 seater Tom Finney Stand. The new stand was opened on 16th March for the visit of Darlington.

FACTFILE 1995-96

Manager: Gary Peters

LEAGUE STATISTICS

Final position: Champions of Division Three
Games played: 46   **Points:** 86
Biggest Victory: 6-0 vs Mansfield Town (H)
Biggest Defeat: 0-3 vs Northampton Town (H)
Leading Goalscorer: Andy Saville (29 goals)
Ever-Presents: None
Hat-Trick Heroes: Andy Saville (on two occasions) and Steve Wilkinson (once)
Average Home Attendance: 10,012
Highest Home Crowd: 18,700 vs Exeter City
Lowest Home Crowd: 6,837 vs Wigan Athletic

CUPS

F.A. Cup: Round 2
League Cup: Round 1

1996-97

With the exception of John Vaughan (who joined Lincoln City), Gary Peters kept faith with the promotion squad at the start of 1996-97. The early results were fairly encouraging, with three of the first nine League fixtures ending in victory. By that time Peters had realised that he needed to bring some new faces into the squad. Experienced goalie Bobby Mimms, midfielder Mark Rankine and, in October, striker David Reeves were all drafted in. The later replaced the 1995-96 goalscoring hero Andy Saville (who returned to the basement by signing for Wigan Athletic), who had only found the net once in 12 Second Division appearances.

Reeves' first goal helped his new side end a poor trot of four successive defeats by beating Shrewsbury Town. However, the side's confidence did not really return until they won four out of five League matches in November and early December. Making his League debut for the Lilywhites in the last of those wins (3-0 against Blackpool) was midfielder Sean Gregan. The £350,000 signing from Darlington made an immediate impression on the fans. The signing of Gregan, Reeves (who ended up as the top scorer with 11 goals) and, in March, Michael Jackson probably saved Preston from falling straight back into the Third Division. The season ended with three successive victories to leave Peters' side comfortably placed in 15th, 14 points above the relegation line.

Among the departures in the summer of 1997 was former skipper Ian Bryson (who joined Rochdale) and Steve Wilkinson (who joined Chesterfield). Going in a different direction though was Kevin Kilbane. The local lad's impressive displays on the wing earned him a £1.25 million move to WBA. It was a record fee for the club. The 1996-97 campaign was the last in which fans stood on the Spion Kop as progressive Preston looked to the future.

FACTFILE 1996-97

Manager: Gary Peters

LEAGUE STATISTICS

Final position: 15th place in Division Two
Games played: 46   **Points**: 61
Biggest Victory: 3-0 vs Blackpool (H)
Biggest Defeat: 1-5 vs Luton Town (A)
Leading Goalscorer: David Reeves (11 goals)
Ever-Presents: None
Hat-Trick Heroes: None
Average Home Attendance: 9,411
Highest Home Crowd: 14,626 vs Blackpool
Lowest Home Crowd: 7,004 vs Luton Town

CUPS

F.A. Cup: Round 2
League Cup: Round 2

1997-98

The arrival of three young Manchester United players – Jonathan Macken, Colin Murdock and Michael Appleton – ensured Preston kicked off 1997-98 with a bit of a buzz about them. Three of the first five League games were won and Rotherham United were comfortably side-stepped in the League Cup. Even a 6-0 hammering in the next round of the League Cup at Blackburn did not seem to affect the spirit of the side.

A run of four successive defeats in the autumn did give cause for concern, though. However, North End bounced back with victories at Luton and Wigan, and at home to Northampton Town. But Gary Peters had started to feel the pressure of the job and, after another sticky patch of three defeats from four fixtures, he resigned in the January. Although caretaker player-manager David Moyes oversaw two Auto Windscreen Shield successes, it was not until the end of February (at Bournemouth) that the side won for him in the League. Relegation still looked quite possible, though, but Moyes' own fighting spirit rubbed off on the players and they ended the season by losing just two of their last 13 matches. With Preston finishing 15th, nine points above the relegation zone, Moyes earned himself a permanent contract.

Lee Ashcroft top scored with 14 goals in 1997-98, a campaign which saw Sean Gregan, Gary Parkinson, Mark Rankine, Murdoch and keeper Tepi Moilanen all impressing on a regular basis. Ashcroft, Simon Davey, Sean Barrick, David Reeves and the retiring Moyes were among the men who pulled on a Preston shirt for the last time in 1997-98.

FACTFILE 1997-98

Managers: Gary Peters and David Moyes

LEAGUE STATISTICS

Final position: 15th place in Division Two
Games played: 46 **Points:** 59
Biggest Victory: 4-1 vs Wigan Athletic (A)
Biggest Defeat: 0-3 vs Carlisle United (H)
Leading Goalscorer: Lee Ashcroft (14 goals)
Ever-Presents: None
Hat-Trick Hero: Lee Ashcroft
Average Home Attendance: 9,460
Highest Home Crowd: 13,500 vs Blackpool
Lowest Home Crowd: 6,992 vs Luton Town

F.A. Cup: Round 3
League Cup: Round 2

1998-99

The Lilywhites made an excellent start, losing only one of their first 12 fixtures. That defeat came when they were shaded out at home by Stoke City in a seven goal thriller. Incredibly, David Moyes' side bounced back by winning 4-3 at Lincoln seven days later. It was obvious early on in the campaign that Preston were genuine promotion contenders with Kurt Nogan scoring on a regular basis and the defence looking very solid.

Home victories over Rymans League outfit Ford United and Walsall gave Preston a third round F.A. Cup tie at home to Arsenal. This Monday night thriller was captured live on Sky TV. North End battled brilliantly in the first half and sent the fans wild with two goals from Nogan. However, the Premiership side's extra class eventually told. The Gunners halved the deficit before half-time and scored three more times (after David Eyres was sent-off) in the second half, to win 4-2.

Meanwhile, in the League, the first five matches after Christmas brought maximum points to lift Moyes' men to the top of the table. The prospects of promotion still looked bright, despite defeat at Bournemouth, when Preston bounced back with a 5-0 win at Wrexham. The arrival of Steve Basham, on loan from Southampton, gave the side fresh impetus and he ended up bagging ten goals in just 17 appearances. Yet, North End missed out on an automatic promotion place after only winning one of their final nine games. However, having finished fifth, they still held promotion hopes via the play-off route.

Moyes' side were paired with fourth placed Gillingham in the semi-final. It looked as if a goal by Eyres would proved good enough to give the Lilywhites victory at Deepdale, but the Kent side levelled with just 11 minutes remaining. The Gills opened the scoring early on in the second leg and, despite all Preston's efforts, it proved to be the only goal. All thoughts of Wembley had evaporated.

FACTFILE 1998-99

Manager: David Moyes

LEAGUE STATISTICS

Final position: 5th place in Division Two
Games played: 46   **Points**: 79
Biggest Victory: 5-0 vs Wrexham (A) and also vs Lincoln City (H)
Biggest Defeat: 0-3 vs Fulham (A)
Leading Goalscorer: Kurt Nogan (18 goals)
Ever-Presents: None
Hat-Trick Heroes: None
Average Home Attendance: 11,926
Highest Home Crowd: 20,857 vs Manchester City
Lowest Home Crowd: 8,656 vs York City

CUPS

F.A. Cup: Round 3
League Cup: Round 1

1999-2000

Preston won their first two matches in 1999-2000, but then experienced a five match winless spell which embraced home defeats against Wigan Athletic and Chesterfield. However, David Moyes' side then stepped up a gear and embarked on an 18 match unbeaten run. Jonathan Macken was in lethal form up front and went on to score 22 League goals. Sean Gregan and Mark Rankine worked tirelessly in midfield, while the defence as a unit formed a solid wall in front of Tepi Moilanen (who regained the goalie's jersey early in the campaign from David Lucas).

The third League defeat of the term came as late as 14th January at Stoke. Preston responded positively by defeating Wycombe Wanderers 3-2 at home and then thrashed Oxford United 4-0 on their own pitch. The Lilywhites were by now playing the best football in the Second Division and had the title firmly in their sights.

With striker Kurt Nogan returning to his native Wales to join Cardiff City, Moyes brought in Brett Angell on loan from Stockport County. Angell contributed 8 goals from his 15 appearances, while another late season signing, Iain Anderson, weighed in with the winning goals against Luton Town and Wrexham as North

End cemented their place at the top of the table. Ten of the final 15 fixtures ended in triumph and Preston collected the championship pennant with a club record 95 points – seven more than the runners-up Burnley.

After a gap of 19 campaigns, Preston North End were back in the second-flight of English football. Macken netted 22 times to be the top scorer, but just as crucial were the consistent displays by defenders Colin Murdock, Michael Jackson, Rob Edwards and Graham Alexander. All-told, Moyes' well-organised defence kept clean sheets in 24 of the 46 League games. Only seven games were lost, ironically the last defeat came at Cambridge on the night that they were confirmed as champions. A bumper 19,407 crowd was in carnival mood during the final home game against Millwall (which ended in a 3-2 victory).

In addition to their great exploits in the League, Preston embarked on two decent cup runs in 1999-2000. They reached the third round of the League Cup, but then found Arsenal too strong for them at Highbury. While Bristol Rovers, Enfield, Oldham Athletic, Plymouth Argyle were all side-stepped before Moyes' side exited the F.A. Cup 2-0 at Everton.

FACTFILE 1999-2000

Manager: David Moyes

LEAGUE STATISTICS

Final position: Champions of Division Two
Games played: 46 **Points:** 95
Biggest Victory: 4-0 vs Cardiff City (A) and also vs Oxford United (A)
Biggest Defeat: 1-4 vs Wigan Athletic (H)
Leading Goalscorer: Jonathan Macken (22 goals)
Ever-Presents: Graham Alexander and Michael Jackson
Hat-Trick Heroes: None
Average Home Attendance: 12,589
Highest Home Crowd: 19,407 v Millwall
Lowest Home Crowd: 8,506 v Chesterfield

CUPS

F.A. Cup: Round 5
League Cup: Round 3

2000-01

David Moyes kept faith with the championship winning squad in 2000-01 and the Deepdale faithful enjoyed another wonderful campaign, in which their side never slipped below ninth place. Four successive victories at the end of September and early October kept North End amongst the promotion contenders and, in spite of six defeats in seven matches around the turn of the year, Moyes' men continued to hold a chance of participating in the play-offs. This was eventually achieved with four victories from the final five fixtures, to finish in fourth place (with 78 points).

Jonathan Macken was again the leading scorer (with 19 goals), while another ex-Manchester United forward, David Healy, chipped in with nine goals after joining the Lilywhites mid-season. No Preston player was ever-present in 2000-01, but the consistent Paul McKenna, Mark Rankine, Rob Edwards and Sean Gregan all featured in at least 41 games.

With Wembley Stadium closed, the venue of the Play-off Final was Cardiff's superb Millennium Stadium. To get there Preston had to by-pass Birmingham City (who finished fifth) in a two-legged semi-final. Moyes' side fought like Lions at St Andrews, but lost to single goal (scored early in the second half). Four days later a crowd of 16,928 witnessed a sensational second leg at Deepdale. Healy equalised the aggregate scores midway through the first half. However, the Blues levelled on the night (to nose ahead again) just before the hour mark. Preston threw everything bar the kitchen sink at Birmingham, but it looked like being a night of frustration until Mark Rankine popped up with a goal in the last minute.

Extra-time brought no further goals and the place in the Cardiff Final had to decided by a penalty shoot-out. Astonishingly, the City manager Trevor Francis twice took his side off the pitch in protest at the end that the referee had chosen to hold the shoot-out. Francis felt that close proximity of the Preston supporters would give Moyes' men an extra advantage. He might even had a point, but it was certainly obvious that the City manager's actions had a negative affect on his own men. Anyhow Preston kept their nerve and won the shoot-out 4-2 to seal a trip to South Wales. After an interval of 40 years, the door to top-flight football was only 90 minutes away.

Preston's opponents at the Millennium Stadium, were Bolton Wanderers (who had finished third in the table). Moyes' side never stopped running, but the Trotters had the edge from the moment they scored in the 17th minute. The

Lilywhites lacked their usual cutting-edge and Bolton continued to hold sway in the second half. Near the end, Moyes pushed forward extra men and the Trotters cashed in with two breakaway goals to clinch promotion. Some Preston supporters left Cardiff in tears; however, over the length of the 2000-01 campaign, their team had certainly done them proud.

The National Football Museum opened at Deepdale during 2000-01. Costing £12 million, and housed beneath the Bill Shankly Kop and the Sir Tom Finney Stand, the NFM opened its doors in the February.

FACTFILE 2000-01

Manager: David Moyes

LEAGUE STATISTICS

Final position: 4th place in Division One
Games played: 46   **Points**: 78
Biggest Victory: 5-0 vs Queen's Park Rangers (H)
Biggest Defeat: 0-4 vs Gillingham (A)
Leading Goalscorer: Jonathan Macken (19 goals)
Ever-Presents: None
Hat-Trick Heroes: None
Average Home Attendance: 14,617
Highest Home Crowd: 17,355 vs Burnley
Lowest Home Crowd: 12,632 vs Crewe Alexandra

CUPS

F.A. Cup: Round 3
League Cup: Round 2

2001-02

The season opened disastrously with a 5-0 hammering at Gillingham and it was not until the sixth fixture, at home to Millwall, that David Moyes' side posted their first victory. However, the Lilywhites cut through the pack with an 11 match unbeaten run to put themselves in contention for another promotion push. However, too many matches were lost in the second half of the season and they finished three points short of a play-off berth in eighth place. The average attendance for League games at Deepdale, in 2001-02, was 14,883 – the highest level for 30 years.

Both Jonathan Macken and David Moyes were enticed away from Deepdale in the March. Macken joined First Division champions-elect Manchester City for a club record fee of upwards of £4 million. The 39 year-old Moyes became the new manager of Everton after a £1 million compensation package was worked out. Assistant manager Kelham O'Hanlon acted as caretaker for the remainder of the campaign. Then, just over a week after the season ended, the board appointed former Scotland boss Craig Brown as the new manager. Preston North End's immediate future appeared to be in very capable hands. And, with the opening of the Alan Kelly Town End Stand the previous November, Deepdale was looking better than ever.

FACTFILE 2001-02

Manager: David Moyes

LEAGUE STATISTICS

Final position: 8th place in Division One
Games played: 46   **Points:** 72
Biggest Victory: 6-0 vs Stockport County (H)
Biggest Defeat: 0-5 vs Gillingham (A)
Leading Goalscorer: Richard Cresswell (13 goals)
Ever-Presents: None
Hat-Trick Hero: David Healy
Average Home Attendance: 14,883
Highest Home Crowd: 21,014 vs Manchester City
Lowest Home Crowd: 11,371 vs Millwall

CUPS

F.A. Cup: Round 5
League Cup: Round 2

THE FUTURE

With a new manager about to make his mark, there were parallels with 25 years before at Deepdale at the start of the 2002-03 campaign. Perhaps Craig Brown will emulate Nobby Stiles and take Preston North End up a division in his first term at the helm. Certainly, the club's board and the management has their eyes set firmly on the Premiership. Given that the 2002-03 is the 42nd consecutive campaign that the Lilywhites have been confined to the lower divisions, it is likely that majority of their fans have never seen their side play top-flight football. That is unwanted distinction that the world's first League champions are determined to put right.

Brown has inherited a group of players squad rich in quality, losing only skipper Sean Gregan, who stepped up to the Premiership with WBA in the summer, and Jonathan Macken (who joined Manchester City in March) from David Moyes' powerful squad. In their place, the new manager drafted in Jamaican striker Ricardo Fuller (who was on loan at Hearts in 2001-02) and two extra defenders, Marlon Broomes (from Sheffield Wednesday) and Tyrone Mears (from Manchester City).

With just one more side of the ground still to be redeveloped, Preston North End and Deepdale appear to be going in the right direction. The club is no longer in decline and there is a strong belief that Preston North End will be a Premiership name in the not so distant future.

PRESTON NORTH END
25 SEASONS 1977-78 TO 2001-02

THE PLAY-OFF FINALS

Preston North End last participated in a major Cup Final in 1964, when they lost 3-2 to West Ham United in the F.A. Cup Final. However, during the quarter of a century up to the summer of 2002, the Lilywhites appeared in two Play-off Finals. Unfortunately, on both occasions they were defeated and missed out on promotion. Those matches were:

1993-94	THIRD DIVISION	vs WYCOMBE WANDERERS	LOST
2000-01	FIRST DIVISION	vs BOLTON WANDERERS	LOST

THIRD DIVISION PLAY-OFF FINAL 1993-94
PRESTON NORTH END V WYCOMBE WANDERERS

Preston North End appeared in a Play-off Final for the first time in their history in 1993-94. They reached it by squeezing past Torquay United over two legs at the semi-final stage. The Gulls won the first leg 2-0; however, Tony Ellis headed an early goal to put the pressure on the Devon side at Deepdale. But Preston's participation in the Final looked a long way off when Torquay regained their two goal advantage. Yet, things swayed North End's way following two incidents close to half-time. The visitors had a man sent-off for fighting. Then David Moyes headed in to make it 2-1 on the night. Another header by Stuart Hicks took the game into extra-time and yet another header (by Paul Raynor) ensured North End triumphed 4-3 on aggregate.

So, for the first time in 30 years, Preston North End supporters travelled south to see their team play at Wembley Stadium. Around 24,000 Preston fans made the trip to swell the gate to 40,109 – a record for a basement Play-off Final. The Final was a splendid game and for more than 45 minutes it looked as if Preston would clinch promotion. However, the Football League's original champions ended up being defeated 4-2 by its newest recruits – Wycombe Wanderers.

John Beck's side belied their long-ball reputation to play some attractive football and scored two classy first half goals. Ian Bryson's outrageous bicycle-kick was immediately equalised by a Steve Thompson effort which Jamie Squires could only help into the net. However, at that stage of the game, Preston were playing the better football and their lead was restored by a majestic header by Raynor.

Sadly, it all went wrong in the second half. In fairness, Martin O'Neill's Wanderers were scintillating. Wycombe netted three more times – through Simon Garner and Dave Carroll (twice) – to consign the Lilywhites to a longer stay in the basement.

PRESTON NORTH END 2-4 WYCOMBE WANDERERS

Date: 28th May 1994
Manager: John Beck
Team: Steve Woods, Andy Fensome, David Moyes, Ryan Kidd, Jamie Squires, Gareth Ainsworth, Lee Cartwright, Neil Whalley, Ian Bryson, Paul Raynor, Tony Ellis
Attendance: 40,109 (Wembley Stadium)
Club defeated in the Semi-final: Torquay United (aggregate 4-3 AET)

FIRST DIVISION PLAY-OFF FINAL 2000-01
PRESTON NORTH END V BOLTON WANDERERS

With Wembley Stadium closed, the venue of the 2000-01 Play-off Finals was Cardiff's superb Millennium Stadium. Preston had reached there by squeezing past Birmingham City in a two-legged semi-final. David Moyes' side lost the away leg to single second half goal. But in the return at Deepdale, David Healy equalised the aggregate scores midway through the first half. And, after City regained their goal advantage, Mark Rankine scored in the last minute to extend the excitement into extra-time. Preston kept their nerve and won the shoot-out 4-2. After a gap of 40 years, top-flight football was only 90 minutes away.

The Final took place exactly seven years to the day after Preston's previous Play-off Final. Their opponents at the Millennium Stadium, in front of an evenly split 54,328 crowd, were Bolton Wanderers – enabling Sir Tom Finney and Nat Lofthouse to renew their rivalry from their seats in the stand. Moyes' side never stopped working, but it was Bolton who had the edge from the moment Gareth Farrelly fired them into the lead in the 17th minute. With Jon Macken, Paul McKenna and Lee Cartwright all subdued, North End lacked their usual cutting-edge. Bolton continued to create the better chances and both Bo Hansen and Dean Holdsworth wasted clear-cut chances to kill the game.

While there was only one goal in it there was still hope and, near the end, Moyes pushed forward extra men in search of an equaliser. However, it was to no avail and the Trotters cashed in with two breakaway goals from substitute Michael Ricketts and Ricardo Gardner (in the 89th and 90th minutes). Bolton, managed by former North End player (and caretaker manager), Sam Allardyce had regained their Premiership place. Preston were beaten, but certainly not disgraced. And few, even as recently as nine months before, would have predicted that there would have been so much progress so quickly.

PRESTON NORTH END 0-3 BOLTON WANDERERS

Date: 28th May 2001
Manager: David Moyes
Team: David Lucas, Graham Alexander, Colin Murdock, Ryan Kidd, Rob Edwards, Lee Carwright (sub. Iain Anderson), Mark Rankine, Sean Gregan, Paul McKenna (sub. Richard Cresswell), David Healy, Jon Macken
Attendance: 54,328 (Millennium Stadium)
Club defeated in the Semi-final: Birmingham City (aggregate 2-2 AET). Preston North End won the penalty shoot-out 4-2

PRESTON NORTH END
25 SEASONS 1977-78 TO 2001-02

A-Z OF THE 25 MOST INFLUENTIAL PLAYERS

LEE ASHCROFT

Lee Ashcroft had two spells in the 1990's for his home town club. He is a versatile performer who can play in midfield, behind the front two or in attack. He possesses a powerful shot and was once described as a "scorer of great goals rather than a great goalscorer". Yet, in his last season at Deepdale, he bagged 14 goals to be the club's leading scorer. He moved to Grimsby Town for £500,000 in August 1998. He was hampered by injuries during his time at Blundell Park and moved again, two years later, to Wigan Athletic (for £250,000). Sadly, more injuries have denied him the chance to make a huge impact at the JJB Stadium.

Ashcroft made his debut for the Lilywhites in 1990-91 aged 18. After two full terms in the first-team he joined WBA for £250,000 in the summer of 1993. However, he cost Gary Peters twice that amount to bring him back three years later in a bid to strengthen his Third Division championship winning squad. Lee Ashcroft won one England Under-21 cap.

FACTFILE

Born: Preston, 7th September 1972
Position: Striker/Midfield
PNE 25 Seasons League Record: 155 appearances – 35 goals
PNE Career League Record: As above
Other League apps (Between spells with PNE): WBA (90 apps. – 17 goals),
Notts County (on loan 6 apps. – 0 goals)
Other League apps (Post-PNE): Grimsby Town (61 apps. – 15 goals),
Wigan Athletic (46 apps. – 8 goals)

25 SEASONS PNE LEAGUE RECORD

Season	Apps	Goals
1990-1991	14	1
1991-1992	38	5
1992-1993	39	7

1996-1997	27	8
1997-1998	37	14
25 Seasons Total	155	35

BOB ATKINS

Bob Atkins joined Preston in 1984-85, originally on loan, from Sheffield United and played in exactly 200 League games. The classy midfielder was a model professional, who never put in less than 100% effort, and was one of the club's better performers during the dark days of the mid-1980's. He was originally on the books of Leicester City, but joined the Blades from Non-League Enderby Town in the summer of 1982. He cost Preston £12,500 when he signed on a permanent basis.

Bob was a key member of John McGrath's promotion winning squad of 1986-87 and was the club's 'Player of the Season' in 1987-88. He is one of only seven men to appear in as many as 200 League games for Preston during the quarter of a century up to the summer of 2002.

FACTFILE

Born: Leicester, 16th October 1962
Position: Midfield
PNE 25 Seasons League Record: 200 appearances – 5 goals
PNE Career League Record: As above
Other League apps (Pre-PNE): Sheffield United (40 apps. – 3 goals)

25 SEASONS PNE LEAGUE RECORD

Season	Apps	Goals
1984-1985	13	0
1985-1986	34	2
1986-1987	41	1
1987-1988	45	1
1988-1989	39	0
1989-1990	28	1
25 Seasons Total	200	5

MICK BAXTER

It was Bobby Charlton who gave Mick Baxter his League debut in April 1975. The youngster grew into a wonderfully solid centre-half, who went on to play top-flight football with Middlesbrough. Sadly, Mick was to die at Deepdale at the very young age of 32, after returning to North End to work behind the scenes.

From his days as an apprentice, it was clear that Baxter had bags of potential. A fine header of the ball, he made the centre-half spot his own in 1977-78, when he helped the Lilywhites regain their Second Division status. He continued to show excellent form in the second-flight and was the club's 'Player of the Season' in the relegation campaign of 1980-81 (when he was ever-present). He was transferred to Middlesbrough in the summer of 1981 for £425,000. Boro were relegated from the First Division at the end of Mick's first campaign there. He moved to Portsmouth, in the summer of 1984, but did not make a League appearance for the south coast club.

Mick was appointed community officer at Deepdale and it was shortly after working with some children that he collapsed and died in January 1989. The death of this well-liked man came as a great shock. However, many Preston supporters hold happy memories of him keeping the defence in check during Nobby Stiles' reign.

FACTFILE

Born: Birmingham, 30th December 1956
Position: Defender
PNE 25 Seasons League Record: 161 appearances – 15 goals
PNE Career League Record: 210 appearances – 17 goals
Other League apps (Pre-PNE): Middlesbrough (122 apps. – 7 goals)

25 SEASONS PNE LEAGUE RECORD

Season	Apps	Goals
1977-1978	45	5
1978-1979	37	4
1979-1980	37	2
1980-1981	42	4
25 Seasons Total	161	15

GARY BRAZIL

Gary Brazil was a consistent scorer for Preston during his four-year spell during the second half of 1980's. He was the club's second top scorer in both their re-election campaign and again in 1986-87, when promotion from the Fourth Division was achieved. Gary was top scorer (with 14 goals) the following campaign, which proved to be his last full term at Deepdale. His last League goals in open play for the Lilywhites were in the 5-0 defeat of Gillingham in October 1988, when he bagged a hat-trick.

Brazil joined Preston in February 1985 (for £12,500) from Sheffield United. He made his Football League debut for the Blades in 1980-81, but had previously been a junior at Crystal Palace.

Gary left Preston for Newcastle United in February 1989. He struggled to hold down a first-team place as the Magpies tumbled out of the top-flight. He moved on to Fulham in September 1990 and stayed at Craven Cottage for six happy seasons. He briefly played for Cambridge United, in 1996-97, before switching to Barnet. He later played for Non-League St Albans and afterwards had two brief spells as Notts County's manager. Gary Brazil was a strong running forward with enough skill to give a lot of lower division defenders difficult afternoons.

FACTFILE

Born: Tunbridge Wells, 19th September 1962
Position: Striker
PNE 25 Seasons League Record: 166 appearances – 58 goals
PNE Career League Record: As above
Other League apps (Pre-PNE): Sheffield United (62 apps. – 9 goals),
Port Vale (on loan 6 apps. – 3 goals)
Other League apps (Post-PNE): Newcastle United (23 apps. – 2 goals),
Fulham (214 apps. – 48 goals), Cambridge United (1 apps. – 1 goal),
Barnet (19 apps. – 2 goals)

25 SEASONS PNE LEAGUE RECORD

Season	Apps	Goals
1984-1985	17	3

1985-1986	43	14
1986-1987	45	18
1987-1988	36	14
1988-1989	25	9
25 Seasons Total	166	58

ALEX BRUCE

In two spells at Deepdale, Alex Bruce scored 157 League goals. The last 96 of them were scored during the quarter of a century up to the summer of 2002. His tally was 22 goals more than the next highest scorer (Tony Ellis) for North End during those 25 seasons. A period when only three men (Lee Cartwright, Ryan Kidd and Andy McAteer) pulled on a Preston jersey more times than Bruce.

The little Scot made his debut for the Lilywhites in the last game of the 1971-72 campaign. Having claimed a regular place in the side he was the top scorer the following season and again headed Preston's list of scorers in 1973-74 despite moving to Newcastle United for £150,000 in the January. Alex could not carve out a regular first team place for himself at St James' Park and returned to Deepdale in early 1975-76 in a player-exchange deal that saw John Bird go the other way. Manager Bobby Charlton objected to the sale of Bird and resigned. However, it did prove to be a good deal for Preston as the ginger-haired striker went on to bag another 135 League goals for them.

Bruce was Preston's leading scorer on eight occasions (once jointly), with the 27 he scored in 1977-78, when his side won promotion to the Second Division, being his best seasonal haul. He was ever-present in that triumphant campaign and again in 1981-82. Alex Bruce left Deepdale during the summer of 1983 and joined Wigan Athletic. He won one Under-23 cap for Scotland.

FACTFILE

Born: Dundee, 23rd December 1952
Position: Striker
PNE 25 Seasons League Record: 215 appearances – 96 goals
PNE Career League Record: 363 appearances – 157 goals
Other League apps (Between spells at PNE): Newcastle United (20 apps. – 3 goals)
Other League apps (Post-PNE): Wigan Athletic (43 apps. – 7 goals)

25 SEASONS PNE LEAGUE RECORD

Season	Apps	Goals
1977-1978	45	27
1978-1979	40	21
1979-1980	26	10
1980-1981	31	13
1981-1982	46	18
1982-1983	27	7
25 Seasons Total	215	96

IAN BRYSON

Ian Bryson was an integral member of the Preston squad for four seasons during the mid-1990's. He was skipper of the side which lifted the Third Division title in 1995-96 and opened the scoring with a marvellous over-head kick in the 1994 Third Division Play-off Final. The experienced Scot was bought by John Beck in November 1993 for a bargain £42,500. His favoured role was on the left-hand side of midfield and was a very accurate passer of the ball. He also contributed a significant number of goals. His best tally for North End came in the championship campaign, when he netted nine times to be fourth top scorer.

Bryson signed for his home town side Kilmarnock in 1981 from Hurlford. He made 215 League appearances (scoring 40 goals) for Killie before signing for Sheffield United, in the summer of 1988, for £40,000. The Blades recouped half that fee when he joined Barnsley five years later. He quickly moved on again to Preston, just over three months after that. Ian Bryson had two seasons at Rochdale, after being freed by North End in the summer of 1997. He was dogged by injury, but was still one of the most influential performers at Spotland.

FACTFILE

Born: Kilmarnock, 26th November 1962
Position: Midfield
PNE 25 Seasons League Record: 151 appearances – 19 goals
PNE Career League Record: As above
Other League apps (Pre-PNE): Sheffield United (155 apps. – 36 goals),

Barnsley (16 apps. – 3 goals)

Other League apps (Post-PNE): Rochdale (54 apps. – 1 goals)

25 SEASONS PNE LEAGUE RECORD

Season	Apps	Goals
1993-1994	25	2
1994-1995	41	5
1995-1996	44	9
1996-1997	41	3
25 Seasons Total	151	19

LEE CARTWRIGHT

Nobody made more appearances for Preston North End in the quarter of a century up to the summer of 2002 than Lee Cartwright. He made his debut as an 18 year-old in 1990-91 and, up to the end of 2001-02, had registered 363 League appearances. He is a consistent performer who has been equally effective in both the centre of midfield and wide on the right. He is a solid tackler, despite being short of stature, and is an accurate passer.

Lee Cartwright has been heavily involved in all Preston's most recent magic moments. He was a key member of the 1995-96 and 1999-2000 championship winning squads. In addition, he also played in both Preston's Play-off Finals, at Wembley (in 1994) and in Cardiff (in 2001). Lee was awarded a testimonial match (against Middlesbrough) in early 2001-02.

FACTFILE

Born: Rawtenstall, 19th September 1972
Position: Midfield
PNE 25 Seasons League Record: 363 appearances – 22 goals
PNE Career League Record: As above

25 SEASONS PNE LEAGUE RECORD

Season	Apps	Goals
1990-1991	14	1
1991-1992	33	4

1992-1993	34	3
1993-1994	39	1
1994-1995	36	1
1995-1996	26	3
1996-1997	14	1
1997-1998	36	2
1998-1999	27	4
1999-2000	30	1
2000-2001	38	0
2001-2002	36	1
25 Seasons Total	**363**	**22**

GORDON COLEMAN

Gordon Coleman was a key member of Preston's squad throughout the second half of the 1970's and early 1980's. Somewhat of an underrated player, he always gave 100% effort and weighed in with some useful goals.

Coleman was given his debut by Bobby Charlton, when aged 19, in 1973-74. However, he did not tie down a regular role in midfield until 1976-77, when he missed just one game. He also played 45 times the following campaign to help the Lilywhites return to the Second Division. Even though he was effected by injury towards the end of his ten year stay, Gordon amassed 269 League appearances for the club. His best role was in midfield, but at times he also performed capably at full-back. Gordon Coleman joined Bury after leaving Deepdale in 1983.

FACTFILE

Born: Nottingham, 11th February 1954
Position: Midfield/Defender
PNE 25 Seasons League Record: 181 appearances – 18 goals
PNE Career League Record: 269 appearances – 25 goals
Other League apps (Post-PNE): Bury (29 apps. – 0 goals)

25 SEASONS PNE LEAGUE RECORD

Season	Apps	Goals
1977-1978	45	4
1978-1979	37	7
1979-1980	30	3
1980-1981	36	3
1981-1982	15	0
1982-1983	18	1
25 Seasons Total	181	18

SIMON DAVEY

Simon Davey was an important member of the squad which won the Third Division championship in 1995-96, when he netted ten times from midfield to be the club's joint second top scorer. He was a hard-working tenacious player who weighed in with a number of vital goals and some memorable ones too! He was an excellent passer and a great dead-ball specialist.

Gary Peters paid Carlisle United £125,000 for his services in February 1995; but Simon had commenced his League career with his home town side Swansea City. He moved to the Cumbrians in the summer of 1992 and played 25 times, in 1994-95, to put them on the road to the Third Division title before he moved south to Deepdale.

Simon lost more than a stone in weight during one week in 1995-96 after contracting food poisoning. The energetic box-to-box performer was loaned to Darlington, but returned to win his place back in David Moyes' side. He made his final appearance for the Lilywhites on the last day of the 1997-98 campaign. A back injury forced him to retire early and he is now Preston's youth-team manager.

FACTFILE

Born: Swansea, 1st October 1970
Position: Midfield
PNE 25 Seasons League Record: 106 appearances – 21 goals
PNE Career League Record: As above
Other League apps (Pre-PNE): Swansea City (49 apps. – 4 goals),

Carlisle United (105 apps. – 18 goals)
Other League apps (on loan from PNE): Darlington (11 apps. – 0 goals)

25 SEASONS PNE LEAGUE RECORD

Season	Apps	Goals
1994-1995	13	3
1995-1996	38	10
1996-1997	37	6
1997-1998	18	2
25 Seasons Total	106	21

STEVE ELLIOTT

Only Alex Bruce and Tony Ellis scored more League goals for Preston during the 25 seasons up to the summer of 2002 than Steve Elliott. He was the club's leading League scorer on three occasions and all-told, in just a little more than five campaigns, netted 70 times.

Steve's first club was Nottingham Forest. He appeared to be the first choice to replace the departed Peter Withe in 1978-79, but after just three game Brian Clough gave the nod to Gary Birtles. Elliott only made one more League appearance for Forest and joined Preston towards the end of the 1977-78 promotion campaign (for a club record fee of £90,000). He made his mark in 1978-79, netting 16 times when ever-present in the Second Division.

Elliott and Bruce formed a formidable partnership for North End in the early 1980's. The cash-strapped club sold Steve to Luton Town for £95,000 in the summer of 1984. However, he quickly made the switch to Walsall. He later returned north to serve Bolton Wanderers, Bury and Rochdale. Without doubt, though, Steve Elliott's most memorable campaigns were while he wore the white of Preston North End.

FACTFILE

Born: Haltwhistle, 15th September 1958
Position: Striker
PNE 25 Seasons League Record: 208 appearances – 70 goals

PNE Career League Record: As above

Other League apps (Pre-PNE): Nottingham Forest (4 apps. – 0 goals)

Other League apps (Post-PNE): Luton Town (12 apps. – 3 goals), Walsall (69 apps. – 21 goals), Bolton Wanderers (60 apps. – 11 goals), Bury (31 apps. – 11 goals), Rochdale (52 apps. – 9 goals)

25 SEASONS PNE LEAGUE RECORD

Season	Apps	Goals
1978-1979	7	0
1979-1980	42	16
1980-1981	35	9
1981-1982	35	10
1982-1983	45	19
1983-1984	44	16
25 Seasons Total	208	70

TONY ELLIS

Only Alex Bruce netted more League goals for Preston North End during the 25 seasons up to the summer of 2002 than Tony Ellis. In his two spells at the club he netted 74 League goals, all his Deepdale strikes coming on the plastic pitch! Having joined senior football late (aged nearly 22), Ellis was determined to make the most of his career and was still active in the First Division when aged 37, in 2001-02.

Tony made his League debut for Oldham Athletic in 1986-87, after moving from Non-League Horwich RMI. He joined Preston for £23,000 in October 1987 and came good in his second campaign at the club, when he was the top scorer with 19 goals (to help his side reach the Third Division play-offs). He signed for Stoke City (for £250,000) towards the end of 1989, shortly after playing in the F.A. Cup defeat against Whitley Bay. However, he returned to Deepdale in the summer of 1992 for £140,000 and was the top scorer in two consecutive campaigns. He netted 22 times in the relegation season of 1992-93 and scored 26 more League goals to help his side reach the Third Division play-offs the following term. Fittingly he scored in the last match on the Deepdale plastic to help the Lilywhites defeat Torquay United, on aggregate, after extra-time to reach Wembley. The losing Final, against Wycombe Wanderers, proved to be his last appearance for Preston. He moved to Blackpool for £165,000 two months later.

Tony Ellis later played for Bury, Stockport County and Rochdale. However, his last League club was First Division Burnley. He made 11 League appearances, all from the bench, and scored a superb winner against Bradford City. He left Turf Moor in 2002 to play in Australia.

FACTFILE

Born: Salford, 20th October 1964
Position: Striker
PNE 25 Seasons League Record: 158 appearances – 74 goals
PNE Career League Record: As above
Other League apps (Pre-PNE): Oldham Athletic (8 apps. – 0 goals)
Other League apps (Between spells at PNE): Stoke City (77 apps. – 19 goals)
Other League apps (Post-PNE): Blackpool (146 apps. – 54 goals),
Bury (38 apps. – 8 goals), Stockport County (20 apps. – 6 goals),
Rochdale (59 apps. – 17 goals), Burnley (11 apps. – 0 goals)

25 SEASONS PNE LEAGUE RECORD

Season	Apps	Goals
1987-1988	24	4
1988-1989	45	19
1989-1990	17	3
1992-1993	35	22
1993-1994	37	26
25 Seasons Total	158	74

SEAN GREGAN

For the six seasons up to the summer of 2002, Sean Gregan was one of the most important members of the Preston squad. He was an inspirational captain who always put in 100% effort. He left Deepdale during the summer of 2002 to join Premiership new boys WBA, for a £1.5 million fee.

The six foot two inch Sean made his League debut for his local club Darlington in 1991-92. His impressive displays for the Quakers attracted wider attention and, in November 1996, Gary Peters paid £350,000 for him. His most effective role for the Lilywhites was in the centre of midfield, but he is also a very useful central defender. He is an uncompromising tackler and an excellent man-marker. He is also a powerful header of the ball and perhaps should have netted more than the 12 times that he did for the club. He captained the 1999-2000 Second Division championship side and led Preston out at the Millennium Stadium for the 2001 First Division Play-off Final. Sean Gregan is one of the most popular men ever to pull on a Preston shirt.

FACTFILE

Born: Guisborough, 29th March 1974
Position: Midfield/Defender
PNE 25 Seasons League Record: 212 appearances – 9 goals
PNE Career League Record: As above
Other League apps (Pre-PNE): Darlington (136 apps. – 4 goals)

25 SEASONS PNE LEAGUE RECORD

Season	Apps	Goals
1996-1997	21	1
1997-1998	35	2
1998-1999	41	3
1999-2000	33	3
2000-2001	41	2
2001-2002	41	1
25 Seasons Total	212	12

MICHAEL JACKSON

Michael Jackson lost his first team place during 2001-02, but for much of the five seasons beforehand was one of the first names to be written on the Preston team-sheet. He is an uncomplicated no-frills defender who was worth every penny of the £125,000 fee that Gary Peters paid Bury in March 1997.

Jackson made his Football League debut for Crewe Alexandra in 1991-92 as an 18 year-old before Dario Gradi allowed him to join the Shakers in August 1993. He blossomed even more after joining Preston and was a key member of the squad which lifted the Second Division crown in 1999-2000. Michael was ever-present that campaign, when he weighed in with five valuable goals.

FACTFILE

Born: Runcorn, 4th December 1973
Position: Defender
PNE 25 Seasons League Record: 180 appearances – 16 goals
PNE Career League Record: As above
Other League apps (Pre-PNE): Crewe Alexandra (5 apps. – 0 goals), Bury (125 apps. – 9 goals)

25 SEASONS PNE LEAGUE RECORD

Seasons	Apps	Goals
1996-1997	7	0
1997-1998	40	2
1998-1999	44	8
1999-2000	46	5
2000-2001	30	1
2001-2002	13	0
25 Seasons Total	180	16

WARREN JOYCE

Warren Joyce was a key component of Preston's midfield for five seasons at the end of the 1980's and early 1990's. He was an influential skipper who contributed a clutch of valuable goals. A dead-ball expert, Warren netted 11 times in the League to be North End's leading scorer in 1989-90.

Joyce, the son of ex-Burnley wing-half (and ex-Preston coach) Walter, made his Football League debut for Bolton Wanderers in 1982-83. He joined Preston for £35,000 in October 1987. He immediately added bite to John McGrath's side and was the club's 'Player of the Season' in 1989-90.

Warren joined Plymouth Argyle (for £160,00) in May 1992. He moved on again to Burnley (for £140,000) in the summer of 1993. He had a spell on loan at Hull City in 1994-95 and moved to Boothferry Park on a permanent contract in the summer of 1996. He became the player-manager of the Tigers in November 1998, but was sacked in April 2000 after failing to guide the cash-strapped club to promotion from the Third Division.

FACTFILE

Born: Oldham, 20th January 1965
Position: Midfield
PNE 25 Seasons League Record: 177 appearances – 34 goals
PNE Career League Record: As above
Other League apps (Pre-PNE): Bolton Wanderers (184 apps. – 17 goals)
Other League apps (Post-PNE): Plymouth Argyle (30 apps. – 3 goals),
Burnley (70 apps. – 9 goals), Hull City (147 apps. – 15 goals)

25 SEASONS PNE LEAGUE RECORD

Season	Apps	Goals
1987-1988	22	0
1988-1989	40	9
1989-1990	44	11
1990-1991	42	9
1991-1992	29	5
25 Seasons Total	177	34

RYAN KIDD

Only Lee Cartwright made more League appearances for the Lilywhites in the quarter of a century up to the summer of 2002 than Ryan Kidd. When a neck injury forced him to retire, in 2001-02, he had clocked up 259 League appearances. He was a very reliable left-sided defender, who gave service both at full-back and in the heart of the defence.

Ryan was a member of Preston's championship winning sides of 1995-96 and 1999-2000. He also played against Bolton Wanderers in the 2000-01 Play-off Final at the Millennium Stadium. He was a fine over-lapping full-back, who was also a good tackler and a powerful header of the ball. A popular figure at Deepdale he fully deserved his testimonial in 2001-02. Ryan Kidd joined North End on a free transfer from Port Vale during the summer of 1992.

FACTFILE

Born: Radcliffe, 6th October 1971
Position: Defender
PNE 25 Seasons League Record: 259 appearances – 9 goals
PNE Career League Record: As above
Other League apps (Pre-PNE): Port Vale (2 apps. – 0 goals)

25 SEASONS PNE LEAGUE RECORD

Season	Apps	Goals
1992-1993	15	0
1993-1994	36	1
1994-1995	32	3
1995-1996	30	0
1996-1997	35	0
1997-1998	33	2
1998-1999	28	3
1999-2000	29	0
2000-2001	15	0
2001-2002	6	0
25 Seasons Total	259	9

JONATHAN MACKEN

Jonathan Macken was Preston's most effective striker during the five seasons up to the summer of 2002. He was the club's leading scorer (with 22 goals) in the promotion winning campaign of 1999-2000, and repeated this feat in the second-flight, in 2000-01, when his tally was 19 goals. He left Deepdale for Manchester City, in a club record deal worth more than £4 million, in March 2002.

Macken was a trainee at Old Trafford, but did not make a League appearance for the Red Devils. The English youth international cost Gary Peters a £250,000 fee in July 1997. He was a member of the Preston side that played in the 2001 First Division Play-off Final in Cardiff. Jon Macken scored five times to help Manchester City win the First Division title.

FACTFILE

Born: Manchester, 7th September 1977
Position: Striker
PNE 25 Seasons League Record: 184 appearances – 63 goals
PNE Career League Record: As above
Other League apps (Post-PNE): Manchester City (8 apps. – 5 goals)

25 SEASONS PNE LEAGUE RECORD

Season	Apps	Goals
1997-1998	29	6
1998-1999	42	8
1999-2000	44	22
2000-2001	38	19
2001-2002	31	8
25 Seasons Total	184	63

ANDY McATEER

Andy McAteer was a cultured left-back who made 251 League appearances for North End, during two spells with the club, in the 1980s. The local lad made an instant impact (and kept his place for the rest of the campaign) after making his debut in the 3-0 Boxing Day triumph over Shrewsbury Town in 1979.

A tireless performer, he joined Blackpool for £17,500 in December 1988. However, he returned to Preston in May 1988 on a free transfer and made another 13 League appearances before a series of injuries forced him to retire.

FACTFILE

Born: Preston, 24th April 1961
Position: Defender

PNE 25 Seasons League Record: 251 appearances – 9 goals

PNE Career League Record: As above

Other League apps (Between spells at PNE): Blackpool (41 apps. – 0 goals)

25 SEASONS PNE LEAGUE RECORD

Season	Apps	Goals
1979-1980	21	0
1980-1981	20	0
1981-1982	41	0
1982-1983	44	5
1983-1984	34	0
1984-1985	33	2
1985-1986	29	0
1986-1987	16	1
1988-1989	13	1
25 Seasons Total	251	9

TEUVO MOILANEN

Teuvo Moilanen made League appearances for Preston in each of the last seven of the 25 seasons up to the summer of 2002. Although he has often had to share the jersey, only one other keeper, Roy Tunks, stood between the posts more times than Tepi during these 25 seasons.

The six foot five inch goalie was signed from FF Jaro in December 1995. He kept a clean sheet on his League debut the following month at Lincoln. He started 1996-97 in the first-team but lost his place to new signing Bobby Mimms. Tepi enjoyed spells at Darlington and Scarborough, on loan, and made the Preston keeper's jersey his own when making 40 League appearances in 1997-98. An injury to his breast-bone, sustained at Northampton, curtailed his first-team action to the first games of 1998-99.

The big Finn missed only five League games as Preston lifted the Second Division crown, in 1999-2000. He missed the crucial run-in and play-off games the following campaign through injury. Tepi gets down very well for a big man and is very good at collecting crosses. He made 63 League appearances for his first club, Ilves, before joining Jaro (for whom he appeared 26 times), in 1995. By the summer of 2002, Tepi had won three caps for his country.

FACTFILE

Born: Oulu (Finland), 12th December 1973
Position: Goalkeeper
PNE 25 Seasons League Record: 143 appearances – 0 goals
PNE Career League Record: As above
Other League apps (on loan from PNE): Scarborough (4 apps. – 0 goals), Darlington (16 apps. – 0 goals)

25 SEASONS PNE LEAGUE RECORD

Season	Apps	Goals
1995-1996	2	0
1996-1997	4	0
1997-1998	40	0
1998-1999	15	0
1999-2000	41	0
2000-2001	17	0
2001-2002	24	0
25 Seasons Total	143	0

KURT NOGAN

Kurt Nogan's spell at Deepdale embraced four seasons at the end of the 1990's. Despite moving on to Cardiff City in the second half of the campaign, Kurt collected a Second Division championship medal with the Lilywhites in 1999-2000. However, his most memorable season with the club was 1998-1999 when he netted 18 times to be the leading scorer.

The younger brother of Lee Nogan, Kurt made his League debut for Luton Town in 1989-90. He joined Peterborough United in September 1992, but quickly moved on again to Brighton & Hove Albion without making a League appearance at London Road. He scored 49 League goals for the Seagulls, at a rate of a goal every other game, before making a £250,000 move to Burnley in April 1995. Gary Peters signed him for half that fee two years later. Kurt will always be remembered for the brace he scored for North End in the F.A. Cup against Arsenal in January 1999, in front of the Sky TV cameras. He left Preston for his home town side, Cardiff City, in March 2000 (for £50,000). Kurt Nogan collected one Welsh B cap and two Under-21 caps.

FACTFILE

Born: Cardiff, 9th September 1970
Position: Striker
PNE 25 Seasons League Record: 93 appearances – 27 goals
PNE Career League Record: As above
Other League apps (Pre-PNE): Luton Town (33 apps. – 3 goals),
Brighton & Hove (97 apps. – 49 goals), Burnley (92 apps. – 33 goals)
Other League apps (Post-PNE): Cardiff City (18 apps. – 1 goal)

25 SEASONS PNE LEAGUE RECORD

Season	Apps	Goals
1996-1997	7	0
1997-1998	22	5
1998-1999	42	18
1999-2000	22	4
25 Seasons Total	93	27

MARK RANKINE

Mark Rankine was a key member of the squads which won the Second Division title and reached the First Division Play-off Final in consecutive campaigns. A tireless worker in midfield, what Mark lacks in pace he makes up for with his tackling and passing.

He first made his name in the Doncaster Rovers side which reached the F.A. Youth Cup Final in 1987-88. He made his League debut earlier that same season for his home town club and stayed at Belle Vue until Wolves bid £70,000 for him in January 1992. Gary Peters paid £100,000 to bring this ball-winner to Deepdale

Despite sterling service for the Lilywhites as a player in the 1950's, Tommy Docherty's failure as manager at Deepdale during 1981 meant that he was quickly sacked.

Gordon Lee (pictured during his time as Everton manager) put the club back on it's feet after the departure of Tommy Docherty.

After playing over 50 games for the club, Les Chapman hung up his boots and took up a coaching role at Deepdale. He later worked as assistant to John McGrath and became manager after McGrath resigned in 1990.

Alan Kelly was a talented goalkeeper who made a record-breaking 447 League appearances during his time at the club (keeping 126 clean sheets). He later became manager and he was honoured in 2001-02 when a bit of Deepdale was named after him. The 6,000 seater Alan Kelly Town End Stand opened in November 2001.

Steve Elliott kept up a strike rate of a goal every three games during his 5 full seasons at the club during the 1980's.

Nobby Stiles – a hero in 1966 – made almost 50 League appearances for the Lilywhites after being brought to the club by former England team-mate Bobby Charlton. After retiring from playing, he joined the coaching staff and he was promoted to manager in July 1977.

Alex Bruce maintained an excellent strike rate of almost a goal every two games during two spells at North End and was top-scorer at the club for 8 seasons.

John Kelly made 129 League appearances and scored 27 goals from midfield in his 4 seasons at the club.

in September 1996.

His favoured position is central midfield, where he formed a particularly fruitful partnership with Sean Gregan. Never a prolific scorer, he did net four times during the 2001-02 campaign despite missing a chunk of games through injury. However, his most important goal for the Lilywhites came right at the end of the previous season's play-off semi-final second leg. That strike gave North End the chance to shoot-out for a place at the Millennium Stadium.

FACTFILE

Born: Doncaster, 30th September 1969
Position: Midfield
PNE 25 Seasons League Record: 214 appearances – 12 goals
PNE Career League Record: As above
Other League apps (Pre-PNE): Doncaster Rovers (164 apps. – 20 goals), Wolverhampton Wanderers (132 apps. – 1 goal)

25 SEASONS PNE LEAGUE RECORD

Season	Apps	Goals
1996-1997	23	0
1997-1998	35	1
1998-1999	42	3
1999-2000	44	0
2000-2001	44	4
2001-2002	26	4
25 Seasons Total	214	12

ANDY SAVILLE

The much-travelled Andy Saville only stayed at Deepdale for one and a quarter seasons; but made a huge impact by scoring 29 times in 1995-96 to help the Lilywhites lift the Third Division crown. Preston were the sixth of ten League clubs he represented; but was the only one in which he won a championship medal. He and his co-striker Steve Wilkinson were a formidable force in that title-winning season. Saville, the Division's joint leading scorer, twice netted hat-tricks – one of which was in the game with Mansfield Town, in which Wilkinson also bagged three to make it a unique afternoon.

Andy played his early football for his home town club Hull City. Afterwards he spent a year at Walsall and two years at Barnsley, who paid £100,000 and £80,0000, respectively, for him. He joined Hartlepool United in March 1992 (for £60,000), but just over a year later was on the move again to Birmingham City for £155,000. Gary Peters obtained him for a bargain £100,000 during the summer of 1995. He was rampant in helping the Lilywhites gain promotion to the Second Division, but looked out of his depth in the higher sphere the following campaign. The 31 year-old was allowed to join Wigan Athletic for £125,000 after adding just one Second Division goal to his first term tally.

He later played for Cardiff City, Hull City (on loan) and, very briefly, Scarborough. During the quarter of a century up to the summer of 2002 no Preston player scored more goals in a single campaign than Andy Saville's 1995-96 tally of 29.

FACTFILE

Born: Hull, 12th December 1964
Position: Striker
PNE 25 Seasons League Record: 56 appearances – 30 goals
PNE Career League Record: As above
Other League apps (Pre-PNE): Hull City (101 apps. – 18 goals),
Walsall (38 apps. – 5 goals), Barnsley (82 apps. – 21 goals),
Hartlepool United (37 apps. – 14 goals), Birmingham City (59 apps. – 17 goals),
Burnley (on loan 4 apps. – 1 goal)
Other League apps (Post-PNE): Wigan Athletic (25 apps. – 4 goals),
Cardiff City (35 apps. – 12 goals), Hull City (on loan 3 apps. – 0 goals),
Scarborough (9 apps. – 0 goals)

25 SEASONS PNE LEAGUE RECORD

Season	Apps	Goals
1995-1996	44	29
1996-1997	12	1
25 Seasons Total	56	30

GRAHAM SHAW

Graham Shaw topped Preston's list of goalscorers for two successive campaigns at the club in the early 1990's. Shaw was signed from his home town side, Stoke City, in the summer of 1989 and made an immediate impact at Deepdale by scoring in each of his first four games.

Graham's initial blitz of goals for North End included a hat-trick against Tranmere Rovers, in the League Cup, which proved to be his only one for the club. After such a great start it came as a surprise when the goals dried up. He only netted three more times in the League during 1989-90. However, he re-found his scoring touch in his last two seasons at the club, netting 24 more Third Division goals, often with only limited support up front. After being ever-present in 1991-92, Graham Shaw left Deepdale and returned to the Potters. He later played for Plymouth Argyle (on loan) and Rochdale.

FACTFILE

Born: Newcastle-under-Lyme, 7th June 1967
Position: Striker
PNE 25 Seasons League Record: ???
PNE Career League Record: As above
Other League apps (Pre-PNE): Stoke City (99 apps. – 18 goals)
Other League apps (Post-PNE): Stoke City (38 apps. – 5 goals),
Plymouth Argyle (on loan 6 apps. – 0 goals), Rochdale (22 apps. – 0 goals)

25 SEASONS PNE LEAGUE RECORD

Season	Apps	Goals
1989-1990	31	5
1990-1991	44	10
1991-1992	46	14
25 Seasons Total	121	29

GARY SWANN

Gary Swann was important member of the Preston squad in the second half of the 1980's and early 1990's. The classy performer had the knack of scoring vital goals from midfield. His biggest haul was the 12 goals he netted in 1987-88. That was the club's first season back in the Third Division, Gary having helped the Lilywhites to promotion in his first campaign at Deepdale.

John McGrath signed Swann from Hull City for £10,000 in November 1986. He was ever-present in both 1987-88 and 1989-90. He left in 1992 after making 199 League appearances for the Lilywhites. Gary Swann had two seasons with his home town club, York City, and later played for Scarborough.

FACTFILE

Born: York, 11th April 1992
Position: Midfield/Defender
PNE 25 Seasons League Record: 199 appearances – 37 goals
PNE Career League Record: As above
Other League apps (Pre-PNE): Hull City (186 apps. – 9 goals)
Other League apps (Post-PNE): York City (82 apps. – 4 goals), Scarborough (27 apps. – 3 goals)

25 SEASONS PNE LEAGUE RECORD

Season	Apps	Goals
1986-1987	30	5
1987-1988	46	12
1988-1989	18	2
1989-1990	46	8
1990-1991	30	5
1991-1992	29	5
25 Seasons Total	199	37

JOHN THOMAS

The much travelled John Thomas was a great favourite of the Deepdale faithful during his two spells (in the mid-1980's and early 1990's). In his first spell he slotted home 38 goals in 78 Fourth Division fixtures and was the club's leading scorer two seasons on the trot.

John's first League club was Everton, but he did not appear in the League for them. He made his Football League debut on loan with Tranmere Rovers and also had a temporary stint at Halifax Town. He joined Bolton Wanderers on a free transfer in the summer of 1980, but two years later was freed to Chester City. Thomas netted 20 times for the Sealand Road side and a year later signed for Lincoln City for £22,000. Preston paid £15,000 for his services in 1985 and he certainly did not disappoint. The 5 foot 8 inch striker netted 17 times in the campaign that the Lilywhites had to apply for re-election and then hit another 21 goals to help John McGrath's side earn promotion to the Third Division.

Thomas returned to Burnden Park for a £30,000 fee in the summer of 1987, but was back at Deepdale in 1989-90 after a spell at WBA. He helped Les Chapman's side avoid relegation to the basement, but unfortunately broke a leg, at Bolton, early in 1990-91. John Thomas left Deepdale for a second time in March 1992 when he joined Hartlepool United. He later played for Halifax again.

FACTFILE

Born: Wednesbury, 5th August 1958
Position: Striker
PNE 25 Seasons League Record: 105 appearances – 44 goals
PNE Career League Record: As above
Other League apps (Pre-PNE): Tranmere Rovers (on loan 11 apps. – 2 goals), Halifax Town (on loan 5 apps. – 0 goals), Bolton Wanderers (22 apps. – 6 goals), Chester City (44 apps. – 20 goals), Lincoln City (67 apps. – 18 goals)
Other League apps (Between spells at PNE): Bolton Wanderers (73 apps. – 31 goals), West Bromwich Albion (18 apps. – 1 goal)
Other League apps (After second spell with PNE): Hartlepool U (7 apps. – 1 goal), Halifax Town (12 apps. – 0 goals)

25 SEASONS PNE LEAGUE RECORD

Season	Apps	Goals
1985-1986	40	17
1986-1987	38	21
1989-1990	11	3
1990-1991	5	1
1991-1992	11	2
25 Seasons Total	105	44

ROY TUNKS

No-one spent more time between Preston's goalposts in the 25 seasons up to the summer of 2002 than Roy Tunks. The 6 foot 1 inch custodian played for the club in two spells and later became a member of the coaching staff. He made his Football League debut for Rotherham United and cost Bobby Charlton £7,000 in November 1974. Roy took over from John Brown and made an immediate impact with his high level of concentration and consistency.

Tunks was an ever-present member of Nobby Stiles' side which earned promotion to the Second Division in 1977-78. He was also ever-present during the following two seasons as Nobby Stiles' side consolidated in the second-flight. He left Deepdale for Springfield Park, on a free transfer, in November 1981 and, served Wigan for seven years. before returning to Deepdale, via a brief spell at Hartlepool, in January 1989. This time the Brown who made way for the almost 39 year-old was David. Roy Tunks later coached for the Lancashire FA.

FACTFILE

Born: Worthing, 21st January 1951
Position: Goalkeeper
PNE 25 Seasons League Record: 194 appearances – 0 goals
PNE Career League Record: 302 appearances – 0 goals
Other League apps (Pre-PNE): Rotherham United (138 apps. – 0 goals),
York City (on loan 4 apps. – 0 goals)
Other League apps (Between spells at PNE): Wigan Athletic (245 apps. – 0 goals),
Hartlepool United (5 apps. – 0 goals)

25 SEASONS PNE LEAGUE RECORD

Season	Apps	Goals
1977-1978	46	0
1978-1979	42	0
1979-1980	42	0
1980-1981	39	0
1988-1989	23	0
1989-1990	2	0
25 Seasons Total	194	0

PRESTON NORTH END
25 SEASONS 1977-78 TO 2001-02

JUST ABOUT MANAGING!

Eleven men held the post of manager of Preston North End FC during the quarter of a century up to the summer of 2002. The first of these men, Nobby Stiles was the only one to stay in the job for four full seasons, although the last permanent incumbent David Moyes stayed for a couple of months longer. Conversely, Tommy Booth, Tommy Docherty and Brian Kidd left within a year of accepting the challenge. Docherty never made it to Christmas after taking the job in the summer of 1981. Kidd lasted only two months during Preston's worst ever campaign, in which they ended up having to apply for re-election. The reigns of the Preston managers embraced the following periods.

JULY 1977 TO MAY 1981	NOBBY STILES
JUNE 1981 TO DECEMBER 1981	TOMMY DOCHERTY
DECEMBER 1981 TO DECEMBER 1983	GORDON LEE
DECEMBER 1983 TO FEBRUARY 1985	ALAN KELLY
FEBRUARY 1985 TO JANUARY 1986	TOMMY BOOTH
JANUARY 1986 TO MARCH 1986	BRIAN KIDD
MAY 1986 TO FEBRUARY 1990	JOHN McGRATH
FEBRUARY 1990 TO SEPTEMBER 1992	LES CHAPMAN
DECEMBER 1992 TO DECEMBER 1994	JOHN BECK
DECEMBER 1994 TO JANUARY 1998	GARY PETERS
JANUARY 1998 TO MARCH 2002	DAVID MOYES

NOBBY STILES
JULY 1977 TO MAY 1981

It was Bobby Charlton who brought his old Manchester United and England team-mate Nobby Stiles to Preston, as a player, in 1973. Stiles made 46 League appearances before joining the coaching staff and he was promoted to manager in July 1977, after Harry Catterick resigned.

Although two very promising youngsters (Mark Lawrenson and Gary Williams) were sold pre-season, Nobby took the Lilywhites back to the Second Division in his first campaign at the helm. Preston finished third, going up courtesy of a better goal difference than Peterborough United. Despite having to sell off some of his better performers, Stiles steered North End into the top half of the second-flight in their first two campaigns back at that level.

However, the side's failure to score goals proved expensive in 1980-81. They netted only 41 times to finish third from bottom and were relegated. The tension lasted all the way to the final day of the season. Stiles' side won at Derby, but Cardiff's point at home sent Preston down on goal difference. Relegation cost Stiles his job.

As a player, Stiles was a combative midfielder who won 28 caps and, of course, was a member of the 1966 World Cup winning side. He played for Middlesbrough after his long and successful career with Manchester United ended. He collected two Championship medals and an European Cup winners' meal at Old Trafford. After leaving Deepdale, Nobby coached Vancouver Whitecaps before returning to England in 1984 and joining WBA as youth-team coach. He acted as caretaker manager at the Hawthorns after his brother-in-law Johnny Giles left the club. Nobby later returned to Old Trafford to coach Manchester United's youth-team.

FACTFILE

Born: Manchester, 18th May 1942

PNE MANAGERIAL RECORD

	Played	Won	Drew	Lost
League	172	55	67	50
F.A. Cup	6	2	0	4
League Cup	16	6	4	6
Total	194	63	71	60

Honours/Promotions: Third Division Promotion in 1977-78
Highest League finish: 7th in the Second Division in 1980-81
Lowest League finish: 3rd in the Third Division in 1977-78
Best F.A. Cup Run: Round 4 in 1978-79
Best League Cup Run: Round 4 in 1980-81

First Match in charge: 13th August 1977 vs Port Vale League Cup (lost 1-2)
Last Match: 6th May 1981 vs Derby County Second Division (won 2-1) (drew 0-0)

TOMMY DOCHERTY
JUNE 1981 TO DECEMBER 1981

Tommy Docherty, the player, gave excellent service to Preston North End for much of the 1950s. However, his spell in change of the team, as manager, lasted only six months in 1981. With the benefit of hindsight, the Doc was far too long in the tooth when he took over from Nobby Stiles. He lasted just 17 League games (of which only three were won), with his side playing a poor style of football. He was sacked in early December after a run of four successive defeats (including an F.A. Cup exit at Chesterfield).

Docherty won 25 caps for Scotland. He signed for North End as a wing-half from Glasgow Celtic (for £4,000) towards the end of 1949. He was ever-present when the Lilywhites won the Second Division title in 1950-51, and missed only one game two seasons later when they were pipped to the League title (on goal average) by Arsenal. He joined the Gunners in the summer of 1958 (for £28,000) after falling out with Preston's directors. He wanted to play for Scotland in the World Cup tournament in Sweden, but the board insisted he went on a pre-season tour of Switzerland. After leaving Highbury he became player-coach of Chelsea. Later he became manager at Stamford Bridge.

Chelsea were relegated and promoted under the Doc. He led them to success in the League Cup and took them to their first F.A. Cup Final. After resigning as the Blues' boss in October 1967 he managed Rotherham United, QPR (for just 29 days) and Aston Villa.

After being sacked by Villa, in January 1970, he managed Porto. He returned from Portugal to become assistant-manager at Hull City. However, after just two months, he became manager of the Scottish national side. After some good work with Scotland, Tommy became manager of Manchester United (in December 1972). He took them down to Division Two, but they bounced straight back again. The Red Devils won the F.A. Cup in 1977, but he lost his job a few months later because of his affair with the wife of United's physio.

Docherty became Derby County's manager in September 1977. He resigned after two seasons to return to Loftus Road. History seemed to be repeating itself in Shepherd's Bush when he was quickly sacked. However, this time he was reinstated and stayed for more than a season before his contract was terminated. He then managed Sydney Olympic before taking up the challenge to manage Preston. After his failure at Deepdale, Tommy returned to Australia and again managed Olympic, and also South Melbourne.

The Doc returned to England in 1984 to manage Wolves, his last League club. He was sacked in the summer of 1985, but later managed Non-League Altrincham. Tommy's son Michael (born in Preston) also played and managed in the Football League.

FACTFILE

Born: Glasgow, 24th August 1928

PNE MANAGERIAL RECORD

	Played	Won	Drew	Lost
League	17	3	6	8
F.A. Cup	1	0	0	1
League Cup	4	2	1	1
Total	22	5	7	10

Honours/Promotions: None
Highest League finish/Lowest League finish: Did not finish his first season (Third Division in 1981-82)
Best F.A. Cup Run: Round 1 in 1981-82
Best League Cup Run: Round 2 in 1981-82
First Match in charge: 29th August 1981 vs Millwall Third Division (lost 1-2)
Last Match in charge: 28th November 1981 vs Oxford United Third Division (lost 0-3)

GORDON LEE
DECEMBER 1981 TO DECEMBER 1983

Gordon Lee was given the task of putting Preston on its feet after the low months of Tommy Docherty's reign at the end of 1981. He brought in some new players and restored some confidence to the squad. They gradually climbed the table and finished 14th in 1981-82. Lee was hampered by a clutch of injuries and a run of bad luck in 1982-83. His side started very badly, but finished the campaign in better form and was placed 16th.

Preston started very brightly in 1983-84, going seven League and cup games without defeat. However, a disastrous run of seven League matches on the trot, coupled with exits from both the cups, sounded the death knell for Lee. He was sacked just prior to Christmas 1984.

In his playing days, Lee was a full-back with Aston Villa and Shrewsbury Town. He managed Port Vale, Blackburn Rovers, Newcastle United and Everton before taking the reins at Preston. After leaving Deepdale he went to Iceland to coach KR Reykjavik and he later coached in the Middle East and at Leicester City.

FACTFILE

Born: Hednesford, 13th July 1934

PNE MANAGERIAL RECORD

	Played	Won	Drew	Lost
League	93	32	26	35
F.A. Cup	4	2	0	2
League Cup	5	1	1	3
Total	102	35	27	40

Honours/Promotions: None
Highest League finish: 14th in the Third Division in 1981-82
Lowest League finish: 16th in the Third Division in 1982-83
Best F.A. Cup Run: Round 3 in 1982-83
Best League Cup Run: Round 3 in 1983-84
First Match in charge: 5th January 1982 vs Chesterfield Third Division (drew 0-0)
Last Match: 17th December 1983 vs Bolton Wanderers Second Division (drew 2-2)

ALAN KELLY
DECEMBER 1983 TO FEBRUARY 1985

Alan Kelly holds the record for the number of League appearances made by a Preston player. He appeared in 447 League games and kept 126 clean sheets before joining the coaching staff after a shoulder injury ended his career in 1973. He was promoted to assistant-manager under Nobby Stiles and acted as caretaker manager for one match after Tommy Docherty was sacked. He reverted to a coaching role under Gordon Lee, but was again give caretaker control after Lee was sacked in December 1983. Preston won their next two games by four goal margins (4-0 at home and 5-1 away) and, by the end of 1983-84, Kelly was appointed manager on a permanent basis.

The Lilywhites finished 16th in the Third Division in 1983-84. Unfortunately, with little money available to him, Kelly was unable to lift the club the following season. Deep in relegation trouble, matters went from bad to worse with a 4-1 humbling at home in the F.A. Cup by Non-League Telford United. More bad results followed over the Christmas period and Kelly resigned in February 1985. Preston were relegated at the end of the season.

Alan was a wonderful keeper, who joined North End from Drumcondra (with whom he won an Irish Cup winners' medal). He made his first-team debut at Swansea, in the F.A. Cup, in 1960-61. His first League game (at Hillsborough) ended in a 5-1 defeat, but he became Preston's regular keeper in 1961-62 (their first season back in the Second Division). He played in the F.A. Cup Final in 1964, but missed much of the following campaign through injury.

He was ever-present for two consecutive seasons, the second being when Preston won the Third Division title in 1970-71. He was still the first choice keeper when he was injured during the home game with Bristol City in September 1973 and unfortunately, failed to regain sufficient fitness to resume his Football League duties. Alan won 47 caps for the Republic of Ireland. He briefly managed his country's side in 1980.

Alan Kelly's sons, Gary and Alan, are both plying their trade as League goalkeepers. Republic of Ireland international Alan junior started his career with Preston, making 142 League appearances, before leaving in 1992.

Preston's greatest goalkeeper was honoured in 2001-02 when a bit of Deepdale was named after him. The 6,000 seater Alan Kelly Town End Stand opened in November 2001.

FACTFILE

Born: Dublin, 5th July 1936

PNE MANAGERIAL RECORD (NOT INCLUDING FIRST CARETAKER SPELL)

	Played	Won	Drew	Lost
League	98	30	17	51
F.A. Cup	2	1	0	1
League Cup	4	1	2	1
Total	104	32	19	53

Honours/Promotions: None
Highest League finish: 16th in the Third Division in 1983-84
Lowest League finish: 16th in the Third Division in 1983-84
Best F.A. Cup Run: Round 2 in 1984-85
Best League Cup Run: Round 2 in 1984-85
First Match in charge: 26th December 1983 vs Port Vale Third Division (won 4-0)
Last Match in charge: 2nd February 1985 vs Plymouth Argyle Third Division (lost 1-2)

TOMMY BOOTH
FEBRUARY 1985 TO DECEMBER 1985

Tommy Booth took over the responsibility of managing Preston after Alan Kelly resigned in February 1985. Originally it was on a temporary basis, but he was persuaded to stay on permanently. He brought in Brian Kidd as his assistant and tried hard to change things around. However, with very little spare cash available to buy new players, it proved to be an impossible task.

Preston spiralled towards relegation and, their first taste of Division Four football, in 1984-85. They finished second from bottom, having conceded exactly 100 goals. Booth's side fared little better in the basement during the early months of 1985-86. They opened the campaign by losing 4-2 at home to Peterborough United, were hammered 6-0 at Northampton and lost 6-3 at Deepdale to Chester City. There was no joy in the F.A. Cup either as they lost 7-3 at Walsall. Booth resigned in the December and has not managed another club since.

As a player, Booth was one of the First Division's most efficient centre-halves of the 1970's. He joined Manchester City as an apprentice in 1967 and remained at Maine Road until he joined Preston as a player in October 1981. He won F.A.

Cup, European Cup Winners' Cup and two League Cup winners' medals with the Citizens and was awarded four England Under-23 caps. Tommy Docherty signed him for Preston for £30,000 and he went on to make 53 League appearances, the last being at Millwall in November 1985.

FACTFILE

Born: Langley, 9th November 1949

PNE MANAGERIAL RECORD

	Played	Won	Drew	Lost
League	40	12	5	22
F.A. Cup	1	0	0	1
League Cup	4	2	1	1
Total	45	14	6	24

Honours/Promotions: None

Highest League finish: 23rd in the Third Division in 1985-86

Lowest League finish: 23rd in the Third Division in 1985-86

Best F.A. Cup Run: Round 2 in 1985-86

Best League Cup Run: Round 1 in 1985-86

First Match in charge: 9th February 1985 vs Rotherham United Third Division (lost 0-3)

Last Match: 18th January 1986 vs Peterborough United Fourth Division (drew 1-1)

BRIAN KIDD
DECEMBER 1985 TO MARCH 1986

Brian Kidd joined North End as assistant-manager to Tommy Booth during the second half of 1984-85. He was thrust into the hot-seat when Booth resigned in December 1985 after Preston's appalling start to their first campaign in the Fourth Division. Kidd was unable to stop the rot and was sacked after only two months.

As a player, Kidd was one of the last of Matt Busby's 'babes'. He helped Manchester United win the 1968 European Cup Final, scoring one of the goals himself. He won two England caps and later played for Arsenal, Manchester City, Everton and Bolton Wanderers. He was assistant-manager at Swindon Town before joining Preston.

Apart from a brief spell as manager of Non-League Barrow, Kidd's only other spell as a manager, outside Deepdale, was when he was in charge of Blackburn Rovers (in 1998-99). The limelight did not seem to suit him, though and Blackburn sacked him in November 1999, six months after he took them down into the Football League. He certainly seemed much better suited in his previous role as assistant-manager to Alex Ferguson at Old Trafford (having returned there initially on the youth development side). He has also looked a lot more comfortable in his role as coach of Leeds United, under David O'Leary and Terry Venables.

FACTFILE

Born: Manchester, 29th May 1949

PNE MANAGERIAL RECORD

	Played	Won	Drew	Lost
League	17	1	5	11
F.A. Cup	0	0	0	0
League Cup	0	0	0	0
Total	17	1	5	11

Honours/Promotions: None

Highest League finish/Lowest League position: Did not finish his first season (Fourth Division in 1985-86).

Best F.A. Cup Run: None

Best League Cup Run: None

First Match: 24th January 1986 vs Stockport County Fourth Division (lost 1-2)

Last Match: 18th March 1986 vs Cambridge United Fourth Division (lost 1-2)

JOHN McGRATH
MAY 1986 TO FEBRUARY 1990

John McGrath became Preston's manager in May 1986 (after Jonathan Clark had briefly held the reins on a caretaker basis). He made a immediate impression bringing some much needed zest to the club. He also appointed two new coaches in the form of Walter Joyce and Les Chapman. The latter was one of several new players who helped make the side more buoyant. With its spirit renewed, the team performed splendidly under McGrath and claimed promotion as runners-up to Northampton Town.

Preston made a poor start to 1987-88, but recovered to finish 16th. The following season was much more fruitful, with a 6th place finish and qualification for the play-offs. Unfortunately, McGrath's side found Port Vale too strong for them and lost the semi-final 4-2, on aggregate. North End made an awful start to 1989-90, losing six of their first seven League and cup matches. McGrath resigned during the following February. His side had been humbled 2-0 in the F.A. Cup by Whitley Bay and had clocked up another run of dire results in the League.

As a player, John McGrath was a tough-tackling centre-half who made League appearances for Bury (winning the Third Division title), Newcastle United, Southampton and Brighton & Hove Albion (on loan). He joined Southampton's back-room staff when he hung up his boots. His first managerial appointment was with Port Vale. He led Vale into the Third Division at the end of 1982-83, but was sacked during the following campaign. He managed Fourth Division Chester City between January 1984 and May 1985. After his spell at Deepdale, he managed Halifax Town between October 1991 and November 1992.

FACTFILE

Born: Manchester, 23rd August 1938

PNE MANAGERIAL RECORD

	Played	Won	Drew	Lost
League	166	68	45	53
F.A. Cup	12	5	3	4
League Cup	12	2	4	6
Total	190	75	52	63

Honours/Promotions: Division Four Promotion in 1986-87
Highest League finish: 6th in the Third Division in 1988-89

Lowest League position: 2nd in the Fourth Division in 1986-87

Best F.A. Cup Run: Round 4 in 1986-87

Best League Cup Run: Round 2 in 1986-87 and 1988-89

First Match: 23rd August 1986 vs Tranmere Rovers Fourth Division (drew 1-1)

Last Match: 13th February 1990 vs Leyton Orient Third Division (lost 0-3)

LES CHAPMAN
FEBRUARY 1990 TO SEPTEMBER 1992

Les Chapman stepped up from his role as assistant to manage Preston on a caretaker basis after John McGrath resigned in February 1990. His first match was a disaster – a 6-0 hammering at Reading. His second game proved just how funny the game can be – Preston defeated Cardiff City 4-0. Results improved under Chapman and North End just avoided relegation to the Fourth Division, in 1989-90, finishing 19th.

Preston did not progress much under Chapman, although the manager put in a terrific amount of hard work. His side finished 17th in both his full seasons at the helm. He was sacked after the Lilywhites made a poor start start to 1992-93.

As a player, Chapman was a cultured midfielder who played for six clubs and in total made 746 League appearances. Only 16 players have played more League games than Les since the Second World War. He made his League debut for Oldham Athletic, and also played for Huddersfield Town, Stockport County and Bradford City. He became player-manager of struggling Rochdale (in 1985-86) before John McGrath brought him to Deepdale in the summer of 1986. He combined his coaching duties with playing, making his last 53 League appearances for North End before hanging up his boots at the end of 1987-88. Les achieved the rare feat of making appearances on the grounds of all '92' clubs when he played for Preston at Swansea City's Vetch Field in January 1987.

He has been involved in football in various capacities since leaving Deepdale, working for several clubs including Manchester City and Huddersfield Town. Les is the father of actress Tiffany Chapman (Brookside's Rachel Dixon).

FACTFILE

Born: Oldham, 27th September 1948

PNE MANAGERIAL RECORD

	Played	Won	Drew	Lost
League	72	24	17	31
F.A. Cup	3	2	0	1
League Cup	4	2	0	2
Total	79	28	17	34

Honours/Promotions: None
Highest League finish: 17th in the Third Division in 1990-91 and 1991-92
Lowest League position: 19th in the Third Division in 1989-90
Best F.A. Cup Run: Round 3 in 1991-92
Best League Cup Run: Round 1 in 1990-91 and 1991-92
First Match: 17th February 1990 vs Reading Third Division (lost 0-6)
Last Match: 26th September 1992 vs Hartlepool United Third Division (lost 0-2)

JOHN BECK
DECEMBER 1992 TO DECEMBER 1994

John Beck was manager of Cambridge United when Preston sacked Les Chapman in September 1992. He (and his assistant Gary Peters) eventually joined the Lilywhites in early December. In the interim period Sam Allardyce steered North End on a caretaker basis. Beck brought in a flood of new players and got the side playing more directly. Results started to improve and relegation looked to be avoided. However, Preston lost their last five fixtures to slip into the basement in 21st place.

Beck injected even more fresh blood into the squad in 1993-94 and his side maintained their promotion challenge through to the spring. They eventually finished fifth and qualified for the play-offs. They overcame a 2-0 first leg deficit to squeeze past Torquay United in the semi-final to set up a day out at Wembley against Wycombe Wanderers. Preston twice led, but the Buckinghamshire side stepped up a gear in the second half to break a lot of Lancashire hearts.

Despite the promotion near miss, there was growing concern about some Beck's long-ball methodology and he resigned in early December 1994.

As a player, John was a hard-working midfielder. He was a fine passer and crosser, who made excellent use of a dead-ball. He played for QPR, Coventry City, Fulham, Bournemouth and Cambridge United. He became Cambridge's assistant-manager in 1988 and later took over as manager on a caretaker basis. He was a great success and was given the job permanently. He led Cambridge to the quarter-final of the F.A. Cup in 1990 and up two divisions to the second-flight (in 1989-90 & 1990-91). Cambridge were still in the First Division when Beck left them, but were relegated at the end of the season. Ironically, in tandem with Preston's demise from the Second Division.

Beck was manager of Lincoln City between 1995 and 1998. He returned to manage Cambridge again towards the end of the 2000-01 campaign. However, he resigned after just eight months at the helm, in November 2001.

FACTFILE

Born: Edmonton, 25th May 1954

PNE MANAGERIAL RECORD

	Played	Won	Drew	Lost
League	87	31	19	37
F.A. Cup	7	4	1	2
League Cup	4	0	1	3
Total	98	35	21	42

Honours/Promotions: None
Highest League finish: 21st place in the Second Division in 1992-93
Lowest League position: 5th place in the Third Division in 1993-94
Best F.A. Cup Run: Round 4 in 1993-94
Best League Cup Run: Round 1 in 1992-93 and 1993-94
First Match: 12th December 1992 vs Port Vale Second Division (lost 2-5)
Last Match: 26th December 1994 vs Chesterfield Third Division (lost 0-1)

GARY PETERS
DECEMBER 1994 TO JANUARY 1998

Gary Peters was appointed as caretaker manager following John Beck's resignation in December 1994. He was eventually given the job on a permanent basis and did well to lead the Lilywhites to the play-offs at the end of the season. Preston finished fifth, but suffered the disappointment of losing both play-off semi-finals 1-0 to Bury.

Peters strengthened the squad during the summer of 1995 and it paid dividends. The 1995-96 campaign was a wonderful one for Preston supporters as their team lifted the Third Division championship playing attractive football. Peters kept things moving in the right direction in 1996-97 and Preston consolidated in 15th place. However, the Lilywhites hit a goal drought in 1997-98 and, after a run of bad results, Peters resigned in the January. He remained at Deepdale and is the Director of the Centre of Excellence.

Gary came relatively late to League football via Non-League Guildford City. He was an enthusiastic and determined right-back who saw service with Reading (two spells, where he won Third and Fourth Division Championship medals), Fulham (two spells), Wimbledon and Aldershot. He was assistant-manager at Fulham before becoming John Beck's assistant at Cambridge in 1989. They both joined Preston in December 1992.

FACTFILE

Born: Carshalton, 3rd August 1954

PNE MANAGERIAL RECORD

	Played	Won	Drew	Lost
League	143	63	37	43
F.A. Cup	8	5	0	3
League Cup	10	3	4	3
Total	161	71	41	49

Honours/Promotions: Third Division Championship in 1995-96
Highest League finish: 15th place in the Second Division in 1996-97
Lowest League position: 5th place in the Third Division in 1994-95
Best F.A. Cup Run: Round 3 in 1997-98
Best League Cup Run: Round 2 in 1996-97 and 1997-98
First Match: 3rd December 1994 vs Walsall F.A. Cup (drew 1-1)
Last Match: 10th January 1998 vs Gillingham Second Division (lost 1-3)

DAVID MOYES
JANUARY 1998 TO MARCH 2002

David Moyes first joined Preston as a player in September 1993. He was appointed assistant-manager under Gary Peters in 1994 although he continued playing. He took over the team on a temporary basis, when Peters resigned in January 1998, and then permanently after proving he was the ideal man for the task. Relegation was staved off at the end of 1997-98 and 12 months later North End just missed out on promotion. Having finished fifth they qualified for the play-offs, but found Gillingham too strong for them over the two-legged semi-final.

Moyes installed an extra element of fighting spirit into the squad, and a year after their play-off failure, they bounced back to lift the Second Division title playing wonderfully attractive football. Moyes became the first manager since Nobby Stiles (in 1977-78) to take Preston up to the second-flight. North End's revival under Moyes did not stop there and 12 months later they came within one victory of playing Premiership football. Having finished fourth in the First Division, North End qualified for the play-offs. The dramatically squeezed past Birmingham City (after a shoot-out) to meet Bolton Wanderers in the final at Cardiff's Millennium Stadium. The Trotters proved too good for Moyes' side; but 2000-01 had still been a wonderful campaign.

Preston were in contention to reach the play-offs again in 2001-02, but after much soul-searching David Moyes accepted an offer to become Everton's new manager. Preston received £1 million compensation for their loss. Moyes' assistant Kelham O'Hanlon took over as caretaker manager. O'Hanlon did a fine job, although North End just missed out on the play-offs in eighth place. Before the end of April 2002 it was announced that the new manager of Preston North End was to be ex-Scotland boss Craig Brown.

Meanwhile Moyes made an immediate impact at Goodison Park, leading his side to victory in his first two games at the helm. His honest style of management quickly won over the players and the fans. Everton finished in 15th place.

As a player, Moyes was a very useful centre-half in the lower divisions. He actually won a League Championship medal with his first club, Glasgow Celtic, in 1981-82. He then played for Cambridge United, Bristol City and Shrewsbury Town before moving back to Scotland in 1990 and signing for Dunfermline. He briefly played for Hamilton Academical before moving to Deepdale where he was a key member of the side which lifted the 1995-96 Third Division title. In all, he played 143 League games (netting 15 times) for Preston.

FACTFILE

Born: Glasgow, 25th April 1963

PNE MANAGERIAL RECORD

	Played	Won	Drew	Lost
League	196	95	53	48
F.A. Cup	13	8	1	4
League Cup	13	5	3	5
Total	212	108	57	57

Honours/Promotions: Second Division Championship in 1999-2000
Highest League finish: 4th place in the First Division in 2000-01
Lowest League finish: 15th place in the Second Division in 1997-98
Best F.A. Cup Run: Round 5 in 1999-2000 and 2001-02
Best League Cup Run: Round 3 in 1999-2000
First Match: 17th January 1998 vs Watford Second Division (lost 1-3)
Last Match: 9th March 2002 vs Rotherham United First Division (won 2-1)

THE MUSEUM THAT SCORES

England's National Football Museum is located at Deepdale, the home of Preston North End FC. Thousands of visitors have enjoyed their pilgrimage to the NFM since it opened its doors for the first time in February 2001. So, don't miss out – make sure you incorporate football's number one museum into your itinerary if you are visiting the north-west of England.

The ambitious idea of a national football museum was devised by Ben Casey, a long time Preston North End supporter and Bryan Gray (who was then North End's chairman). Thus it is not a surprise that the £12 million project is based at the home of the club who won the first two Football League Championships. The Invincibles, as they were known, won the 'Double' in that historic initial 1888-89 League campaign. The museum is housed under two of Deepdale's stands – the Bill Shankly Kop and the Sir Tom Finney Stand. There are plans to extend the project to all four sides after the ground is completely redeveloped in a few years time.

The NFM is split into two halves. The first half tells the story of the game's development from its early origins to the present day. The second half includes an art gallery and also an interactive area where it's possible to take an active part in finding out more about football.

There is a lot on offer, with good use made of TV footage and audio clips. The displays are generally bright and well presented, and there is certainly no hint of the stuffiness associated with some other museums. The great achievements of the bigger clubs are naturally well covered, but the whole project is extremely well balanced with many aspects of the game lower down the Leagues given excellent coverage.

The museum aims to both entertain and inform – with so many artefacts on display, and so much information being fired around, it was impossible not to come away enlightened.

Around 1,000 exhibits are displayed (on a rotation basis from a store of around 20,000) and on match-days special fact-sheets pertinent to the away club are provided to visitors free of charge.

The National Football Museum has its own cafe and is completed by the obligatory souvenir shop. You should allow at least two hours to do the museum adequate justice, so if you are combining it with a North End game make sure you budget sufficient time. It is well worth the visit and value-for-money at less than £7 per head.

Location: Deepdale Stadium, Sir Tom Finney Way, Preston, Lancashire.

There is a regular bus service from the town centre to Deepdale. The National Football Museum is approximately 30 minutes walk from the railway station via Fishergate, Church Street and Deepdale Road.

OPENING TIMES

Tuesday – Saturday   10:00 – 17:00
Midweek matchdays   10:00 – 19:30
Sundays   11:00 – 17:00
Closed every Monday (except Bank Holidays)
Closed Christmas Day

ADMISSION CHARGES

Adults   £6.95
Children (ages 5-15)   £4.95
Children (under-5)   Free of charge
Groups of 10 people of more receive a 20% discount.

Note: On match days only – if you show your match-ticket you are eligible for discounted admission to the museum.

For more information telephone the NFM at: 017772 908442

or E-mail them at: enquiries@nationalfootballmuseum.com

PRESTON NORTH END – 1977-78 TO 2001-02

THE 25 MEN WHO HAVE APPEARED MOST FREQUENTLY

LEAGUE APPEARANCES 1977-1978 TO 2001-2002

25 SEASONS TOTAL

1	Lee Cartwright	363
2	Ryan Kidd	259
3	Andy McAteer	251
4	Alex Bruce	215
5	Mark Rankine	214
6	Sean Gregan	212
7	Steve Elliott	208
8	Bob Atkins	200
9	Gary Swann	199
10	Roy Tunks	194
11	Jonathan Macken	184
12	Gordon Coleman	181
13	Michael Jackson	180
14	Warren Joyce	177
15=	Gary Brazil	166
15=	Jeff Wrightson	166
17	Willie Naughton	162
18	Mick Baxter	161
19=	Tony Ellis	158
19=	Don O'Riordan	158
21=	Lee Ashcroft	155
22	Colin Murdock	153
23	Paul McKenna	152
24	Ian Bryson	151
25=	Graham Bell	143
25=	Tepi Moilanen	143
25=	David Moyes	143

EVER-PRESENTS (15)

3 campaigns: Roy Tunks

2 campaigns: Gary Swann*

1 campaign: Graham Alexander, Mick Baxter, Alex Bruce, Steve Elliott, Mike Elwiss, Andy Fensome, Michael Jackson, Alex Jones, Don O'Riordan and Graham Shaw*

* includes one game as substitute

THE 25 LEADING GOALSCORERS

LEAGUE GOALS 1977-1978 TO 2001-2002

25 SEASONS TOTAL

1	Alex Bruce	96
2	Tony Ellis	74
3	Steve Elliott	70
4	Jonathan Macken	63
5	Gary Brazil	58
6	John Thomas	44
7	Gary Swann	37
8	Lee Ashcroft	35
9	Warren Joyce	34
10	Andy Saville	30
11	Graham Shaw	29
12	John Kelly	27
13	Kurt Nogan	23
14=	Lee Cartwright	22
14=	Mike Conroy	22
16	Simon Davey	21
17	Brian Mooney	20
18=	Ian Bryson	19
18=	David Eyres	19
18=	David Healy	19
18=	Darren Patterson	19
22=	Gordon Coleman	18

22=	Nigel Greenwood	18
24=	Graham Alexander	17
24=	Ricky Thomson	17

SEASON-BY-SEASON: LEADING GOALSCORERS

1977-1978	27 – Alex Bruce
1978-1979	21 – Alex Bruce
1979-1980	16 – Steve Elliott
1980-1981	13 – Alex Bruce
1981-1982	18 – Alex Bruce
1982-1983	19 – Steve Elliott
1983-1984	16 – Steve Elliott
1984-1985	7 – John Kelly
1985-1986	17 – John Thomas
1986-1987	21 – John Thomas
1987-1988	14 – Gary Brazil
1988-1989	19 – Tony Ellis
1989-1990	11 – Warren Joyce
1990-1991	10 – Graham Shaw
1991-1992	14 – Graham Shaw
1992-1993	22 – Tony Ellis
1993-1994	26 – Tony Ellis
1994-1995	10 – Mike Conroy
1995-1996	29 – Andy Saville
1996-1997	11 – David Reeves
1997-1998	14 – Lee Ashcroft
1998-1999	18 – Kurt Nogan
1999-2000	22 – Jonathan Macken
2000-2001	19 – Jonathan Macken
2001-2002	13 – Richard Cresswell

LEADING SCORERS (15 DIFFERENT MEN)

4 campaigns: Alex Bruce

3 campaigns: Steve Elliott, Tony Ellis
2 campaigns: Jonathan Macken, Graham Shaw, John Thomas
1 campaign: Lee Ashcroft, Gary Brazil, Mike Conroy, Richard Cresswell, Warren Joyce, John Kelly, Kurt Nogan, David Reeves and Andy Saville

INDIVIDUAL MATCH SCORING FEATS

FOUR GOALS IN A MATCH

The only Preston player to net four times in a League game during the 25 seasons up to the summer of 2002 was Alex Bruce. The little Scot achieved this feat in a Third Division fixture in 1977-78.

Alex Bruce
vs Colchester United (H) 28th February 1978

OTHER HAT-TRICKS (15 IN TOTAL)

Fifteen other hat-tricks were bagged by players wearing Preston colours in League football during the quarter of a century since the summer of 1977. Three were registered by Tony Ellis, while Steve Elliott and Andy Saville hit two. Eight other men were hat-trick heroes on one occasion.

Tony Ellis (3 hat-tricks)
vs Blackpool (A) 10th October 1992
vs Rotherham United (A) 27th March 1983
vs Chesterfield (H) 9th October 1993

Steve Elliott (2 hat-tricks)
vs Millwall (H) 28th August 1982
vs Scunthorpe United (A) 27th December 1983

Andy Saville (2 hat-tricks)
vs Mansfield Town (H) 21st October 1995
vs Leyton Orient (H) 4th November 1995

John Thomas (1 hat-trick)   vs Halifax Town (H) 16th September 1986

Gary Brazil (1 hat-trick)   vs Gillingham (H) 25th October 1988

Brian Mooney (1 hat-trick)   vs Chester City (H) 23rd September 1989

Steve Harper (1 hat-trick)   vs Cardiff City (H) 24th February 1990

Mike Conroy (1 hat-trick)   vs Shrewsbury Town (H) 28th August 1993

Steve Wilkinson (1 hat-trick)   vs Mansfield Town (H) 21st October 1995

Lee Ashcroft (1 hat-trick)   vs Fulham (H) 29th November 1997

David Healy (1 hat-trick)   vs Stockport County (H) 3rd November 2001

SEASON-BY-SEASON GOALS AND AVERAGE SCORING RATES

	Games	Scored		Conceded	
		Goals	Average	Goals	Average
1977-1978	46	63	1.37	38	0.83
1978-1979	42	59	1.40	57	1.36
1979-1980	42	56	1.33	52	1.24
1980-1981	42	41	0.98	62	1.48
1981-1982	46	50	1.09	56	1.22
1982-1983	46	60	1.30	69	1.50
1983-1984	46	66	1.43	66	1.43
1984-1985	46	51	1.11	100	2.17
1985-1986	46	54	1.17	89	1.93
1986-1987	46	72	1.57	47	1.02
1987-1988	46	48	1.04	59	1.28
1988-1989	46	79	1.72	60	1.30
1989-1990	46	65	1.41	79	1.72
1990-1991	46	54	1.17	67	1.46
1991-1992	46	61	1.33	72	1.56

1992-1993	46	65	1.41	94	2.04
1993-1994	42	79	1.88	60	1.43
1994-1995	42	58	1.38	41	0.98
1995-1996	46	78	1.70	38	0.83
1996-1997	46	49	1.07	55	1.20
1997-1998	46	56	1.22	56	1.22
1998-1999	46	78	1.69	50	1.09
1999-2000	46	74	1.61	37	0.80
2000-2001	46	64	1.39	52	1.13
2001-2002	46	71	1.54	59	1.28

LEAGUE ATTENDANCES AT DEEPDALE

The largest crowd for a League game at Deepdale during the quarter of a century up to the summer of 2002 was the 21,014 who watched Manchester City's visit in 2001-02. Both Blackpool and Burnley attracted the largest crowds in four of the 25 seasons. The lowest gate was registered in 1985-86, when only 2,007 witnessed Scunthorpe United's visit.

The highest average Deepdale gate over a season, during the 25 seasons up to the summer of 2002, was the 18,883 recorded in 2001-02. The lowest average was recorded as 3,502 in 1985-86.

Season	Average	Highest	Lowest
1977-1978	8,799	16,078 vs Shrewsbury T	5,319 vs Cambridge United
1978-1979	12,117	17,820 vs Wrexham	8,500 vs Charlton Athletic
1979-1980	9,751	13,069 vs Chelsea	7,407 vs Notts County
1980-1981	7,631	18,970 vs Swansea City	4,746 vs Wrexham
1981-1982	5,496	7,527 vs Burnley	4,162 vs Brentford
1982-1983	4,941	7,565 vs Wigan A	3,363 vs Wrexham
1983-1984	4,571	8,745 vs Burnley	3,144 vs Orient
1984-1985	3,749	5,478 vs Bolton W	2,653 vs Cambridge United
1985-1986	3,502	5,585 vs Burnley	2,007 vs Scunthorpe United
1986-1987	8,079	16,456 vs Northampton T	4,362 vs Swansea City
1987-1988	6,194	11,155 vs Blackpool	4,192 vs Fulham

1988-1989	7,737	14,126 vs Wolves	4,963 vs Cardiff City
1989-1990	6,313	9,135 vs Bolton W	4,480 vs Leyton Orient
1990-1991	5,214	9,844 vs Bolton W	3,245 vs Mansfield Town
1991-1992	4,722	7,738 vs Birmingham C	2,932 vs Hull City
1992-1993	5,689	10,403 vs Blackpool	3,329 vs Reading
1993-1994	7,377	12,790 vs Chester City	4,941 vs Shrewsbury Town
1994-1995	8,469	11,867 vs Carlisle U	6,377 vs Colchester United
1995-1996	10,012	18,700 vs Exeter City	6,837 vs Wigan Athletic
1996-1997	9,411	14,626 vs Blackpool	7,004 vs Luton Town
1997-1998	9,460	13,500 vs Blackpool	6,992 vs Luton Town
1998-1999	11,926	20,857 vs Manchester C	8,656 vs York City
1999-2000	12,589	19,407 vs Millwall	8,506 vs Chesterfield
2000-2001	14,617	17,355 vs Burnley	12,632 vs Crewe Alexandra
2001-2002	14,883	21,014 vs Manchester C	11,371 vs Millwall

1977-78

1	Aug	20	(a)	Plymouth Argyle	D	0-0		7,154
2		27	(h)	Rotherham U	W	3-2	Thomson, Doyle, Bruce	5,964
3	Sep	3	(a)	Oxford U	L	0-1		4,804
4		10	(a)	Carlisle U	L	1-3	Bruce	5,743
5		13	(h)	Swindon T	D	1-1	Robinson	6,014
6		17	(h)	Hereford U	D	0-0		5,447
7		24	(a)	Colchester U	D	0-0		4,978
8		27	(a)	Walsall	D	0-0		5,138
9	Oct	1	(h)	Cambridge U	W	2-0	Bruce, Baxter	5,319
10		4	(h)	Sheffield W	W	2-1	Elwiss, Cross	7,627
11		8	(a)	Bradford C	D	1-1	Smith	5,815
12		15	(h)	Gillingham	W	2-0	Elwiss, Smith	7,212
13		22	(a)	Exeter C	L	0-2		5,444
14		25	(h)	Tranmere R	W	2-1	Baxter, Elwiss	7,906
15		29	(h)	Chester	W	2-1	Bruce 2	7,550
16	Nov	5	(a)	Port Vale	D	0-0		4,208
17		12	(h)	Wrexham	L	1-3	Bruce	10,342
18		19	(a)	Lincoln C	D	2-2	Bruce 2	3,924
19	Dec	3	(h)	Portsmouth	W	3-1	Bruce, Elwiss, Smith	5,936
20		10	(a)	Shrewsbury T	D	0-0		3,764
21		26	(h)	Bury	W	4-0	Bruce 2 (1 pen), Elwiss, Coleman	10,297
22		27	(a)	Chesterfield	W	1-0	Bruce	6,484
23		31	(a)	Peterborough U	L	0-1		7,134
24	Jan	2	(h)	Port Vale	W	2-0	Thomson, Bruce	10,930
25		6	(a)	Tranmere R	L	0-1		7,250
26		14	(h)	Plymouth Argyle	W	5-2	Baxter, Bruce, Coleman, Thomson, Elwiss	6,500
27	Feb	4	(h)	Carlisle U	W	2-1	Bruce (2 pen)	9,095
28		11	(a)	Hereford U	D	0-0		4,791
29		21	(h)	Oxford U	W	3-2	Thomson 2, Bruce	6,189
30		25	(a)	Cambridge U	D	1-1	Thomson	5,766
31		28	(h)	Colchester U	W	4-0	Bruce 4 (2 pen)	9,225
32	Mar	4	(h)	Bradford C	W	3-1	McMahon, Elwiss 2	11,920
33		7	(a)	Swindon T	W	2-0	Baxter, Bruce	10,211
34		11	(a)	Gillingham	L	1-2	Coleman	9,568
35		18	(h)	Exeter C	D	0-0		9,189
36		24	(a)	Chester	W	2-1	Bruce, Elwiss	7,864
37		25	(h)	Chesterfield	D	0-0		10,922
38		27	(a)	Bury	D	1-1	Thomson	9,783
39	Apr	1	(h)	Peterborough U	L	0-1		9,695
40		4	(h)	Walsall	W	1-0	Paul (og)	11,239
41		8	(a)	Wrexham	D	0-0		19,008
42		15	(h)	Lincoln C	W	4-0	Robinson, Baxter, Bruce, Coleman	11,208
43		18	(a)	Sheffield W	L	0-1		12,426
44		22	(a)	Portsmouth	W	2-0	Bruce, Elwiss	6,866
45		25	(a)	Rotherham U	L	1-2	Bruce	6,646
46		29	(h)	Shrewsbury T	D	2-2	Elwiss, Bruce	16,078

FINAL LEAGUE POSITION: 3rd in Division Three

Appearances

Sub. Appearances

Goals

Tunks	McMahon	Wilson	Doyle	Baxter	Cross	Coleman	Brown	Thomson	Elwiss	Bruce	Burns	Cameron	Smith	Robinson	Haslegrave	Uzelac	Spavin	
1	2	3	4*	5	6	7	8	9	10	11	12							1
1	2	3	4	5	6		8	9	10	11	7							2
1		3	4	5	6	7		9*	10	11	8	2	12					3
1	2	3	4	5	6	7		9	10	11	8							4
1	2	3	4	5	6	7		9	10	11	8*		12					5
1	2	3	4	5	6	7		12	10	11	8*		9					6
1	2	3	4	5	6	7			10	11	8		9					7
1		3	4	5	6	7			10	11	8	2	9					8
1		3	4	5	6	7			10	11		2	9		8			9
1		3	4	5	6	7			10	11		2	9		8			10
1		3	4	5	6	7			10	11		2	9		8			11
1		3	4	5	6	7			10	11*		2	9	12	8			12
1		3	4	5	6	7		9*	10		12	2	11		8			13
1		3	4	5	6	7			10	11		2	9		8			14
1		3	4	5	6	7			10	11		2	9		8			15
1		3	4	5		7			10	11		2	9		8	6		16
1		3	4	5		7			10	11		2	9*		8	5	12	17
1		3*	4	5		7			10	11	6	2	9		8	12		18
1	2		4	5		7			10	11	6	3	9		8			19
1	2		4	5		7			10	11	6	3	9		8			20
1	2			5	6	7		9	10	11	4*	3			8	12		21
1	2			5	6	7		9	10	11	4	3			8			22
1	2			5	6	7		9	10	11	4	3			8			23
1	2			5	6	7		9	10	11	4	3			8			24
1	2			5	6	7		9	10	11	4	3			8			25
1	2	12		5	6*	7		9	10	11	4	3			8			26
1	2			5	6	7		9	10	11	4	3			8			27
1		7		5	6	2		9	10	11	4	3			8			28
1		7		5	6	2		9	10	11	4	3			8			29
1		4		5	6	2		9	10	11	7	3			8			30
1		7		5	6	2		9	10	11	4	3			8			31
1	2			5	6	7		9	10	11	4	3			8			32
1	2			5	6	7		9	10	11	4	3			8			33
1	2			5	6	7		9	10	11	4	3			8			34
1	2			5	6	7		9*	10	11	4	3			8	12		35
1	2			5	6	7		9	10	11	4	3			8			36
1	2	12		5*	6	7		9	10	11	4	3			8			37
1	2	5			6			9	10	11	4	3			8		7	38
1	2*	12		5	6	7		9	10	11	4	3			8			39
1	2			5	6	7			10	11	4	3		9	8			40
1	2			5	6	7			10	11	4	3		9	8			41
1	2	12		5	6	7			10	11	4*	3		9	8			42
1	2*	12		5	6	7			10	11	4	3		9	8			43
1	2			5	6	7			10	11	4	3		9	8			44
1	2	12		5	6*	7			10	11	4	3		9	8			45
1	2	12		5	6	7			10	11	4	3		9*	8			46
46	30	18	25	45	40	45	2	25	46	45	36	40	14	8	38	2	1	
		7						1			2		1	2		1		
	1		1	5	1	4		7	11	27			3	2				

1978-79

1	Aug	19	(a)	Cardiff C	D	2-2	Bruce 2	7,812
2		22	(h)	Blackburn R	W	4-1	Robinson, Doyle, Bruce 2	15,412
3		26	(h)	Sheffield U	D	2-2	Robinson 2	13,208
4	Sep	2	(a)	Sunderland	L	1-3	Robinson	16,819
5		9	(h)	Millwall	D	0-0		8,926
6		16	(a)	Oldham Ath	L	0-2		9,766
7		23	(h)	Stoke C	L	0-1		14,057
8		30	(a)	Brighton & HA	L	1-5	Cochrane	19,217
9	Oct	7	(a)	Cambridge U	L	0-1		5,398
10		14	(h)	Crystal Palace	L	2-3	Haslegrave, Thomson	10,795
11		21	(a)	Fulham	L	3-5	Bruce, Baxter, Coleman	8,719
12		28	(h)	Burnley	D	2-2	Thomson, Bruce	15,014
13	Nov	4	(a)	West Ham U	L	1-3	Thomson	23,579
14		11	(h)	Cardiff C	W	2-1	Robinson 2	9,268
15		18	(a)	Sheffield U	W	1-0	Bruce	14,807
16		21	(h)	Sunderland	W	3-1	Thomson, Robinson, Bruce	13,204
17		25	(a)	Orient	L	0-2		4,702
18	Dec	9	(a)	Luton T	W	2-1	Robinson (pen), Baxter	7,036
19		12	(h)	Charlton Ath	W	6-1	Coleman, Potts 2, Bruce 2, Robinson	8,500
20		16	(h)	Notts Co	D	1-1	Baxter	10,728
21		23	(a)	Leicester C	D	1-1	Bruce	10,481
22		26	(h)	Wrexham	W	2-1	Bruce, Jones (og)	17,820
23		30	(h)	Bristol R	D	1-1	Bruce	12,660
24	Feb	10	(h)	Brighton & HA	W	1-0	Bruce	11,649
25		24	(a)	Crystal Palace	D	0-0		17,592
26		28	(a)	Stoke C	D	1-1	Bruce	18,177
27	Mar	3	(h)	Fulham	D	2-2	Bruce, Potts	10,890
28		10	(a)	Burnley	D	1-1	Bruce	15,175
29		17	(h)	West Ham U	D	0-0		15,376
30		20	(h)	Oldham Ath	D	1-1	Coleman	12,535
31		24	(a)	Blackburn R	W	1-0	Bruce	17,790
32		31	(h)	Orient	D	1-1	Coleman	9,494
33	Apr	4	(a)	Newcastle U	L	3-4	Robinson 2, Bruce	12,157
34		7	(a)	Charlton Ath	D	1-1	Coleman	5,836
35		14	(a)	Wrexham	L	1-2	Robinson	13,419
36		16	(h)	Newcastle U	D	0-0		12,960
37		17	(h)	Leicester C	W	4-0	Robinson, Bruce 2, Coleman	10,394
38		21	(a)	Notts Co	D	0-0		7,009
39		24	(h)	Cambridge U	L	0-2		10,136
40		28	(h)	Luton T	D	2-2	Doyle, Coleman	8,927
41	May	5	(a)	Bristol R	W	1-0	Baxter	5,814
42		22	(a)	Millwall	W	2-0	Bell, Potts	2,833

FINAL LEAGUE POSITION: 7th in Division Two

Appearances

Sub. Appearances

Goals

Tunks	McMahon	Cameron	Doyle	Baxter	Cross	Burns	Haslegrave	Thomson	Robinson	Bruce	Wilson	Smith	Spavin	Potts	Coleman	Cochrane	Uzalac	O'Riordan	Taylor	Elliott	Bell	No.
1	2	3	4	5	6	7	8	9	10	11												1
1		2*	4	5	6	7	8	9	10	11	3	12										2
1			4	5	6	7	2	9*	10	11	3		8	12								3
1			4	5	6	7	2	9	10	11	3		8*	12								4
1	2		6	5		4	8	10*	9	11	3	12		7								5
1	2		4	5		7	8	9	10*	11	3	12			6							6
1	2*		4	5		6	8			11	3	10		7	9	12						7
1		2*		5	6	4	8	9		11	3			10	7	12						8
1			4	5		10*	8	12		11	3			7	2	9	6					9
1	2	3	4	5			8	10	9	11					7			6				10
1	2	3	4	5			8	10	9	11					7			6*	12			11
1	2	3	4	5			8	10	9	11					7			6				12
1	2	3	4	5			8	10	9	11					7			6				13
1		3		5		4	8	10	9	11					7			6	2			14
1		3	12	5		4	8*	10	9	11					7			6	2			15
1		3	12	5		4	8	10*	9	11					7			6	2			16
1		3	4	5		10	8		9	11	12				7			6	2*			17
1		3		5		4	8		9	11				10	7			6	2			18
1		3		5		4	8*		9	11	12			10	7			6	2			19
1		3		5		4	8		9	11				10	7			6	2			20
1		3		5		4	8		9	11				10	7			6	2			21
1		3		5		4	8		9	11				10	7			6	2			22
1		3		5		4	8		9	11				10	7			6	2			23
1		3		5		4	8		9	11				10	7			6	2			24
1		3	12	5		4*	8		9	11				10	7			6	2			25
1		3	4	5			8		9	11				10	7			6	2			26
1		3	4	5			8		9	11				10	7			6	2			27
1		3	4	5			8		9	11				10	7			6	2			28
1		3	4*	5			8			11	12			10	7			6	2	9		29
1		3	4	5			8			11	12			10	7			6	2*	9		30
1		3	8	5						11				10	7			6	2	9	4	31
1		3	4*	5			8	12		11				10	9	7		6	2			32
1		3		5			8	12	9	11				10*	7			6	2		4	33
1		3		5			8		9	11				10	7			6	4		2	34
1		3		5			8		9	11*				10	7			6	2	12	4	35
1		3	12				8		9					10*	7		5	6	2	11	4	36
1		3	4				8		9	11					7		5	6	2		10	37
1		3	4				8		9*	11				12	7		5	6	2		10	38
1		3	4				8*		9	11				12	7		5	6	2		10	39
1		3	10				8*		9	11					7		5	6	2		4	40
1		3	4	5			8		9	11				10	7			6	2*	12		41
1		3		5			8	12	9					10*	7		6		2	11	4	42
42	8	36	25	37	5	21	41	13	36	40	8	1	2	25	37	2	7	32	29	5	10	
			4					4			4	3		4		2			1	2		
			2	4		1	4	13	21					4	7	1				1		

1979-80

1	Aug	18	(a)	Charlton Ath	W	3-0	Elliott, Bell, Thomson	6,148
2		21	(h)	Newcastle U	W	1-0	Potts	12,707
3		25	(h)	Swansea C	D	1-1	Bartley (og)	12,116
4	Sep	1	(a)	Fulham	L	0-1		7,922
5		8	(h)	West Ham U	D	1-1	Coleman	10,460
6		15	(a)	Oldham Ath	L	2-3	Thomson 2	9,849
7		22	(h)	Bristol R	W	3-2	Bruce 2, Elliott	7,555
8		29	(a)	Sunderland	D	1-1	Elliott	24,594
9	Oct	6	(h)	Birmingham C	D	0-0		10,740
10		10	(a)	Newcastle U	D	0-0		24,985
11		13	(a)	Q.P.R.	D	1-1	Thomson	14,316
12		20	(h)	Burnley	W	3-2	Bruce, Thomson 2	12,300
13		27	(a)	Luton T	D	1-1	Elliott	11,648
14	Nov	3	(h)	Charlton Ath	D	1-1	Elliott	9,950
15		10	(a)	Notts Co	L	1-2	Bruce	8,602
16		17	(h)	Leicester C	D	1-1	Bruce	10,038
17		24	(h)	Orient	D	2-2	Bruce, Elliott	7,835
18	Dec	1	(a)	Chelsea	L	0-2		21,192
19		8	(h)	Cambridge U	D	2-2	Bruce, Elliott	7,585
20		15	(a)	Cardiff C	W	2-0	Bruce 2	6,419
21		21	(h)	Watford	L	1-2	Elliott (pen)	8,956
22		26	(h)	Shrewsbury T	W	3-0	Elliott, Bruce, Bell	8,875
23		29	(a)	Swansea C	L	0-1		11,401
24	Jan	1	(a)	Wrexham	L	0-2		14,738
25		12	(h)	Fulham	W	3-2	Elliott 2 (1 pen), McGee	7,912
26		19	(a)	West Ham U	L	0-2		17,603
27	Feb	2	(h)	Oldham Ath	L	0-1		8,932
28		16	(h)	Sunderland	W	2-1	Hindmarch (og), Coleman	12,165
29		23	(h)	Q.P.R.	L	0-3	.	10,350
30	Mar	1	(a)	Burnley	D	1-1	McGee	10,843
31		8	(h)	Luton T	D	1-1	McGee	7,862
32		11	(a)	Bristol R	D	3-3	Baxter, McGee, Aitken (og)	6,022
33		15	(a)	Birmingham C	D	2-2	Elliott, McGee	19,548
34		22	(h)	Notts Co	W	2-0	McGee, Taylor	7,407
35		29	(a)	Leicester C	W	2-1	Elwiss 2	15,293
36	Apr	1	(a)	Shrewsbury T	W	3-1	Keay (og), Elliott 2	8,643
37		5	(h)	Wrexham	D	0-0		9,430
38		9	(a)	Watford	D	0-0		11,967
39		12	(h)	Chelsea	D	1-1	Baxter	13,069
40		19	(a)	Orient	D	2-2	McGee, Elliott	4,509
41		26	(h)	Cardiff C	W	2-0	McGee, Coleman	7,481
42	May	3	(a)	Cambridge U	L	2-3	Elliott, Elwiss	5,395

FINAL LEAGUE POSITION: 10th in Division Two

Appearances

Sub. Appearances

Goals

Tunks	Taylor	Wilson	Bell	Baxter	Blackley	Elliott	Haslegrave	Thomson	Doyle	Potts	Coleman	Cameron	O'Riordan	Bruce	Burns	McGee	McAteer	Naughton	Anderson	Houston	Elwiss	No.
1	2	3	4	5	6	7	8	9	10	11												1
1	2	3	7	5	6	9		11*	4	10	12											2
1	2	3	7	5	6	9		11	4	10	8											3
1		3	7	5	6*	9	8	11	4	10	12	2										4
1	2			5		9	8	11	4	10	7	3	6									5
1	2			5		9	8	11	4	10*	7	3	6	12								6
1	2		12	5	6	9	8			10	4*	3		11	7							7
1	2		7	5	6	9	8	12		10*		3		11	4							8
1	2		7	5	6	9	8			10		3		11	4							9
1	2		7	5	6	9	8			10		3		11	4							10
1	2		7	5	6	9	8			10		3		11	4							11
1	2		7	5	6	9*	8			10	12	3		11	4							12
1	2		7	5	6	9	8			10		3*		11	4	12						13
1	2	3	7	5	6	9	8			10				11	4							14
1	2	3	7	5	6	9	8			10				11	4							15
1	2	3*	7	5		9	8			12			6	11	4	10						16
1	2	3	7	5		9	8			10			6	11	4							17
1	2	3	7	5		9	8			12			6	11	4*	10						18
1	2	3	7	5		9	8			12			6	11	4	10*						19
1	2	3	7	5		9	8			10			6	11	4							20
1	2	3	7	5		9	8			10			6	11	4*	12						21
1	2		7	5		9				10	8		6	11	4		3					22
1	2		7	5		9	12			10*	8		6	11	4		3					23
1	2		7	5		9	8		4		11		6			10*	3	12				24
1	2		7			9	8		4				6	11		10	3		5			25
1	2		7			9	8		4		12		6	11		10*	3		5			26
1	2		7			9	8		4		12		6	11		10*	3		5			27
1	2		7		6	9			4		8	12		11		10*	3		5			28
1	2*		7		6	9			4		8			11		10	3	12	5			29
1			4	5	6	9	8			10	7	2				11	3					30
1	12		7	5	6	9			4*	10	8	2				11	3					31
1	2		7	5	6*	9				10	8		12		4	11	3				12	32
1	2		7	5	6	9				10*	8		6		4	11	3				12	33
1	2		7	5	6	9				10*	8				4	11	3				12	34
1	2		7*	5	6	9				12	8				4	11	3				10	35
1	2			5	6	9				7	8				4	11	3				10	36
1	2*			5	6	9				7	8		12		4	11	3				10	37
1				5	6	9				7	8	2			4	11	3				10	38
1				5	6	9				7	8	2	4			11	3				10	39
1			7	5	6*	9					8	2	12		4	11	3				10	40
1			7	5	6	9					8	2			4	11	3				10	41
1			7	5	6	9					8	2	12		4	11*	3				10	42
42	34	12	35	37	27	42	24	11	14	22	24	17	16	22	27	20	21	2	5		8	
	1		1				1	1		3	6		2	4		2		1		1	2	
	1		2	2		16		6		1	3			10		8					3	

101

1980-81

#	Month	Date		Opponent	Result		Scorers	Attendance
1	Aug	16	(h)	Bristol C	D	1-1	Elliott	6,058
2		19	(a)	Grimsby T	D	0-0		10,461
3		23	(h)	West Ham U	D	0-0		9,063
4		30	(a)	Sheffield W	L	0-3		16,724
5	Sep	6	(h)	Cambridge U	W	2-0	McGee 2	5,516
6		13	(a)	Watford	L	1-2	Coleman	11,275
7		20	(a)	Chelsea	D	1-1	Elliott	13,755
8		27	(h)	Shrewsbury T	D	0-0		6,309
9	Oct	4	(a)	Orient	L	0-4		4,295
10		7	(h)	Newcastle U	L	2-3	Coleman, Bruce	5,301
11		11	(h)	Luton T	W	1-0	Elliott	5,620
12		18	(a)	Wrexham	W	1-0	Bruce	5,775
13		21	(a)	Bolton W	L	1-2	Bruce	10,713
14		25	(h)	Bristol C	D	0-0		5,807
15	Nov	1	(a)	Oldham Ath	D	1-1	Bruce	6,739
16		8	(h)	Cardiff C	W	3-1	Baxter, Bruce, Stevens (og)	5,458
17		15	(a)	Bristol C	D	0-0		8,042
18		22	(h)	Q.P.R.	W	3-2	Naughton 2, Baxter	6,725
19		28	(a)	Swansea C	L	0-3		9,115
20	Dec	2	(h)	Grimsby T	L	2-4	Elliott (pen), Baxter	5,289
21		6	(h)	Derby Co	L	0-3		6,118
22		13	(a)	Luton T	L	2-4	Elliott, Bruce	7,874
23		20	(h)	Wrexham	D	1-1	Elliott	4,746
24		26	(a)	Blackburn R	D	0-0		17,726
25		27	(h)	Notts Co	D	2-2	Baxter, Elliott (pen)	6,547
26	Jan	10	(a)	Q.P.R.	D	1-1	Bell	8,415
27		31	(a)	West Ham U	L	0-5		26,413
28	Feb	7	(h)	Watford U	W	2-1	McGee, Coleman	5,107
29		14	(a)	Cambridge U	L	0-1		4,228
30		21	(a)	Shrewsbury T	L	0-3		4,660
31		28	(h)	Chelsea	W	1-0	Bruce	8,129
32	Mar	7	(h)	Orient	W	3-0	Taylor (og), Doyle, McGee	5,448
33		14	(a)	Newcastle U	L	0-2		11,946
34		24	(h)	Bolton W	L	1-2	Bruce	8,505
35		28	(a)	Bristol R	L	0-2		4,427
36	Apr	4	(h)	Oldham Ath	L	1-2	Bruce	6,154
37		11	(a)	Cardiff C	W	3-1	Haslegrave, Bruce, Elliott	4,991
38		14	(h)	Sheffield W	W	2-1	Elliott, Houston	9,537
39		18	(a)	Notts Co	D	0-0		8,485
40		21	(h)	Blackburn R	D	0-0		18,742
41	May	2	(h)	Swansea C	L	1-3	Bruce	18,970
42		6	(a)	Derby Co	W	2-1	Bruce 2	15,050

FINAL LEAGUE POSITION: 20th in Division Two

Appearances

Sub. Appearances

Goals

Tunks	Taylor	Carmeron	Burns	Baxter	Blackley	Bell	Coleman	Elliott	Potts	McGee	Doyle	McAteer	Bruce	Sayer	O'Riordan	Houston	Westwell	Haslegrave	Naughton	Anderson	Litchfield	
1	2	3	4	5	6	7	8	9	10	11												1
1	2*	3	4	5	6	7	8	9	10	11	12											2
1		2	4	5	6*	7	8	9	10	11	12	3										3
1		2	4*	5	6	7	8			11	12	3	9	10								4
1		2	4	5		7	8			9		3	11		6	10						5
1		2	4	5		7	8	12		9		3	11	10*	6							6
1		3		5		7	8	10		9	4				6	11	2					7
1				5		7	8	12		9	4	3	10		6	11	2*					8
1	2			5	12		8	10		9	4	3	7		6	11*						9
1	2	3	4	5			8	9		12	7		10		6	11*						10
1		3	4	5	6		8	9		11	7		10		2							11
1		3	4	5	6		8	9		11	7		10		2							12
1			4	5	6	8		9		11	7	3	10		2							13
1	2		4	5	6		8	9		11	7*		10		3			12				14
1			4	5	6	7	8	9*		11		3	10		12		2					15
1	12		4	5		7	8			9		3	11		6		2		10*			16
1	12		4	5	6	7	8*	9		11		3	10				2					17
1	8		4	5	6	7		9		11		3					2		10			18
1	8	3	4	5	6	7		9		11			10				2					19
1	8	3	4	5	6*	7		9		11			10				2		12			20
1	4	3*		5		7		9		11	8		10	12			2			6		21
1	2		4	5		7		9		11*	8		10	12			3			6		22
1	2		4	5			8	9			7	3	10		6	11						23
1	2		4	5		7		9			8	3	10		6	11						24
1	2			5		4	7	9		12	8	3	10*		6	11						25
1				5		4	8	9		10	7	3			6	11	2					26
1				5		4	7	9		10*	8	3		12	6	11	2					27
1				5		4	8	9		10	7	3			6		2		11			28
1				5		4	8	9		10	7	3			6		2		11			29
1				5		4	8	9		10	7*	3	12		6		2		11			30
		3		5		4	8			10	7		12	9*			2		11	6	1	31
		3		5		4	8			10	7		9				2		11	6	1	32
		3		5		4	8	12		10	7		9*				2		11	6	1	33
1		3		5	12	4	8			10	7		9				2		11	6*		34
1				5	6	12	8	9		11	7	3	10			2*		4				35
1	2			5	6	8	3			9	7		11			10		4				36
1	2	3		5	6	8	7	9					11			10		4				37
1	2	3		5	6	8	7	9					11			10		4				38
1	2	3		5	6	8	7	9					11			10		4				39
1	2	3		5	6	8	7	9					11			10		4				40
1	2	3*		5	6	8	7	9					11			10		4		12		41
1	2			5	6	8	7	9					11		12	10*		4		3		42
39	20	13	29	42	21	34	36	32	3	32	24	20	29	5	19	17	20	8	9	7	3	
	2				2	1		3		2	3		2	3	2			1	1	1		
				4		1	3	9		4	1		13			1			1	2		

1981-82

1	Aug	29	(a)	Millwall	L 1-2	Walsh	4,549
2	Sep	5	(h)	Portsmouth	W 1-0	Bruce	6,112
3		12	(a)	Swindon T	L 0-4		5,695
4		19	(h)	Gillingham	D 1-1	Bruce (pen)	4,563
5		22	(h)	Huddersfield T	D 1-1	Naughton	6,483
6		26	(a)	Newport Co	D 1-1	Doyle	5,064
7		29	(a)	Doncaster R	L 0-1		7,513
8	Oct	3	(h)	Bristol R	L 0-1		4,964
9		10	(a)	Bristol C	D 0-0		5,389
10		17	(h)	Reading	D 0-0		5,671
11		20	(h)	Burnley	D 1-1	O'Riordan	7,527
12		24	(a)	Exeter C	L 3-4	Bruce 2 (1 pen), Doyle	3,642
13		31	(h)	Southend U	W 1-0	Pountney (og)	4,285
14	Nov	4	(a)	Lincoln C	W 2-1	Buckley, Elliott	3,587
15		7	(h)	Chester	L 0-1		5,181
16		14	(a)	Wimbledon	L 2-3	Dunn, Bruce	2,428
17		28	(a)	Oxford U	L 0-3		3,798
18	Dec	5	(h)	Brentford	L 1-3	Bruce	4,162
19	Jan	5	(a)	Chesterfield	D 0-0		3,964
20		16	(h)	Plymouth Argyle	W 1-0	Bruce	4,936
21		23	(h)	Millwall	W 1-0	Elliott (pen)	5,085
22		30	(a)	Gillingham	W 2-0	Naughton, Bruce	5,379
23	Feb	2	(a)	Carlisle U	L 0-1		5,044
24		6	(h)	Swindon T	D 0-0		5,606
25		9	(a)	Huddersfield T	W 3-2	Bruce 2, Elliott	6,674
26		13	(a)	Bristol R	L 0-2		5,003
27		20	(h)	Doncaster R	W 3-1	McGee, Bruce, Elliott (pen)	5,830
28		27	(h)	Bristol C	L 1-3	Kelly	6,411
29	Mar	6	(a)	Reading	L 1-2	Elliott	2,655
30		13	(h)	Exeter C	W 1-0	Elliott	4,770
31		16	(h)	Lincoln C	D 1-1	O'Riordan	4,879
32		19	(a)	Southend U	D 2-2	Elliott, Bruce	3,549
33		27	(a)	Chester	W 1-0	Elliott	2,842
34	Apr	3	(h)	Wimbledon	W 3-2	Bruce 2, O'Riordan	4,964
35		6	(a)	Portsmouth	D 1-1	O'Riordan	6,712
36		10	(h)	Carlisle U	D 0-1		7,802
37		13	(a)	Walsall	W 3-0	Elliott, Bruce 2	3,507
38		17	(a)	Brentford	D 0-0		5,627
39		20	(h)	Fulham	L 1-3	Buckley (pen)	6,009
40		24	(h)	Oxford U	D 2-2	Kelly, Doyle	5,516
41		27	(h)	Walsall	W 1-0	Kelly	4,930
42	May	1	(a)	Plymouth Argyle	W 3-0	Kelly, Bell, Elliott	3,319
43		4	(h)	Newport Co	W 2-1	Bruce, Kelly	4,972
44		8	(h)	Chesterfield	W 2-0	Naughton, Bruce	5,445
45		11	(a)	Burnley	L 0-2		13,871
46		15	(a)	Fulham	L 0-3		7,985

FINAL LEAGUE POSITION: 14th in Division Three

Appearances

Sub. Appearances

Goals

Litchfield	Taylor	Coleman	Clark	O'Riordan	Blackley	Walsh	Houston	Bruce	Doyle	Naughton	Elliott	Westwell	McGee	McAteer	Anderson	Bell	Farrelly	Booth	Kelly	Buckley	Dunn	Mullen	Sayer	Hodge	
1	2	3	4	5	6	7	8	9	10	11*	12														1
1		2	4	5	6	12	7*	10	8	11			3	9											2
1	2		4	5	6	12	7	10	8*	11			3	9											3
1		2	4	5		12	7	9		11	10*			3	6	8									4
1		2	4	5		7	8	9		11*				3	6	10	12								5
1		2	4	5		11	7	9	8					3	6	10									6
1		2	6	5		7*	12	9	8			11		3	4	10									7
1		2	4	5		12	7	9	8*			11		3	6	10									8
1		2	4	6				9						3	10*	12	5	7	8	11					9
1		2	4	6				9						3	10*	12	5	7	8	11					10
1	12	2	4	6				9	10					3			5	7	8	11*					11
1	8		4	6				9	10		2			3	12		5*		7	11					12
1		2	4	6				9	10					3	5	12		7*	8	11					13
1		2	4	6				9	10		8			3	12		5*		7	11					14
1	2*		4	6				9	10		8			3	5				12	7	11				15
1	2*		4	6				9	10	12	8			3	5				7	11					16
1	12	2	4				7	8*	10	11	9			3				5			6				17
1	2	8	4					9	6		10			3	7			5				11			18
	2		6					11	8	10	9			3	7*	4		5		12			1		19
	2		6					11	8	10	9			3	7	4		5					1		20
	2		6					11	8	10	9			3	7	4		5					1		21
	2		6					11	8	10	9			3	7*	4		5	12				1		22
			6				12	11	8	10	9		2	3	4*			5	7				1		23
			6				12	11	8	10	9		2*	3	4			5	7				1		24
	2		6					11	8	10	9			3	4			5	7				1		25
			6					11		10*	9		8	3	2	4		5	7	12			1		26
	2		6					11		10	9		8	3	5	4			7				1		27
	2*		6					11		10	9		8	3	12	4		5	7				1		28
			6					11		12	9		8	3	2	4		5*	7	10			1		29
			6					11			9		8	3	2	4		5	7	10			1		30
			6					11			9		8	3	2	4		5	7	10			1		31
			6				12	11	8	3	9			2	4*			5	7	10			1		32
			6					11	8	3	9		4	2				5	7	10			1		33
			6					11	8	4	9			3	2			5	7	10			1		34
			6				12	11	8	4	9			3	2*			5	7	10			1		35
			6				12	11	8	4	9			3	2			5	7	10*			1		36
			6					11	8	4	9			3	2			5	7	10			1		37
			6					11	8	4	9			3	2			5	7	10			1		38
			6				12	11	8	4	9			3	2			5*	7	10			1		39
			6				12	11	8	4	9	5		3	2				7	10*			1		40
			6				12	11	8	4	9*	5		3	2	10			7				1		41
			6					11	8	4	9	5			2	10			7				1		42
			6			4		11	8	3	9	5			2	10			7				1		43
			6					11	8	4	9	5		3	2	10			7				1		44
			6				12	11	8	4	9	5		3	2	10*			7				1		45
			6				12	11	8	4	9	5		3	2	10			7*				1		46
18	10	15	18	46	3	4	9	46	36	31	34	12	10	41	35	22	3	27	28	20	8	1	1	28	
	2					6	9			2	1				3		4		2	2					
			4			1		18	3	3	10		1		1				5	2					

105

1982-83

1	Aug	28	(h)	Millwall	W	3-2	Elliott 3 (1 pen)	4,483
2	Sep	4	(a)	Sheffield U	L	1-2	Kelly	14,527
3		7	(a)	Walsall	L	1-2	McAteer	2,060
4		11	(h)	Oxford U	L	1-2	Elliott	4,481
5		18	(a)	Exeter C	L	1-5	Elliott (pen)	2,310
6		25	(h)	Bristol R	D	2-2	Bell, Elliott	3,880
7		28	(h)	Wrexham	W	3-0	O'Riordan, Elliott 2	3,363
8	Oct	2	(a)	Reading	W	3-2	Elliott 2, Bruce	1,713
9		9	(a)	Gillingham	L	1-2	Bruce	4,390
10		16	(h)	Huddersfield T	D	0-0		5,570
11		19	(h)	Newport Co	D	0-0		3,747
12		23	(a)	Portsmouth	L	1-3	Bruce	10,331
13		30	(h)	Bournemouth	L	0-1		3,589
14	Nov	2	(a)	Brentford	L	1-3	Elliott	6,142
15		6	(a)	Cardiff C	L	1-3	O'Riordan	5,546
16		13	(h)	Chesterfield	D	1-1	Houston	3,574
17		27	(h)	Plymouth Argyle	D	2-2	McAteer, Elliott	3,633
18	Dec	3	(a)	Southend U	W	3-2	Elliott, Houston, Walsh	3,749
19		17	(a)	Orient	L	1-2	Coleman	1,668
20		27	(h)	Bradford C	D	0-0		7,238
21		28	(a)	Doncaster R	L	0-2		3,895
22	Jan	1	(h)	Wigan Ath	W	4-1	Bruce 2, McAteer, Kelly (pen)	7,565
23		3	(a)	Lincoln C	L	0-3		5,891
24		15	(a)	Millwall	L	0-1		2,816
25		22	(h)	Exeter C	D	2-2	Elliott, Bruce	3,767
26		29	(a)	Oxford U	L	2-3	Gowling, Naughton	4,441
27	Feb	5	(a)	Wrexham	L	1-3	Bell	1,920
28		15	(a)	Newport Co	L	0-3		2,317
29		19	(h)	Gillingham	D	0-0		3,479
30		26	(a)	Huddersfield T	D	1-1	O'Riordan	8,562
31	Mar	1	(h)	Brentford	W	3-0	Elliott, Bell, Westwell	3,669
32		5	(h)	Portsmouth	D	0-0		5,610
33		12	(a)	Bournemouth	L	0-4		4,407
34		19	(h)	Cardiff C	W	2-1	Bruce, Elliott	4,608
35		26	(a)	Chesterfield	D	1-1	O'Riordan	2,332
36		29	(h)	Walsall	W	1-0	Sayer	4,013
37	Apr	2	(h)	Doncaster R	W	4-1	Hinnigan, McAteer, Elliott, Humphries (og)	5,287
38		4	(a)	Bradford C	W	2-1	Gowling, McAteer (pen)	4,357
39		8	(h)	Southend U	D	1-1	Bell	6,286
40		12	(h)	Sheffield U	W	1-0	Houston S (og)	6,296
41		16	(a)	Bristol R	L	2-3	Elliott, Hinnigan	5,189
42		23	(h)	Orient	W	2-1	Hinnigan, Sayer	5,628
43		30	(a)	Plymouth Argyle	D	1-1	Booth	2,912
44	May	2	(h)	Lincoln C	W	1-0	Gowling	6,537
45		7	(h)	Reading	W	2-0	Gowling, Elliott	7,253
46		14	(a)	Wigan Ath	W	1-0	Gowling	7,191

FINAL LEAGUE POSITION: 16th in Division Three

Appearances

Sub. Appearances

Goals

Litchfield	Walsh	McAteer	O'Riordan	Westwell	Coleman	Kelly	Bell	Elliott	Naughton	Bruce	Houston	Gowling	Buckley	Arnold (L)	Clark	Campbell	Sayer	Booth	Farrelly	Lodge	Hunter	Hodge(L)	Hinnigan	No.
1	2	3	4	5	6	7*	8	9	10	11	12													1
1	2	3	4	5		7	8	9	10	11*	12	6												2
1	2	3	4	5		7	8	9	10	11		6												3
1	2	3	4	5		7	8	9	10	12	11*	6												4
1	2	3	4	5*	12	7	8	9	10		11	6												5
1	2	3	4	5	12	7	8	9	10*		11	6												6
1	2	3	4	5		7	8	9	10		11	6												7
1	2	3		5	4	7	8	9	10	12	11*	6												8
1	2*	3		5	4	7	8	9	10	11		6	12											9
	2	3		5	4*	7	8	9	10	11		6	12	1										10
	2*	3		5		7	8	9	10	11		6	12	1	4									11
	2*	3		5		7	8	9	10	11		6	12	1	4									12
	2*	3	12	5		7	8	9	10	11		6		1	4									13
	5	3*	4	2		7	8	9		11	12	6	10	1										14
			4	2	5	7	8	9	3*	11	12	6	10	1										15
		3	4	2	5	7		9	12		11	6	10*			1	8							16
1	7	3	4	2	5			9	10		11	6					8							17
1	7	3	4	2	5			9	10		11	6					8							18
1	7	3	4	2	5			9	10*		11	6	12				8							19
1	7	3	4	2	5*		12	9	10		11	6					8							20
1	7	3	4	2		10	5	9		12	11	6					8*							21
1	7	3	4	5	2			9		10	11	6					8							22
1	7	3	4	5	2			9		10	11	6					8							23
1		3	2			7	9		10	8	11	4	6					5						24
1		3	4	2		7	11	9	10	8		6						5						25
1		3	4	2		7*	11	9	10	12		8	6					5						26
1		3	4	2		7*	11	9	10	8		5	6						12					27
1	7	3	4	5			11	9	10	8*							2	6	12					28
1	7*	3	4	5	12		11	9	10	8							2	6						29
1	7	3	4	5		12	11	9	10	8							2*	6						30
	7	3	4	5	2*		11	9	10	8	12							6				1		31
	7*	3	4	5	2		11	9	10	8	12							6				1		32
	7*	3	4	5	2	12	11	9	10	8								6				1		33
		3	4	5*			11	9	10	8	12						7			6		1	2	34
		3	4			12	11	9	10	8							7*	5		6		1	2	35
		3	4				11	9	10	8							7	5		6		1	2	36
		3	4				11	9	10	8							7	5		6		1	2	37
		3	4				11	9	10	8							7	5		6		1	2	38
		3	4				11	9	10	12		8					7*	5		6		1	2	39
			4				11	9	10	8							7	5	2	6		1	3	40
		3*	4			12	11	9	10			8					7	5		6		1	2	41
		3	4				11	9	10		12	8*					7	5		6		1	2	42
		3	4			12	11	9	10			8*					7	5		6		1	2	43
		3	4				11	9	10			8					7	5		6		1	2	44
		3	4				11	9	10			8					7	5		6		1	2	45
	5	3				12	8	10	11			9*					7	4		6		1	2	46
23	27	44	40	31	15	23	39	45	40	22	15	37	7	6	3	1	21	15	4	19	0	16	13	
			1		3	6	1		1	5	5	3	5							1	1			
	1	5	4	1	1	2	4	19	1	7	2	5					2	1					3	

1983-84

1	Aug	27	(a)	Bournemouth	W	1-0	Houston	4,163
2	Sep	3	(h)	Brentford	D	3-3	Kelly 2, Sayer	3,799
3		6	(h)	Southend U	W	4-1	Sayer, Kelly, Elliott 2	3,967
4		10	(a)	Sheffield U	D	1-1	Sayer	12,441
5		17	(h)	Hull C	D	0-0		6,661
6		24	(a)	Plymouth Argyle	L	0-1		3,674
7		27	(a)	Newport Co	D	1-1	Elliott (pen)	2,542
8	Oct	1	(h)	Oxford U	L	1-2	Sayer	4,665
9		8	(a)	Gillingham	L	0-2		3,725
10		15	(h)	Wigan Ath	L	2-3	Elliott (pen), Hinnigan	6,622
11		18	(h)	Wimbledon	L	2-3	Elliott 2	3,515
12		21	(a)	Millwall	L	0-1		5,243
13		29	(h)	Lincoln C	L	1-2	Clark	4,458
14	Nov	1	(a)	Bristol R	L	1-3	Farrelly	5,635
15		5	(a)	Burnley	L	1-2	Houghton	7,915
16		12	(h)	Rotherham U	W	1-0	Hinnigan	3,196
17		26	(h)	Exeter C	W	2-1	Kelly 2	3,373
18	Dec	3	(a)	Orient	L	1-2	D Jones	2,679
19		17	(a)	Bolton W	D	2-2	Houghton, Farnworth (og)	6,275
20		26	(h)	Port Vale	W	4-0	Houghton 2, Elliott, Kelly	5,599
21		27	(a)	Scunthorpe U	W	5-1	Elliott 3, Houghton, Kelly	3,986
22		31	(h)	Walsall	L	0-1		6,226
23	Jan	2	(a)	Bradford C	L	2-3	Naughton, Kelly	6,405
24		14	(h)	Bournemouth	W	2-0	Houghton, Clark (pen)	3,476
25		31	(h)	Sheffield U	D	2-2	Farrelly, Walsh	5,023
26	Feb	4	(a)	Oxford U	L	0-2		9,105
27		11	(h)	Plymouth Argyle	W	2-1	Twentyman, Naughton	4,370
28		14	(h)	Bristol R	W	1-0	Clark	3,813
29		18	(a)	Lincoln C	L	1-2	Naughton	2,780
30		25	(h)	Millwall	D	0-0		4,109
31	Mar	3	(a)	Wimbledon	D	2-2	Booth, Hinnigan	2,524
32		6	(h)	Burnley	W	4-2	Elliott, Kelly, Hinnigan, Houghton	8,745
33		10	(a)	Rotherham U	W	1-0	Hinnigan	3,256
34		17	(h)	Gillingham	D	2-2	Twentyman, Elliott	3,874
35		24	(a)	Wigan Ath	L	0-1		4,470
36		30	(h)	Newport Co	W	2-0	Elliott, Kelly	3,534
37	Apr	3	(a)	Brentford	L	1-4	Houston	3,446
38		6	(a)	Southend U	D	1-1	Kelly	1,826
39		10	(a)	Hull C	L	0-3		8,134
40		14	(h)	Orient	W	3-1	Houghton, Kelly, Houston	3,144
41		21	(a)	Port Vale	D	1-1	Houghton	3,574
42		24	(h)	Scunthorpe U	W	1-0	Elliott	3,403
43		28	(a)	Exeter C	L	1-2	Elliott	2,005
44	May	5	(h)	Bradford C	L	1-2	Clark (pen)	3,242
45		7	(a)	Walsall	L	1-2	Kelly	3,273
46		12	(h)	Bolton W	W	2-1	Clark, Elliott	5,077

FINAL LEAGUE POSITION: 16th in Division Three

Appearances

Sub. Appearances

Goals

Litchfield	Hinnigan	McAteer	Jones D	Booth	Lodge	Kelly	Sayer	Elliott	Naughton	Houston	Telfer	Bleasdale	Clark	Walsh	Farrelly	Twentyman	Houghton	Jones M	Murphy	Cameron	#
1	2	3	4	5	6	7	8	9	10	11											1
1	2	3*	4	5	6	7	8	9		11	12	10									2
1	2	3	4	5	6	7	8	9		11*	12	10									3
1		3	4	5	6	7	8	9	12	11*		10	2								4
1		3	4	5	6	7	8	9	12	11		10*	2								5
1	12	3	4*	5	6		8	9	10	11			2	7							6
1	3		4	5	6		8	9	10	11				7	2						7
1	2	3	4	5*	6		8		10	11	12			7		9					8
1	2	3	4		6		8	9	10*	12				7		5	11				9
1	2	3	4		6		8	9	10	12				7*		5	11				10
1		3		5	6			9	12	7			10	8*	2	4	11				11
1		3	4	5	6			9		7			10	8	2*	12	11				12
1	3		4	5	6			9	12	7			10	8	2	11*					13
1	3		4	5	6			9	11	7			10*	8	2	12					14
1	3		4	5	6	7		9	8				10		2		11				15
1	2	3	4	5	6	7		9	8*				10			12	11				16
1	2	3	4		6	7		9	8	12			10			5*	11				17
1	2	3	4	5		7		9	8*	12			10	6			11				18
1	2	3	4	5		7		9	10	12				8	6*		11				19
1	2	3	4	5		7		9	10					8	6		11				20
1	2	3*	4	5		7		9	10	12				8	6		11				21
1	3		4	5		7		9	10	12			2	8	6*		11				22
1	3		4	5		7		9	10				2	8	6		11				23
1	3		4	5*		7		9	10	12			2	8	6		11				24
1	3		4			7*		9	10	12			2	8	6	5	11				25
1	3		4			7		9	10	12			2	8*	6	5	11				26
1	3	12	4			7		9	10				2	8	6	5	11*				27
1	3	12	4			7		9	10	11			2	8*	6	5					28
1	2	3	4		12			9	10	11			6	8	7*	5					29
1	2	3		4				9	10	12			6	8*	7	5	11				30
1	2	3		4		8		9	10	12			6		7	5	11				31
1	2	3	4			7		9	10	12			6		8	5	11*				32
1	2	3	4			7		9	10	12			6		8*	5	11				33
1	2	3	4			7		9	10	12				6*	8	5	11				34
1	2	3	4	5		7		9	10	12				6	8		11*				35
1	2	3	4	5		7	11	9	10	12				6*	8						36
1	2	3	4			7	6*	9	10	11					8	5	12				37
1	2	3		5		7	6*	9	10	11					8	4	12				38
1	2	3	4		12	7		9	10	11				6*		5	8				39
1		3	4	5		7			10	12			6			9*	11	2	8		40
1	2	3	4*	5		7		9	12	11					6		10		8		41
	3*			5		7		9	12	11			6		2	4	10		8	1	42
1	3			5		7		9	12	11			6		2	4	10		8*		43
1	4					7	8	9		11			6		2	5	10	3			44
1		3				7	8*	9	10	11			6		4	5		2	12		45
1		3		5				9	10	11			6		7	4	8	2			46
45	38	32	37	31	17	34	15	44	35	23		4	31	25	31	25	30	4	4	1	
	1	2			2				7	18	2	1				3	2		1		
	5		1	1		13	4	16	3	3			5		2	2	10				

1984-85

1	Aug	25	(h)	Doncaster R	W	2-0	Houston, Wilkins	3,741
2	Sep	1	(a)	Bristol R	L	0-3		5,357
3		8	(h)	Derby Co	W	2-1	Houghton, Kelly	5,425
4		15	(a)	Hull C	W	2-1	Clark, D Jones	7,323
5		18	(a)	Cambridge U	W	3-0	Houston, Houghton, Wilkins	2,310
6		22	(h)	Rotherham U	L	0-3		3,063
7		29	(a)	Plymouth Argyle	L	4-6	Clarke 2, Kelly 2 (1 pen)	4,258
8	Oct	2	(h)	Orient	L	0-1		3,683
9		6	(a)	Lincoln C	L	0-4		1,906
10		13	(h)	Reading	L	0-2		3,656
11		20	(a)	Bolton W	L	0-4		5,691
12		23	(h)	Bradford C	L	1-4	Greenwood	3,588
13		27	(a)	Bournemouth	L	0-2		3,509
14	Nov	3	(h)	Burnley	D	3-3	Greenwood 2, Kelly	5,003
15		6	(h)	Swansea C	W	3-2	Clark, Greenwood, Houston	3,200
16		10	(a)	Millwall	L	0-3		5,680
17		24	(h)	Bristol	W	3-2	Houston, Jones, M Naughton	3,902
18	Dec	1	(a)	Gillingham	L	0-4		455
19		15	(h)	Brentford	D	1-1	Gibson	2,808
20		19	(h)	York C	L	2-4	Johnson (pen), Rudge	2,864
21		26	(a)	Walsall	L	1-2	Greenwood	5,856
22		29	(a)	Wigan Ath	L	0-2		4,503
23	Jan	1	(h)	Newport Co	D	1-1	Kelly	3,375
24		12	(h)	Bristol R	D	2-2	Johnson, Twentyman	3,136
25	Feb	2	(h)	Plymouth Argyle	L	1-2	Kelly	3,248
26		9	(a)	Rotherham U	L	0-3		3,645
27		23	(a)	Burnley	L	0-0		4,740
28		26	(h)	Cambridge U	W	3-1	Brazil, Clark, Farrelly	2,653
29	Mar	2	(h)	Bournemouth	W	2-1	Farrelly, Johnson	2,991
30		6	(a)	Bradford C	L	0-3		6,345
31		9	(h)	Bolton W	W	1-0	Gibson	5,478
32		13	(a)	Derby Co	L	0-2		8,248
33		16	(a)	Reading	L	0-3		3,053
34		23	(h)	Lincoln C	L	0-1		2,926
35		26	(a)	Doncaster R	W	2-1	Kelly, Rudge	2,684
36		30	(a)	Swansea C	L	1-4	Brazil	2,380
37	Apr	6	(h)	Walsall	W	1-0	Houghton	3,776
38		8	(a)	Newport Co	D	3-3	Houghton, McAteer, Twentyman	2,199
39		13	(h)	Millwall	W	2-1	Brazil, Houston	3,855
40		20	(a)	Bristol C	L	0-4		9,637
41		23	(h)	Hull C	L	1-4	Gibson	4,636
42		27	(h)	Gillingham	D	0-0		3,190
43		30	(a)	Orient	D	0-0		3,162
44	May	4	(a)	Brentford	L	1-3	Houghton	3,476
45		6	(h)	Wigan Ath	L	2-5	Houghton, McAteer (pen)	4,875
46		11	(a)	York C	W	1-0	Stevens	4,523

FINAL LEAGUE POSITION: 23rd in Division Three

Appearances

Sub. Appearances

Goals

Litchfield	Jones M	McAteer	Twentyman	Booth	Clark	Kelly	Rudge	Naughton	Houston	Houghton	Jones D	Farrelly	Murphy	Johnson	Gray	Welsh	Campbell	Gidson	Wealands	Atkins	Brazil	Platt	Stevens	Greenwood	Wilkins	
1	2	3	4	5	6	7	8	10*	11	12															9	1
1		3	4	5	12	7	8	10	11		2*	6													9	2
1	2		4	5	6	7	3	10	11	9		8														3
1	2		4	5	6		3	10	11	9		8	7													4
1	2*		4	5	6		3	10	11	9		8	7											12		5
1	2		4	5	6		3	10	11	9		8	7*											12		6
1	2		4	5	6	7	3	10	11	9		8														7
1	3		4	5	6	7	8	10	11	9	2*													12		8
1	2		4	5*		7	3		11	10		6	8											12	9	9
1	2		5			7	3	10	11*		4	6		9										8		10
1	2	3	5		7			10	11	8	4	6		9												11
1	2	3	5		6	7		10	12		4	8		9*										11		12
1	2	3	5		6	7		10	11	12	4													8		13
1	2	3	5		6	7		10	11		4				8									9		14
1	2	3*	5	4	6	7		10	11						8									9		15
1	2	3	5	4	6	7		10	11						8									9		16
1	2	3			6			10	11		4			9	8	5										17
1	2	3			6			10	11		4				8	5										18
		3	4		6	7		10			2			9	8		1	5						12		19
		3	4		6	7	12	10*			2			9	8		1	5						11		20
		3	4		6	7	11	12			2			10	9			5*	1					8		21
		3	5		6	7	8	10			2			9*	4				1					11		22
		3	5		6	7	8	10		9	2				4				1					11		23
		3	4		6	7	8*	10		11	2			12	5				1					9		24
		3	4		6	7	8	10*	12	11	2			9			1	5								25
		3	5		6	7		10	11*		2	8	4	9			1							12		26
	2	3	9		6		8	12				7		10			1	5*		4	11					27
	2	3	5		6	12	8	9				7		10*						4	11	1				28
	2*	3	5		6	12	8	9				7		10						4	11	1				29
		3	5			7	8	9				2		10				6		4	11	1				30
	2	3	5			7	8	9	12			4		10*				6			11	1				31
	2	3	5		6	8	9	10				7						4			11	1				32
	2	3	5		6	7	8	9	12			11		10*				4				1				33
	2	3	5		6	7		9		8		11		10*				4				1	12			34
		3	5		6	7	8*		11	9	2			12	4		1						10			35
		3	5		6	7		9*			2			12	4		1			8	11		10			36
	2	3	9		6				11	7		8					1	4		5	10					37
	2	3	9		6				11	7		8					1	4		5	10					38
		3	9		6	7			11	8		2					1	4		5	10					39
		3	9		6	7			11	8*		2		12			1	4		5	10					40
	2	3	9		6	7			12			8		11*			1	4		5	10					41
	2	3	5		6	7		9*	10	4					8		1				11		12			42
	2	3	5		6	7			9	4	8				10		1				11					43
		3	5		6	7			9	4	8	10					1			2	11					44
	2	3	5		6	7			9	4	8						1			10	11					45
	2		5			7			9	3	6			10*	12		1			4	11		8			46
18	35	33	44	11	38	34	23	31	26	22	13	39	5	20	13	2	17	17	4	13	17	7	3	11	3	
							1	2	1	2	5	2		4				1					1	4	3	
	2	2	2		5	7	2	1	5	6		2		3			3			3		1		5	2	

111

1985-86

#	Month	Date		Opponent	Res	Score	Scorers	Att
1	Aug	17	(h)	Peterborough U	L	2-4	Brazil, Thomas	3,177
2		26	(h)	Tranmere R	D	2-2	Brazil (pen), Thomas	4,206
3		30	(a)	Halifax T	L	1-2	Greenwood	2,011
4	Sep	7	(h)	Torquay U	W	4-0	Brazil 2, Greenwood 2	3,403
5		10	(a)	Northampton T	L	0-6		2,171
6		13	(h)	Stockport Co	L	1-2	Thomas	3,436
7		17	(h)	Burnley	W	1-0	Thomas	5,585
8		28	(h)	Hereford U	W	2-0	Greenwood, Brazil	3,397
9	Oct	2	(a)	Cambridge U	L	0-2		1,500
10		5	(a)	Crewe Alex	D	3-3	Brazil, Gibson, Greenwood	2,454
11		12	(h)	Chester C	L	3-6	Foster, Welsh, Brazil (pen)	4,073
12		19	(a)	Rochdale	D	1-1	Brazil	2,527
13		22	(h)	Hartlepool U	W	2-1	Greenwood, Foster	3,538
14		25	(a)	Southend U	L	1-2	Greenwood	2,787
15	Nov	2	(h)	Port Vale	L	0-1		4,531
16		5	(h)	Scunthorpe U	L	0-1		2,007
17		9	(a)	Orient	L	0-2		2,805
18		23	(h)	Colchester U	W	3-2	Thomas, Gray, Stevens	2,793
19		30	(a)	Exeter C	L	3-0		1,896
20	Dec	7	(a)	Swindon T	L	1-4	Allatt (pen)	3,945
21		14	(h)	Aldershot	L	1-3	Thomas	2,746
22		21	(h)	Northampton T	D	1-1	Thomas	2,570
23		26	(a)	Wrexham	D	1-1	Atkins	2,217
24	Jan	1	(h)	Mansfield T	L	0-2		3,705
25		4	(a)	Port Vale	W	1-0	Jones	3,592
26		11	(h)	Halifax T	L	0-1		3,184
27		18	(a)	Peterborough U	D	1-1	Allatt	2,711
28		24	(a)	Stockport Co	L	1-2	Thomas	3,035
29	Feb	1	(a)	Torquay U	L	0-1		1,215
30		5	(a)	Hartlepool U	L	0-1		3,102
31		8	(h)	Rochdale	D	1-1	Greenwood	3,266
32		22	(h)	Swindon T	L	0-3		3,361
33	Mar	1	(a)	Hereford U	D	1-1	Brazil	1,857
34		8	(h)	Crewe Alex	L	1-2	Thomas	2,922
35		15	(a)	Chester C	L	0-2		3,062
36		18	(h)	Cambridge U	L	1-2	Brazil (pen)	2,840
37		22	(h)	Southend U	W	3-2	Brazil (pen), Thomas 2	2,623
38		25	(a)	Tranmere R	W	3-2	Brazil, Thomas 2	1,574
39		29	(a)	Mansfield T	W	3-2	Foster, Atkins, Allatt	3,733
40		31	(h)	Wrexham	W	1-0	Thomas	5,163
41	Apr	4	(a)	Scunthorpe U	W	3-1	Thomas 2, Greenwood	2,261
42		12	(h)	Orient	L	1-3	Brazil (pen)	4,750
43		18	(a)	Colchester U	L	0-4		2,046
44		22	(a)	Burnley	D	1-1	Brazil (pen)	3,787
45		26	(h)	Exeter C	D	2-2	Thomas, Gibson	3,132
46	May	3	(a)	Aldershot	L	0-4		1,866

FINAL LEAGUE POSITION: 23rd in Division Four

Appearances

Sub. Appearances

Goals

112

Platt	Jones	McAteer	Atkins	Twentyman	Gray	Keen	Foster	Thomas	Rudge	Brazil	Greenwood	Clark	Welsh	Gibson	Martin	Chippendale	Stevens	Rodgers	Tottoh	Allatt	McNeil	Reid	Cooper	Harrington	Kelly	Pilling	Jemson	
1	2	3	4	5	6*	7	8	9	10	11	12																	1
1	2	3	4	5		7	8	9	10	11	12	6																2
1	2	3*	4	5		7	8	9	10	11	12	6																3
1	2	3	4	5		7	8	9*	10	11	12	6																4
1	2	3	4*	5		7	8		10	11	9	6	12															5
1	2		4	3		7		9	10	11	8	6		5														6
1	3		4	2		7	8	9		11	10	6*	12	5														7
1	3		4	2	10	7		9		11	8			5	6													8
1	3		4	2	10	7		9		11*	8		12	5	6													9
1	3		4	2	10	7		9		11	8			5	6													10
1	3		4	2		7*	8	9		11			12	5	6	10												11
1			2	10*	7	8		3		11	9	4		5	6	12												12
1	3		2			7	8			10	11	9	4	5	6													13
1	3			5		2	8			10	11	9	4		6	7												14
1	3	8	2							10	11	9	4	5		7*	12											15
1	3		4	2						10*	11	9		5		7	6	8	12									16
1	3		4	2					12	10	11	9*		5		7	6			8								17
1		3	4	5	8			9	2	11					6		7			10								18
1		3		5	8		12	9	2	11*			6		4		7			10								19
1		3		5	8*		4	9	2	11				12	6		7			10								20
1	8*	3		5				9		11	12				6		7			10	2	4						21
1	8		4	5				9	3	7					6					10	2		11					22
1	3		4	5				9	8	11					6					10	2	7*	12					23
1	3		4	5				9		11					6					10	2	7	8					24
1	3	7	4	5	8			9		11					6					10	2							25
1	3*	7	4	5	8			9		11					6					10	2		12					26
1	3	7	4		5	12		9		11					6*					10	2		8					27
1	8	3	4			7	12	9		11				5	6					10*	2							28
1	8	3	4			7	12	9		11				5	6					10*	2							29
1	8		4		7	2	10	9*		11	12			5	6					3								30
1	4	3			8	7	10	12		11*	9			5	6						2							31
	4	3			8	7	10	12		11	9			5	6*						2			1				32
	4	3			8	7	10	12		11	9	6	5								2			1*				33
	4	3	6		8	7*	10	12		11	9		5								2				1			34
	4	3			8	7	10	5		11	9				6						2				1			35
	4	3			8	7*	10	12		11	9	5			6						2				1			36
	4	3	7		8		12	9		11				5	6					10	2*				1			37
	2	4	7		8		12	10	3	11*				5	6					9					1			38
			2		8	7	9	3	11				4	5	6					10					1			39
			4	2	8	7	9	3	11				12	5*	6					10					1			40
			4	2	8	7	9	3	11	10		5			6										1			41
	2*	4	7		8		9	3	11	10		5			6					12					1			42
	3	4	2		8	7	9		11	10			5	6										1				43
	2	4	3		8	7	9		11	10			5	6										1				44
			4	2	8	7	9	3	11	10*			5	6					12	3				1				45
			3		8	7	9		11	10		5		6*						2				1	4	12	11	46
31	37	29	34	26	27	24	25	34	23	43	25	6	11	25	35	5	6	1		17	19	3	3	2	13	1	1	
						6	6				5		6				1	1	1	2		2				1		
	1		2		1		3	17		14	9		1	2						3								

1986-87

1	Aug	23	(a)	Tranmere R	D	1-1	Thomas	2,108
2		30	(h)	Swansea C	W	2-1	Thomas, Williams	4,362
3	Sep	6	(a)	Lincoln C	D	1-1	Thomas	2,305
4		13	(h)	Hereford U	W	2-1	Williams, Thomas (pen)	4,707
5		16	(h)	Halifax T	W	3-2	Thomas 3	5,259
6		19	(a)	Scunthopre U	L	0-4		2,689
7		27	(h)	Torquay U	D	1-1	Allardyce	5,053
8		30	(a)	Wolverhampton W	L	0-1		4,409
9	Oct	4	(a)	Burnley	W	4-1	Brazil 2, Thomas 2	5,865
10		11	(h)	Cambridge U	W	1-0	Brazil	5,236
11		18	(h)	Aldershot	L	1-2	Thomas (pen)	5,241
12		20	(a)	Stockport Co	W	3-1	Williams 2, Taylor	2,888
13	Nov	1	(h)	Exeter C	W	2-1	McAteer, Williams	5,818
14		4	(h)	Cardiff C	L	0-1		6,614
15		8	(a)	Northampton T	L	1-3	Taylor	6,537
16		22	(h)	Southend U	W	2-0	Hildersley, Thomas	6,033
17		29	(a)	Peterborough U	L	1-2	Williams	3,462
18	Dec	13	(a)	Colchester U	W	2-0	Williams, Hildersley	2,240
19		20	(h)	Orient	W	1-0	Williams	5,925
20		26	(a)	Crewe Alexandra	D	2-2	Thomas, Atkins	3,784
21		27	(h)	Hartlepool U	D	0-0		7,782
22	Jan	1	(h)	Wrexham	W	1-0	Thomas	9,373
23		3	(a)	Southend U	W	2-1	Bennett, Brazil	4,479
24		17	(a)	Swansea C	D	1-1	Jemson	7,677
25		24	(h)	Lincoln C	W	3-0	Brazil, Swann, Jemson	7,821
26	Feb	7	(a)	Halifax T	W	3-1	Brazil, Swann, Jemson	2,968
27		14	(h)	Scunthorpe U	W	2-1	Brazil, Allardyce	7,968
28		21	(a)	Torquay U	W	2-0	Brazil, Jones	1,871
29		25	(a)	Hereford U	W	3-2	Brazil 2, Worthington	2,628
30		28	(h)	Wolverhampton W	D	2-2	Swann, Worthington	12,592
31	Mar	4	(a)	Exeter C	W	2-1	Brazil (pen), Thomas	5,801
32		14	(a)	Aldershot	D	0-0		3,469
33		17	(h)	Stockport Co	W	3-0	Swann, Worthington, Thomas	7,823
34		21	(a)	Cambridge U	L	0-2		2,804
35		28	(h)	Burnley	W	2-1	Williams, Thomas	10,623
36	Apr	3	(h)	Northampton T	W	1-0	Brazil	16,456
37		7	(a)	Rochdale	W	2-0	Brazil, Zelem	4,986
38		11	(a)	Cardiff C	D	1-1	Thomas	2,528
39		14	(h)	Rochdale	L	2-4	Brazil, Thomas	10,185
40		18	(a)	Wrexham	D	1-1	Williams	4,850
41		20	(h)	Crewe Alexandra	W	2-1	Davis (og), Thomas (pen)	11,107
42		25	(a)	Orient	W	2-1	Brazil, Chapman	5,255
43		28	(h)	Tranmere R	W	2-0	Brazil, Thomas	12,109
44	May	2	(h)	Peterborough U	D	0-0		7,919
45		4	(a)	Hartlepool	D	2-2	Thomas, Brazil	2,617
46		9	(h)	Colchester U	W	1-0	Swann	8,757

FINAL LEAGUE POSITION: 2nd in Division Four

Appearances

Sub. Appearances

Goals

Brown	Bulmer	McAteer	Chapman	Jones	Allardyce	Williams O	Clark	Thomas	Hildsley	Brazil	Bennett	Atkins	McNeil	Kelly	Taylor	Swann	Jemson	Miller	Worthington	Williams P	Zelem	No.
1	2	3	4	5	6	7	8	9	10	11												1
1	2	3	4	5	6	7	8	9	10	11												2
1	2		4	5	6	7	8	9	10	11	3											3
1	2*	3	4	5	6	7	8	9	10	11	12											4
1		3	4	5	6	7	8	9	10	11	2											5
1		3	4*	5	6	7	8	9	10	11	2	12										6
1		3		5	6	7	8	9	10	11	2	4										7
1		3	4	5	6	7	8*	9	10	12	2	11										8
1		8	4	5		7		9	10	11	3	6	2									9
		8	4	5		7		9	10	11	3	6	2	1								10
		8		5		7	12	9	4*	11	3	6	2	1	10							11
		10	4	5		7			11	8	3	6	2	1	9							12
1	10	2	5	6		7			11	8	3	4			9							13
1	10	2*	5	6		7	12		11	8	3	4			9							14
1	10		5	6		7		8	11		3	4	2		9							15
1	10	7	5	6			2	9	11	8	3	4										16
1	10*		5	6		7	2	9	11	8	3	4				12						17
1			5	6		7		9	11	8	3	4	2			10						18
1			5	6		7		9	11	10	3	4	2			8						19
1			5	6		7		9	11	10	3	4	2			8						20
1			5	6		7		9	11	10	3	4	2			8						21
1		7	5	6				9	11	10	3	4	2			8						22
1		7	5	6				9	11	10	3	4	2			8						23
1		7	5	6					11	10	3	4	2			8	9					24
		7	5	6						10	3	4	2	1		8	9	11				25
		7	5	6			12			10	3	4	2	1		8	9*	11				26
		7	5	6			12			10	3	4	2	1		8	9*	11				27
		7	5	6						10	3	4	2	1		8		11	9			28
			5	6			7			10	3	4	2	1		8		11	9			29
		7	5	6					11	10	3	4	2	1		8			9			30
		7	5	6			12		11	10	3	4	2	1		8			9*			31
		7	5	6				9	11	10	3	4	2	1		8						32
		7	5	6*				9	11	10	3	4	2	1		8			12			33
		7	5					9	11	10	3	4	2*	1		3			12	6		34
		7	5			11		9		10	3	4	2	1		8			12	6*		35
		7	5			11		9		10	3	4	2	1		8					6	36
		7	5			11		9		10	3	4		1		8		2			6	37
		7	5			11		9		10	3	4		1		8		2			6	38
		7*	5	6		11		9		10	3	4		1		8		2	12			39
		7	5	6		11		9		10	3	4		1		8		2				40
		7	5	6		11		9		10	3	4		1		8		2				41
		7	5	6		11		9		10	3	4		1		8		2				42
		7*	5	6		11		9		10	3	4		1		8		2	12			43
1			5	6				9	11	10		4				8		2	7		3	44
1		12	5	6				9	11	10		4				8		2	7*		3	45
1		7	5	6				9	11	10	3	4				8		2				46
24	4	16	35	46	37	29	10	35	33	44	41	40	24	22	5	29	4	15	6	1	6	
			1					2	3		1	1	1			1			5			
	1	1	1	2	10		21	2	17	1	1				2	5	3		3		1	

1987-88

1	Aug	15	(h)	Chesterfield	L	0-1		6,509
2		22	(a)	Bristol C	L	1-3	Brazil	7,655
3		29	(h)	Wigan Ath	L	0-1		7,057
4	Sep	1	(a)	Southend U	W	2-1	Williams, Atkins	2,600
5		5	(h)	Grimsby T	L	1-3	Swann	5,522
6		12	(a)	York C	D	1-1	Brazil	3,237
7		15	(h)	Northampton T	D	0-0		5,179
8		19	(h)	Rotherham U	D	0-0		5,124
9		26	(a)	Blackpool	L	0-3		8,406
10		29	(h)	Brentford	L	1-2	Lowey	4,241
11	Oct	3	(a)	Walsall	L	0-1		5,467
12		10	(h)	Port Vale	W	3-2	Brazil 2 (1 pen), Ellis	6,274
13		17	(a)	Brighton & HA	D	0-0		6,043
14		20	(h)	Gillingham	D	1-1	Williams	5,676
15		24	(a)	Bury	L	0-4		4,316
16		31	(h)	Chester C	D	1-1	Swann	5,657
17	Nov	4	(a)	Bristol R	W	2-1	Ellis, Jemson	2,804
18		7	(a)	Mansfield T	D	0-0		3,631
19		21	(h)	Doncaster R	L	1-2	Miller	5,178
20		28	(a)	Fulham	W	1-0	Jemson	5,324
21	Dec	12	(h)	Aldershot	L	0-2		4,519
22		19	(a)	Notts Co	L	2-4	Jemson, Swann	5,730
23		26	(h)	Blackpool	W	2-1	Swann, Brazil	11,155
24		28	(a)	Sunderland	D	1-1	Jones	24,814
25	Jan	1	(a)	Wigan Ath	L	0-2		6,872
26		2	(h)	York C	W	3-0	Brazil, Miller, Mooney	6,302
27		9	(h)	Bristol C	W	2-0	Rathbone, Brazil	5,229
28		16	(a)	Rotherham U	D	2-2	Brazil 2	4,011
29		27	(a)	Northampton T	W	1-0	Jemson	5,052
30		30	(h)	Southend U	D	1-1	Mooney	6,180
31	Feb	6	(a)	Grimsby T	W	1-0	Brazil	2,907
32		13	(h)	Sunderland	D	2-2	Swann, Mooney	10,852
33		20	(a)	Chesterfield	D	0-0		2,864
34		27	(h)	Walsall	W	1-0	Brazil (pen)	6,479
35	Mar	1	(a)	Brentford	L	0-2		3,505
36		5	(h)	Brighton & HA	W	3-0	Jemson, Swann 2	5,834
37		12	(a)	Port Vale	L	2-3	Brazil, Swann	4,647
38		19	(a)	Chester C	L	0-1		3,724
39		26	(h)	Bury	W	1-0	Jones	6,456
40	Apr	2	(h)	Mansfield T	W	1-0	Swann	6,254
41		4	(a)	Doncaster R	L	2-3	Swann 2	2,167
42		8	(h)	Bristol R	W	3-1	Ellis, Hildersley, Brazil (pen)	5,386
43		23	(a)	Gillingham	L	0-4		2,721
44		30	(h)	Fulham	W	2-1	Swann, Brazil	4,192
45	May	2	(a)	Aldershot	D	0-0		3,465
46		7	(h)	Notts Co	L	1-2	Ellis	5,822

FINAL LEAGUE POSITION: 16th in Division Three

Appearances

Sub. Appearances

Goals

116

Kelly	Branagan	Rathbone	Atkins	Chapman	Allardyce	Miller	Swann	Lowey	Brazil	Hildersley	Worthington	Brown	Wrightson	Bennett	Jones	Williams	Jemson	Wilkes	Jeffels	Mooney	Ellis	Joyce	Hughes	
1	2	3	4	5	6	7*	8	9	10	11	12													1
	2*	11†	4		6	7	8	9	10		14	1	12	3	5									2
			4	5*	6	2	8		10	11	12	1		3		7	9							3
			4	5	6	2	8		10	11		1		3		7	9							4
			4	5*	6	2	8		10	11	12	1		3		7	9							5
1	11	3	4		6	2	8*		10		14	9†		5		7	12							6
1	2		4		6	7	8			11	10			5	3		9							7
1	2		4		6	7	8		10	11	9			5	3									8
1	2		4		6	7	8			11	9			5	3*		10	12						9
	2		4	14	6	7†	8*	9		11	12			5	3		10							10
	2		4	11	6		8	9			12	1		5	3		10*		7					11
	2		4		6	7*	14		10		12	1	11	3	5					8†	9			12
	2		4		6		11					1	12	3	5		14			8	9†	7		13
1	2		4		6		11							3	5	7				10	9	8		14
1	2*		4		6		11				12		7	3	5					10	9	8		15
1	2		4		6		8			11				3	5		10			7	9			16
1	2		4		6		8			11				3	5		10			7	9			17
1			4		6	2	8			11				3	5		10			7	9			18
1	2*		4	12	6		8		10	11				3	5		9			7				19
1	2		4		6		8		10	11				3	5		9			7				20
1	2		4		6		8		10	11				3	5		9			7*	12			21
1	2		4	12	6		8		10					3	5*		9			7		11		22
1	2		4		6		8		10		12			3	5					7*	9	11		23
1	2		4		6		8		10	11				3	5					7	9			24
1			4	14	6	2	8		10	11				3	5†		12			7	9*			25
			4	5	6	2	8		10			1		3			9			7		11		26
	2*		4	5	6	12	8		10			1		3						7	9	11		27
1	2		4	5	6		8		10			1		3						7	9	11		28
	2		4		6		8		10			1	5	3			9			7		11		29
	2		4		6		8		10			1	5	3			9			7		11		30
	2		4		6		8		10			1	5	3			9			7		11		31
	2		4		6		8		10			1	5	3			9			7		11		32
	2		4		6		8		10			1	5	3			9*			7	12	11		33
	2		4		6		8		10			1	5	3			9			7		11		34
	2		4	12	6		8		10			1	3*	5			9†			7	14	11		35
	2*		4	12	6		8		10			1	3	5			9			7		11		36
			4		6	2	8		10			1		3	5		9			7		11		37
			4		6	2	8		10			1		3	5		11			7	9			38
		3	4			2	8		10	11		1	6	5						7	9			39
		3	4	12		2	8		10	11		1	6	5*						7	9			40
			4	3*	6	2	8		10	11		1		5			14			7	9†	12		41
		3	4		6	2	8		10	11		1		5						7	9			42
			4	6			8		10	11		1		5	12	2				7	9*	3		43
		3	4		6	2	8		10	12		1		5						7	9*	11		44
		3	4		6	2	8		10†	12		1		5			9			7*	14	11		45
		3	4			2	8					1		5			9			7	10	11	6	46
19	3	36	45	15	38	23	45	4	36	21	4	27	23	34	22	9	24	1	1	34	20	21	1	
				2	1	5	1		4	8			2		1	3	2				4	1		
		1	1			2	12	1	14	1					2	2	5			3	4			

1988-89

1	Aug	27	(h)	Port Vale	L	1-3	Williams N	6,718
2	Sep	3	(a)	Huddersfield T	L	0-2		5,622
3		10	(h)	Blackpool	W	1-0	Patterson	8,779
4		17	(a)	Bristol C	D	1-1	Rathbone	7,913
5		20	(h)	Chester C	D	3-3	Patterson 2, Ellis	5,415
6		24	(a)	Notts Co	D	0-0		4,965
7	Oct	1	(h)	Southend U	W	3-2	McAteer, Brazil 2 (1 pen)	5,348
8		5	(a)	Bristol R	L	0-1		3,689
9		8	(h)	Bury	W	1-0	Ellis	5,863
10		15	(a)	Chesterfield	W	3-0	Swann, Mooney, Ellis	2,813
11		22	(a)	Brentford	W	2-0	Brazil 2	5,584
12		25	(h)	Gillingham	W	5-0	Brazil 3 (1 pen), Ellis, Joyce	6,390
13		29	(a)	Swansea C	D	1-1	Ellis	5,370
14	Nov	5	(h)	Mansfield T	W	2-0	Mooney, Rathbone	6,434
15		8	(h)	Wigan Ath	D	2-2	Brazil (pen), Patterson	8,396
16		12	(a)	Reading	D	2-2	Ellis, Patterson	6,225
17		26	(a)	Wolverhampton W	L	0-6		13,180
18	Dec	3	(h)	Cardiff C	D	3-3	Brazil, Ellis 2	4,963
19		17	(a)	Fulham	L	1-2	Patterson	3,858
20		26	(h)	Bolton W	W	3-1	Hughes, Ellis, Joyce	12,104
21		31	(h)	Sheffield U	W	2-0	Patterson, Joyce	11,005
22	Jan	2	(a)	Northampton T	L	0-1		4,219
23		7	(a)	Aldershot	L	1-2	Joyce	2,135
24		14	(h)	Huddersfield T	W	1-0	Patterson	6,959
25		21	(a)	Blackpool	L	0-1		8,951
26		28	(h)	Bristol C	W	2-0	Mooney 2	6,080
27	Feb	3	(a)	Southend U	L	1-2	Mooney	2,948
28		11	(h)	Bristol R	D	1-1	Mooney	7,365
29		18	(a)	Bury	D	1-1	Williams N	6,977
30		25	(h)	Chesterfield	W	6-0	Philliskirk 2, Bloomer (og), Patterson, Ellis 2	7,074
31		28	(a)	Gillingham	W	3-1	Patterson (pen), Ellis 2	3,031
32	Mar	4	(h)	Brentford	W	5-3	Philliskirk, Patterson, Joyce 2, Ellis	8,186
33		11	(a)	Mansfield T	W	3-0	Coleman (og), Philliskirk, Ellis	4,706
34		14	(h)	Swansea C	D	1-1	James (og)	8,975
35		18	(a)	Port Vale	D	1-1	Ellis	8,584
36		25	(h)	Northampton T	W	3-2	Joyce 2, Patterson (pen)	9,137
37		27	(a)	Bolton W	L	0-1		10,281
38	Apr	1	(h)	Fulham	L	1-4	Philliskirk	8,190
39		4	(h)	Aldershot	D	2-2	Bogie, Philliskirk	5,977
40		8	(a)	Sheffield U	L	1-3	Stancliffe (og)	12,718
41		15	(a)	Notts Co	W	3-0	Swann, Joyce, Ellis	6,735
42		22	(a)	Chester C	W	1-0	Jemson	4,617
43		29	(h)	Reading	W	2-1	Patterson 2 (1 pen)	7,003
44	May	1	(a)	Wigan Ath	D	1-1	Jemson	5,671
45		5	(a)	Cardiff C	D	0-0		3,196
46		13	(h)	Wolverhampton W	D	3-3	Ellis 2, Patterson	14,126

FINAL LEAGUE POSITION: 6th in Division Three

Appearances

Sub. Appearances

Goals

Brown	Miller	McAteer	Atkins	Jones	Wrightson	Williams N	Swann	Ellis	Brazil	Patterson	Rathbone	Allardyce	Mooney	Joyce	Hughes	Tunks	Fitzpatrick	Bogie	Philliskirk	Jemson	Harper	#
1	2	3	4	5	6	7	8	9	10	11*	12											1
1	2		4	5		9†	8*	14	10	11	3	6	7	12								2
1	7	3	4	5	6			9	10	11	2			8								3
1	7	3	4	5				9	10	11	2	6		8								4
1	7*	3	4	5			12	9	10	11	2	6		8								5
1	7*	3	4	5			8	9	10	11	2	6	12									6
1	12	3	4	5			8	9*	10	11	2	6	7									7
1	2		4	5*	12	14	8†	9	10	11	3	6	7									8
1	2*		4	5	8	12		9		11	3		7	10	6							9
1			4	5	2		10	9		11	3		7	8	6							10
1			4	5	2		10*	9	12	11	3	14	7	8	6†							11
1	11		4	12	5	2		9	10		3	6*	7	8								12
1	12		4	5	2			9	10	11*	3		7	8	6							13
1			4	5	2			9	10	11	3		7	8	6							14
1			4	5	2			9	10	11	3		7	8	6							15
1			4	5	2			9	10	11	3	6	7	8								16
1			4	5*	2			9	10	11	3	6	7	8	12							17
			4		2			9	7	11	3	6		8	5	1	10					18
		3	4	6	2			9		11			7	8	5	1	10					19
		3	4	5	2			9	10	11			7	8	6	1						20
		3	4	5	2			9	10	11			7	8	6	1						21
	12	3†	4	5	2			9*	10	11	14		7	8	6	1						22
	14		4	12	2			9	10	11	3†	5*	7	8	6	1						23
			4	5	2			9	10	11	3		7	8	6	1						24
	12		4	5	2			9	10	11	3*		7	8	6	1						25
			4	5	2	6		9	10	11	3		7	8		1						26
	10*		4	5	2	6		9	12	11	3		7	8		1						27
			4	5	2	6		12		11	3		7	8*		1		9	10			28
			4	5	2	6		8		11	3		7	12		1		9	10*			29
			4	5	2	6		8		11	3		7*	12		1		9	10			30
			4	5	2	6		8		11	3		7			1		9	10			31
			4	5	2	6		8		11	3		7	12		1		9	10*			32
			4	5	2	6		8		11	3		7			1		9	10			33
			4	5	2	6		8		11	3		7	12		1		9*	10			34
			4	5	2	6		8		11	3		7	9		1		12	10*			35
			4	5	2	6		8		11	3		7	9		1			10			36
			4	5	2	6		8		11	3*		7	9		1		12	10†	14		37
			4	5	2	6	11†	8			3		7*	9		1		12	10	14		38
			4		2	6		8*		11	3		7		5	1		9†	10	12	14	39
			4		2	6		8		11	3		12	9	5	1		7	10*			40
1			4	5	2	3		8		11			7	9	6				10			41
1			4	5	2	3		8					7	9	6			12	10		11*	42
1			4	5	2	3		8		11			7	9	6				10			43
1			4	5	2	3		8		11			7	9	6				10*	12		44
1			4	5	2	3		8		11			7	9	6				10*	12		45
1			4	5	2	3		8		11			7	9	6				12	10*		46
23	9	11	39	29	36	40	16	43	23	42	32	13	38	35	22	23	2	9	13	6	2	
	3	2		1	2	1	2	2	2		2	1	2	5	1			4	1	3	3	
		1			2	2	19	9	15	2			6	9	1			1	6	2		

1989-90

1	Aug	19	(a)	Rotherham U	L	1-3	Shaw	5,951
2		26	(h)	Bury	L	2-3	Shaw, Harper	5,622
3	Sep	2	(a)	Leyton Orient	L	1-3	Ellis	4,871
4		9	(h)	Huddersfield T	D	3-3	Bogie, Swann, Mooney	5,822
5		16	(a)	Bristol R	L	0-3		4,350
6		23	(h)	Chester C	W	5-0	Mooney 3, Harper 2 (1 pen)	5,230
7		26	(h)	Blackpool	W	2-1	Bradshaw (og), Atkins	8,920
8		30	(a)	Walsall	L	0-1		4,045
9	Oct	7	(a)	Northampton T	W	2-1	Harper, Ellis	3,039
10		14	(h)	Brentford	W	4-2	Ellis, Joyce, Harper, Swann	5,956
11		17	(h)	Crewe Alex	D	0-0		7,485
12		21	(a)	Notts Co	L	1-2	Williams	5,284
13		28	(h)	Bolton W	L	1-4	Scully	9,135
14		31	(a)	Mansfield T	D	2-2	Mooney, Joyce	3,129
15	Nov	4	(h)	Shrewsbury T	W	2-1	Swann, Patterson	5,418
16		11	(a)	Swansea C	L	1-2	Patterson	3,843
17		25	(a)	Cardiff C	L	0-3		3,270
18	Dec	2	(h)	Reading	W	1-0	Swann	5,067
19		16	(a)	Birmingham C	L	1-3	Patterson (pen)	6,391
20		26	(h)	Tranmere R	D	2-2	Swann 2	8,300
21		30	(h)	Wigan A	D	1-1	Patterson	7,220
22	Jan	1	(a)	Bristol C	L	1-2	Mooney	11,803
23		6	(h)	Fulham	W	1-0	Shaw	5,055
24		13	(a)	Bury	W	2-1	Joyce, Mooney	4,715
25		20	(h)	Rotherham U	L	0-1		6,088
26	Feb	3	(a)	Chester C	L	1-3	Harper	2,499
27		10	(h)	Bristol R	L	0-1		5,956
28		13	(h)	Leyton Orient	L	0-3		4,480
29		17	(a)	Reading	L	0-6		3,998
30		24	(h)	Cardiff C	W	4-0	Harper 3, Joyce	5,716
31	Mar	3	(a)	Fulham	L	1-3	Shaw	4,207
32		6	(h)	Walsall	W	2-0	Swann, Thomas	5,210
33		13	(a)	Blackpool	D	2-2	Shaw, Mooney	8,108
34		17	(h)	Northampton T	D	0-0		5,681
35		20	(a)	Brentford	D	2-2	Joyce, Williams	4,673
36		24	(a)	Crewe Alex	L	0-1		4,531
37		31	(h)	Notts Co	L	2-4	Joyce 2	5,810
38	Apr	3	(a)	Huddersfield T	W	2-0	Joyce, Bogie	4,381
39		7	(a)	Bolton W	L	1-2	Bogie	8,266
40		10	(h)	Mansfield T	W	4-0	Joyce 2, Foster (og), Hughes	5,035
41		14	(h)	Bristol C	D	2-2	Flynn, Harper	7,599
42		16	(a)	Tranmere R	L	1-2	Joyce	10,187
43		21	(h)	Birmingham C	D	2-2	Thomas, Mooney	7,680
44		24	(a)	Wigan A	W	1-0	Thomas	4,454
45		28	(h)	Swansea C	W	2-0	Swann, Williams	6,695
46	May	5	(a)	Shrewsbury T	L	0-2		5,319

FINAL LEAGUE POSITION: 19th in Division Three

Appearances

Sub. Appearances

Goals

120

Tunks	Miller	Swann	Akins	Jones	Hughes	Mooney	Ellis	Joyce	Shaw	Patterson	Rathbone	Wrightson	Snow	Harper	Kelly	Bogie	Williams	Scully	Bennett	Flynn	Greenwood	Stowell	McLlroy	Thomas	Anderton	
1	2	3	4	5	6	7	8	9	10	11																1
1	11	3	4	5		7		9	10		2	6	8*	12												2
	2*	11	4	5		7	8	9	10		3	6			1	12										3
		3			6	7	8*	9	10		12	4			1	11	2	5								4
		3*	14		6	7	8	9	10		12	4†			1	11	2	5								5
		3	4		6	7	8	9						10	1	11	2	5								6
		3	4		6	7	8	9						10	1	11	2	5								7
		3	4		6	7*	8	9	12					10	1	11	2	5								8
		3	4		6	7	8	9	12					10	1	11*	2	5								9
		3	4			7	8	9					6	10	1	11	2	5								10
		3	4		6	7	8	9						10	1	11	2	5								11
		3	4		6	7	8	9	12					10*	1	11	2	5								12
		3	4		6*	7	8	9	12					10	1	11	2	5								13
		3	4		6	7	8*	5	10	9				12	1	11	2									14
		3	4			7*		5	10	9	12			8	1	11	2	6								15
		3	4		14		8	5	10*	11	12			7†	1	9	2	6								16
		3	4		14	7	8	5	10*	11				12	1	9	2	6†								17
		3	4		6	7	8	5	10	11					1	9	2									18
	9†		4		6*	12	8		10	14	7			11	1		2	3	5							19
	8		4		6	7		9	10					11	1	4	2	3	5							20
	8				6	7		9	10					11	1	4	2	3	5							21
	8				6	7		9	10					11	1	4	2	3	5							22
	8				6	7		9	11	10					1	4	2	3	5							23
			4			7		9	10	8	6			11	1		2	3	5							24
			4		6	7		9*	10	8				11	1	12	2	3	5							25
			4		6*	7		9	10	8				12	1		2	3	5		11					26
		3				7		9	10		6			11			2		5	8		1	4			27
	2					7		9	10*		6			11		12		3	5	8		1	4			28
	2				6	7		9						4	1	11		3	5	8				10		29
		3				7		9	8		6			11	1		2		5				4	10		30
		3			6	7	8				5			11	1	9	2						4	10		31
		3			6	7			10	8	5			11	1		2						4	9		32
		3	5				8							4	1		2		10		11			9		33
		3				7	10		8		6			11	1		2		5				4	9		34
		3	11*		8	7			10	14	6			12	1		2		5				4	9†		35
		3	11*		8†	7			10	9	6			12	1	14	2		5				4			36
		3			12	7		9*	10†		6			11	1	14	2		5	8			4			37
		3	10			7	8	9			6				1	11	2		5				4			38
		3	10			7	8	9			6				1	11	2		5				4			39
		3	10			7	8	9*			6			12	1	11	2		5				4†	14		40
		3	10*			7	8	9			6			12	1	11	2		5				4			41
		3	10		12	7†	8			14	6				1	11	2		5*				4	9		42
		3			12	7	8			14	6			11†	1	10	2		5*				4	9		43
		3	5			7	8				6			11	1	10	2						4	9		44
		3	5			7	8				6			11	1	10	2						4	9		45
		3	5		12	7	8			14	6			11†	1	10	2						4*	9		46
2	3	46	27	3	29	44	17	44	24	12	3	26	1	28	42	30	41	13	10	23	5	2	20	11		
			1		6	1			7	1	5			8		5								1		
		8	1		1	9	3	11	5	4				10		3	3	1		1			3			

1990-91

1	Aug	25	(h)	Grimsby T	L	1-3	Joyce	6,372
2	Sep	1	(a)	Reading	D	3-3	Joyce, Peel, Senior	4,228
3		8	(h)	Tranmere R	L	0-4		5,648
4		14	(a)	Southend U	L	2-3	Joyce, Thomas (pen)	4,614
5		18	(a)	Bolton W	W	2-1	James, Bogie (pen)	5,844
6		22	(h)	Fulham	W	1-0	Hughes	4,691
7		29	(a)	Birmingham C	D	1-1	Bogie	7,154
8	Oct	2	(h)	Brentford	D	1-1	Swann	5,025
9		6	(h)	Exeter C	W	1-0	Bogie	4,716
10		13	(a)	Mansfield T	W	1-0	Rathbone	3,225
11		20	(a)	Rotherham U	L	0-1		4,599
12		23	(h)	Chester C	D	0-0		5,465
13		27	(h)	Bournemouth	D	0-0		4,953
14	Nov	3	(a)	Wigan A	L	1-2	Greenwood	4,728
15		10	(a)	Bradford C	L	1-2	Bogie	7,440
16		24	(h)	Huddersfield T	D	1-1	Joyce	4,646
17	Dec	1	(h)	Shrewsbury T	W	4-3	Bogie 2, Wrightson, Swann	4,515
18		15	(a)	Leyton Orient	L	0-1		3,282
19		22	(h)	Stoke C	W	2-0	Swann 2	7,532
20		26	(a)	Crewe Alex	D	2-2	Bogie, Shaw	4,405
21		29	(a)	Bury	L	1-3	Mooney	5,404
22	Jan	1	(h)	Cambridge U	L	0-2		5,256
23		12	(h)	Reading	L	1-2	Swann	4,470
24		19	(a)	Grimsby T	L	1-4	Mooney	5,391
25		26	(h)	Southend U	W	2-1	Shaw, Wrightson	4,351
26	Feb	2	(h)	Bolton W	L	1-2	Wrightson	9,844
27		5	(a)	Fulham	L	0-1		2,750
28		16	(a)	Huddersfield T	L	0-1		5,504
29		23	(h)	Bradford C	L	0-3		6,878
30	Mar	2	(a)	Shrewsbury T	W	1-0	Shaw	2,989
31		9	(h)	Leyton Orient	W	2-1	Shaw, Thompson	3,651
32		12	(a)	Brentford	L	0-2		4,856
33		16	(h)	Birmingham C	W	2-0	Cartwright, Joyce	5,334
34		19	(h)	Mansfield T	W	3-1	Jepson 2, Joyce (pen)	3,245
35		23	(a)	Exeter C	L	0-4		3,525
36		26	(h)	Swansea C	W	2-0	Shaw 2	3,491
37		30	(h)	Crewe Alex	W	5-1	Joyce, Shaw, Bogie, Thompson, James	4,852
38	Apr	1	(a)	Stoke C	W	1-0	Shaw	11,524
39		6	(h)	Bury	D	1-1	Shaw	5,641
40		13	(a)	Cambridge U	D	1-1	Joyce	6,262
41		16	(a)	Swansea C	L	1-3	Senior	2,507
42		20	(h)	Rotherham U	L	1-2	Flynn	4,069
43		27	(a)	Chester C	D	1-1	Joyce	1,351
44	May	2	(a)	Bournemouth	D	0-0		7,064
45		7	(a)	Tranmere R	L	1-2	Ashcroft	6,006
46		11	(h)	Wigan A	W	2-1	Jepson, Shaw	5,917

FINAL LEAGUE POSITION: 17th in Division Three

Appearances

Sub. Appearances

Goals

Farnworth	Senior	Swann	Greaves	Flynn	Wrightson	Williams	Joyce	Thomas	Shaw	Harper	Peel	Bogie	James	Hughes	Kelly	Fee	Rathbone	Greenwood	Ashcroft	Mooney	Easter	Thompson	Jepson	Cartwright	Lambert	Eaves	Kerfoot	Jackson	
1	2	3	4	5	6	7	8	9	10	11*	12																		1
1	2	3		5	6	7*	10	9		12	8†	4	11	14															2
1	2	3			6	7	10	9		8*	12	4	11	5															3
	2*	8			6	3	11	9	10		7	12	5	1	4														4
1		11			6	2	7	9*	10	12		8	3	5		4													5
1		10			6	2	7		9			8	11	5		4	3												6
1	2	11			6	7	10		9			8	3	5*		4	12												7
1	2	11			6	7*	10		9	12		8	3	5		4													8
1	2	11			6		10		9			8	7	5		4	3												9
1	2	11			6	14*	10		9	12		8	7	5†		4	3												10
1	2	11	12		6		10		9	7*		8	3	5		4													11
1		11	2	5	6		10	7				8	3	9*		4				12									12
1		11	2		6		10	7				8	3	5		4				9									13
1	2	11		4	6		10	7		8*		3	5†	12					14	9									14
	2	7*		4	6		11	10		12		8	14	5	1		3	9											15
	2	10			6	4	9	7*		12		8	11	5	1		3												16
	2	10			6	4	9	11				8		5	1		3			7									17
	2	10		12	6	14	4	9	11			8		5	1		3†			7*									18
	2	11		4	6	3	9		10			8		5	1							7							19
	2	11		4	6	3	9		10			8		5	1							7							20
	2	11		4	6	3†	9		10	12		14	8	5*	1							7							21
	2	11		4	6		9		10	12		14	8†	5*	1		3					7							22
	2	11		4	6		9		10*	14				1	5	3	12					7	8						23
	2	11		4	6		9		10	8				1	5	3						7							24
		11		4	6		9		10	8		3		1	5	2						7							25
1		11		5	6	2	10	8		12		3		4					9			7*							26
1		11		5	6	2	10	8*		12		3		4					9			7							27
1	2	11		5	6	3	10	8†		12		14	4									7*	9						28
1		11		5	6	3	10	8*				2	4						12			7	9						29
1	2	11		5	6		10					3	4									7	9	8					30
1	2			5	6		10	12				3	4						11			7	9*	8					31
1	2			5			10	11				4	6†						12			7		8	3*	9	14		32
1	2			5	6	4	10	11				3										7	9	8					33
1	2			5	6	4	10	11				3										7	9	8					34
1	2			5	6	4	10	11		8†		3							12			7*	9			14			35
	2			5	6	4	10	11		8		3		1								7	9						36
	2			5	6†	4	10*	11		8		3		1								7	9	12			14		37
	2			5	6	4	10	11		8		3		1					12			7*	9						38
	2				6	4	10	11		8		3		1					12			7*	9					5	39
	2				6	4	10	11				3		1								7	9	8				5	40
	2				6	4	10	11		12		3		1								7	9	8*	14			5†	41
	2			5	6	4	10*	11		8		3		1					12			7	9						42
	2			5	6	4	10†	11		12		3		1					14			7*	9	8					43
	2			5		4	10	11				3		1					9			7		8	6				44
	2			5		4	10*	11	14	12		3		1					9†			7		8	6				45
	2			5			10	11		8†		3		1					9*			7	12	4	6	14			46
23	38	30	2	33	40	11	42	5	44	27	1	28	34	25	23	15	11	3	6	9	1	21	13	13	4	1		3	
				2		2				9	9	3	3	1					2	2		8			1	1	1	1	
	2	5		1	3		9	1	10		1	8	2	1		1	1	1	1			2	2	3	1				

123

1991-92

1	Aug	17	(a)	Peterbrough U	L	0-1		6,036
2		24	(h)	Torquay U	W	3-0	Shaw, Ashcroft, Greenwood	3,654
3		30	(a)	Stockport Co	L	0-2		5,405
4	Sep	3	(h)	Bournemouth	D	2-2	James M, Greenwood	3,170
5		7	(h)	Bradford C	D	1-1	Joyce (pen)	4,160
6		14	(a)	Swansea C	D	2-2	Shaw 2	3,170
7		17	(a)	Leyton Orient	D	0-0		3,296
8		21	(h)	Stoke C	D	2-2	Jepson, Swann	6,345
9		28	(a)	Birmingham C	L	1-3	Shaw	8,760
10	Oct	1	(h)	West Brom A	W	2-0	Swann, Senior	5,293
11		12	(a)	Bury	W	3-2	Ashcroft, Greenwood, Shaw	4,265
12		19	(h)	Huddersfield T	W	1-0	James M	6,866
13		26	(a)	Fulham	L	0-1		4,022
14	Nov	2	(a)	Chester C	L	2-3	Shaw, Swann	1,219
15		5	(h)	Wigan A	W	3-0	Swann, Joyce 2 (1 pen)	3,657
16		9	(h)	Darlington	W	2-1	Thomas, Shaw	4,643
17		23	(a)	Bolton W	L	0-1		7,033
18		30	(a)	Hull C	D	2-2	Thomas, Shaw	4,280
19	Dec	14	(h)	Hartlepool U	L	1-4	Ashcroft	5,032
20		20	(a)	Torquay U	L	0-1		2,183
21		26	(h)	Stockport Co	W	3-2	Swann, Shaw (pen), James M	6,782
22		28	(h)	Peterbrough U	D	1-1	Cartwright	5,200
23	Jan	1	(a)	Bournemouth	L	0-1		5,508
24		11	(a)	Shrewsbury T	L	0-2		3,154
25		18	(h)	Exeter C	L	1-3	Lambert	3,585
26		25	(a)	Brentford	L	0-1		7,559
27	Feb	1	(a)	Huddersfield T	W	2-1	Shaw, Cartwright	6,700
28		8	(h)	Fulham	L	1-2	Johnrose	3,878
29		11	(h)	Hull C	W	3-1	Williams, Jepson 2	2,932
30		15	(a)	Hartlepool U	L	0-2		2,140
31		22	(h)	Shrewsbury T	D	2-2	James M, Wrightson	3,342
32		29	(a)	Reading	D	2-2	Lambert, Shaw	3,390
33	Mar	3	(a)	Exeter C	L	1-4	Ashcroft	2,214
34		7	(h)	Brentford	W	3-2	Shaw, Thompson, Ashcroft	3,548
35		10	(a)	Wigan A	L	0-3		3,364
36		14	(h)	Chester C	L	0-3		3,909
37		21	(a)	Darlington	W	2-0	Jepson 2	2,270
38		28	(h)	Bolton W	W	2-1	Joyce (pen), Flynn	7,327
39		31	(h)	Swansea C	D	1-1	Greenall	3,367
40	Apr	4	(a)	Bradford C	D	1-1	Shaw	6,044
41		11	(h)	Leyton Orient	W	2-1	Flynn, Howard (og)	3,926
42		14	(h)	Reading	D	1-1	Cartwright	3,203
43		18	(a)	Stoke C	L	1-2	Thompson	16,151
44		24	(h)	Birmingham C	W	3-2	Cartwright, Flynn, Shaw	7,738
45		25	(a)	West Brom A	L	0-3		11,318
46	May	2	(h)	Bury	W	2-0	Joyce, Finney	6,932

FINAL LEAGUE POSITION: 17th in Division Three

Appearances

Sub. Appearances

Goals

Farnworth	Senior	Swann	Wrightson	Flynn	Berry	Thompson	Joyce	Jepson	Shaw	James M	Williams	Aschroft	Greenwood	Lambert	Kelly	James J	Cartwright	Cross	Thomas	Allpress	Hughes	Kerfoot	Ainsworth	Whitworth	Finney	Johnrose	Greenall	Christie	
1	2	3	4	5	6	7	8	9	10	11																			1
1	2	4	6	5			8	9*	10	3	7	11	12																2
1	2	8*	6	5	7			9	10	3	12	14	11	4†															3
	2	8	3	5	6	7*	4	9	10	11			12		1														4
	2	4	3	5	6*		8	9	10	11			12	7	1														5
	2	4	3	5		12		9	10	11				7	1	6	8*												6
	2	11	6	5		12	8	9	10†	3				7*	1	4	14												7
	2	4	3	5		12	8	9	10	11				7*	1	6													8
	2	4	7	5			8	9	10*	11					1	6		3	12										9
	2	4	7	5			8		10	11			9		1	6		3											10
	2†	4	7	5		12	8		10	14	11		9		1	6	3*												11
	2	4	6	5		12	8		10	11		7	9*		1			3											12
	2	4	6	5		12	8		10	14		7			1		11	3†	9*										13
	2*	4	3	5			9	8	10	11†	14	7			1		12				6								14
		4	3	5			9	8	10	11	2	7			1						6								15
	2	4*	3	5		9†	8		10	11	14	7			1					12	6								16
	2	4	3†	5			8*		10	11	14	7	12		1					9	6								17
	2	4	3	5					10	11		7	12		1		8			9*	6								18
	2	4	3	5					10			7	11*	14	1		8			9	6†	12							19
	2		3	5					10			7	11	6*	1		8			9	12	4							20
	2	4	3	5*					10	11		7	9		1		8			12	6								21
	2	4	3	5					10	11		7	9*		1		8		12		6								22
	2	4	3	5			12		10†			7			1		8		9	11*	6	14							23
1	2	4	3	5					10*			7					8		9		6	12	11						24
1	2	4	3*						10†			7					8		9		6		11	5	14				25
1	2	4							12	11		7	10	3			8				6			5		9*			26
1	2†	4		3					10*	11		7	9	14			8				6	12		5					27
1	2	11	3	5					10		12	7*	9				8			4†	6						14		28
1	2		4	5			9*		10		11	7	3				8				6						12		29
1	2		4	5					10		11	7	9	3			8				6								30
	2		4	5				9	10	3	11	7			1		8				6								31
	2	14	4	5				9	10	11	7*		12	3	1		8				6†								32
	2	8	6	5		14		9†	10	11	12	7	3*		1		4												33
1	2		3	5		9*	8		10	11	12	7					4				6								34
1	2		3	5		9	8		10	11		7	12				4*				6								35
1			3	5		9	8	12	10	11	2*	7					4				6								36
1		6		5		11	8	9	10	3	2	7					4										6		37
1				5		11	8	9	10	3	2	7					4										6		38
1				5		11	8	9	10*	3	2	7					4							12			6		39
1	7*			5		11	8	9	10	3	2						4							12			6		40
1				5		11	8	9	10	3	2	7*					4										6	12	41
1			5			11	8	9	10	3	2	7					4										6		42
1				5		11	8	9*	10	3	2	7					4										6	12	43
1				5		11	8	9	10	3	2	7					4										6		44
1		12	5			11*	8	9†	10	3	2	7					4						14				6		45
1				5		11	8	9*	10	3	2	7					4								12		6		46
23	35	28	36	43	4	18	28	23	45	36	17	35	16	7	23	6	31	5	8	7	14		2	6		1	9		
		1	1			7	1	1	1		9	3	4	4			2		3	2	1	3	3		2	2		2	
	1	5	1	3		2	5	5	14	4	1	5	3	2			4		2						1	1	1		

125

1992-93

1	Aug	15	(h)	Bournemouth	D	1-1	Ellis	4,756
2		22	(a)	Fulham	L	1-2	Ellis	3,641
3		29	(h)	Chester C	W	4-3	Cartwright, Flynn, Ashcroft, Leonard	4,471
4	Sep	5	(a)	Brighton & HA	L	0-2		6,026
5		12	(h)	Burley	W	2-0	Tinker, Ashcroft	7,209
6		15	(a)	Hull C	W	4-2	Ellis 2, Ashcroft, Cartwright	4,463
7		19	(a)	Bradford C	L	0-4		5,882
8		26	(h)	Hartlepool U	L	0-2		4,347
9	Oct	3	(h)	Plymouth A	L	1-2	Davidson	4,401
10		10	(a)	Blackpool	W	3-2	Ellis 3	7,631
11		17	(h)	Stoke C	L	1-2	Callaghan	8,138
12		20	(h)	Reading	W	2-0	Flitcroft, Ashcroft (pen)	3,329
13		24	(a)	Mansfield T	D	2-2	James, Fowler L	3,047
14		31	(h)	Bolton W	D	2-2	James, Cartwright	7,013
15	Nov	3	(a)	Stockport C	L	0-3		4,860
16		7	(h)	Wigan A	W	2-0	Callaghan, James	4,442
17		21	(a)	Rotherham U	L	0-1		4,246
18		28	(h)	West Brom A	D	1-1	Ellis	6,306
19	Dec	12	(h)	Port Vale	L	2-5	James, Ashcroft (pen)	6,038
20		18	(a)	Leyton Orient	L	1-3	Ashcroft	3,436
21		28	(h)	Exeter C	D	2-2	Garnett, Norbury	5,796
22	Jan	9	(h)	Hull C	L	1-2	Garnett	4,719
23		16	(a)	Hartlepool U	D	0-0		2,682
24		23	(h)	Bradford C	W	3-2	Norbury, James, Ellis	5,155
25		26	(a)	Chester C	W	4-2	Norbury, Flynn, Ellis, Flitcroft	2,901
26		30	(h)	Fulham	L	1-2	Ellis	5,858
27	Feb	6	(a)	Bournemouth	L	1-2	Tinker	3,601
28		13	(h)	Brighton & HA	W	1-0	Norbury	4,334
29		16	(a)	Burnley	L	0-2		12,648
30		20	(a)	Reading	L	0-4		3,543
31		27	(h)	Blackpool	D	3-3	Ellis 2, Fowler L	10,403
32	Mar	6	(a)	Plymouth A	L	0-4		5,201
33		9	(h)	Swansea C	L	1-3	Norbury	4,396
34		12	(a)	Wigan A	W	3-2	Norbury, Burton 2	3,562
35		17	(a)	Huddersfield T	L	0-1		4,915
36		20	(h)	Stockport C	L	2-3	Ellis 2	5,255
37		24	(a)	West Brom A	L	2-3	Ellis, Ashcroft	13,270
38		27	(h)	Rotherham U	W	5-2	Norbury 2, Ellis 3	4,859
39	Apr	6	(a)	Port Vale	D	2-2	Ellis, Watson	8,271
40		10	(h)	Huddersfield T	W	2-1	Watson, Ellis	7,647
41		12	(a)	Exeter C	W	1-0	Watson	3,410
42		17	(h)	Leyton Orient	L	1-4	Burton	5,890
43		24	(a)	Stoke C	L	0-1		18,334
44		27	(a)	Swansea C	L	0-2		6,933
45	May	1	(h)	Mansfield T	L	1-5	Ellis	5,889
46		8	(a)	Bolton W	L	0-1		21,270

FINAL LEAGUE POSITION: 21st in Division Two

Appearances

Sub. Appearances

Goals

126

Farnworth	Davidson	Fowler L	Tinkler	Flynn	Callaghan	Ashcroft	Cartwright	Leonard	Ellis	James M	Eaves	Flitcroft	Christie	Burton	Finney	Kidd	Graham	Allardyce S	Taylor	Siddall	Garnett	Moylon	Lucas	Ainsworth	Norbury	Johnstone	Greenall	Fowler J	Whalley	Watson	Allardyce C	
1	2	3	4	5	6	7	8	9	10	11																						1
1	2	3	4*	5	6	7	8	9	10	11†	12	14																				2
1	2	3	4†	5	6	7	8	9	10	11*	14	12																				3
1	2	3		5	6	7	8	9	10*	14	4		11†	12																		4
1	2	3	4	5	6†	7	8	9	10*	11	14			12																		5
1	2	3	4	5	6	7	8	9	10	11																						6
1	2	3	4*	5	6	7	8	9	10	11							12															7
1	2	3	4	5	6*	7	8	9	10	11				12																		8
1	2	3	4	5	6	7	8	9	10	11																						9
1	2	3†	4	5	6	7	8	9	10*	11						12	14															10
1	2	3	4	5	6	7	8	9	10	11*							12															11
1	12	3	4	5	11	7	2	9	10		8*					6																12
1	12	3	4	5	10	7	2	9*		11						6†	8	14														13
1	12	3	4	5	8		2		10	11						6*	7		9													14
1	3	6	4	5	8		2†		10	11	12						7*	14	9													15
1	3	6		5	4	7	2		10	11							8		9													16
1	3	6		5	4	7	2			11				12			8	9	10*													17
1	3	6	7	5	4	9	2		10	11							8															18
	2	3		5	4	9			10	11		8					7			1	6											19
1	3		2†	5	4	12			10	11		8		9			7*				6			14								20
1	2			5	4	7			10					11							6			3	8	9						21
1		12		5	4	7								11	10*						6			3	8	9						22
1		11		5	4	7	2														6			3	8	9						23
1			2	5	4			7		10	11										6			3	8	9						24
1*			2	5†	4		7		10	11	14			12							6			3	8	9						25
		12		4*	7	2			10	11	5										6			3	8	9		1				26
		11*	4			7	2	10						12							6			3	8	9		1	5			27
		12	2	5			7		10	11*											6			3	8	9		1		4		28
		3	2	5		12	7	14	10					11*										4	8	9	6	1				29
		3		5	12	11†	2	14	10															4	8*	9	6	1	7			30
		8		5	4	11			10															3	2	9	6	1	7			31
			5†	12	11	7*	10		14															3	2	9		1	6	8	4	32
1		7		5		11								10										3	2	9		6	8	4		33
		7		5		11			12					10										3	2	9*	1	6	8	4		34
		7*		5	8	11			12					10										3	2	9	1	6		4		35
				5	8	11			10					7										3	2	9	1	6		4		36
1				5	8	11			10					7										3	2	9		6		4		37
1						11	7		10					8		5								3	2	9		6		4		38
1*						11	7		10					8†		5								3	2		6	12	4	9	14	39
1						11	7		10					8		5								3	2			6		4	9	40
1		12				11	7		10*					8		5								3	2			6		4	9	41
1						11	7	10						8		5								3	2			6		4	9	42
1			12			2	11	7*	8					10		5								3	4			6			9	43
1						2	11	14	10*					8		5								3	7	9	6†	6		4	12	44
1		3					12	10*						11		5								7	2	9		6		4	8	45
1		7*				2		11						10		5								3	8	9		6		4	12	46
35	18	29	22	35	33	37	33	19	34	22	1	4	1	17	1	13	8	1	4	1	10			26	26	21	10	20	5	14	6	
3	3	2		2	2	1	3	1	3	3	4	1	4	3	2		2			1								1		2	1	
	1	2	2	2	2	7	3	1	22	5		2		3						2				8						3	1	

127

1993-94

#	Month	Date		Opponent		Result	Scorers	Attendance
1	Aug	14	(h)	Crewe Alex	L	0-2		6,879
2		21	(a)	Scarborough	W	4-3	Ellis 2, Ainsworth 2	2,329
3		28	(h)	Shrewsbury T	W	6-1	Ainsworth 2, Conroy 3, Nebbeling	4,941
4		31	(h)	Bury	W	3-1	Nebbeling, Conroy, Ellis	5,886
5	Sep	4	(a)	Lincoln C	W	2-0	Ellis, Raynor	3,793
6		11	(h)	Doncaster R	W	3-1	Conroy, Matthewson, Raynor	7,294
7		18	(a)	Torquay U	L	3-4	Conroy, Ellis, Ainsworth	3,912
8		25	(a)	Mansfield T	D	2-2	Ellis 2	3,762
9	Oct	2	(h)	Colchester U	W	1-0	Ellis	6,412
10		9	(h)	Chesterfield	W	4-1	Raynor, Ellis 3 (1 pen)	6,581
11		16	(a)	Wigan A	D	2-2	Conroy, Challender	3,741
12		23	(h)	Rochdale	W	2-1	Ellis 2 (1 pen)	8,491
13		30	(a)	Hereford U	W	3-2	Moyes, Ellis 2	3,383
14	Nov	2	(a)	Walsall	L	0-2		4,446
15		6	(h)	Darlington	W	3-2	Nebbeling 2, Cartwright	6,711
16		20	(a)	Carlisle U	W	1-0	Ellis	10,279
17		27	(h)	Wycombe W	L	2-3	Ainsworth, Challender	9,265
18	Dec	11	(h)	Scarborough	D	2-2	Bryson, Ellis (pen)	6,290
19		17	(a)	Crewe Alex	L	3-4	Moyes, Conroy, Raynor	6,035
20		27	(h)	Chester C	D	1-1	Ellis	12,790
21	Jan	1	(h)	Scunthorpe U	D	2-2	Conroy, Norbury	7,669
22		4	(a)	Bury	D	1-1	Norbury	4,164
23		15	(h)	Wigan A	W	3-0	Ellis 2, Conroy	7,728
24		22	(a)	Chesterfield	D	1-1	Moyes	3,804
25	Feb	5	(a)	Rochdale	L	1-2	Conroy	4,317
26		12	(h)	Gillingham	D	0-0		6,167
27		19	(a)	Shrewsbury T	L	0-1		5,391
28		25	(h)	Lincoln C	W	2-0	Conroy, Raynor	5,941
29	Mar	1	(h)	Hereford U	W	3-0	Ellis 2, Bryson	6,641
30		4	(a)	Doncaster R	D	1-1	Yates (og)	3,321
31		12	(h)	Torquay U	W	3-1	Ellis 2, Sulley	6,641
32		15	(a)	Northampton T	L	0-2		3,845
33		19	(h)	Mansfield T	W	3-1	Norbury 2, Ainsworth	6,747
34		26	(a)	Colchester U	D	1-1	Norbury	2,950
35	Apr	2	(a)	Chester C	L	2-3	Ainsworth, Ellis	5,638
36		4	(h)	Northampton T	D	1-1	Ainsworth	7,517
37		9	(a)	Scunthorpe U	L	1-3	Ainsworth, Ellis	3,790
38		12	(a)	Gillingham	D	2-2	Moyes, Green (og)	2,453
39		16	(h)	Walsall	W	2-0	Ainsworth, Fensome	7,020
40		23	(a)	Darlington	W	2-0	Raynor, Ellis	2,739
41		30	(h)	Carlisle U	L	0-3		11,363
42	May	7	(a)	Wycombe W	D	1-1	Kidd	7,442

FINAL LEAGUE POSITION: 5th in Division Three

Appearances
Sub. Appearances
Goals

O'Hanlon	Callaghan	Sulley	Nebbeling	Kidd	Raynor	Ainsworth	Whalley	Norbury	Ellis	Burton	Masefield	Cartwright	Conroy	Matthewson	Lucas	Moyes	Bamber	Challender	Woods	Fensome	Holland	Bryson	Watson	Magee	Kibane	Hicks	Squires	No.
1	2	3	4	5	6	7	8	9	10	11																		1
1		3	4	5	6	7	11	9*	10		2	8	12															2
1		3	5		11	7	4	12	10*		2	8	9	6														3
1		3	5		11	7	4		10		2	8		6														4
1		3	5	12	11	7	4		10		2*	8	9	6														5
1		3	5	2	11	7	4		10			8	9	6														6
1		3	5	2†	11	7	4	12	10			8	9*	6	14													7
1			5		11	7	4		10			8	9*	6	3	2	12											8
1		3	5		11	7		12	10		2	8	9*	6	4†			14										9
		3	5		11	7			10		2	8	9	6				4	1									10
			5	3	11	7			10			8	9	6*				4	1	2	12							11
1			5	3	11	7†	4	12	10			8	9*			6		14		2								12
1			5	3	11		4	9	10			8		7		6				2								13
1			5	3	11		4†	9*	10	12		8		7		6		14		2								14
1			5	3	11		4	12	10*			8	9	7		6				2								15
1			5	3	11	7*	12		10			8	9		4	6				2								16
1*		3			11	7	4		10				9		5	6		8	12	2								17
		3			11	7	4	12	10				9*		5	6		8†	1	2		14						18
1		3	5		11	7	4		10*			14	12		8	6				2†		9						19
1			5	3	11	7*	4†		10			14	12		8	6				2		9						20
1			5	3	11			12	10*			4	9		8	6				2		7						21
1			5	3	11	7*	12					4	9		8	6				2		10						22
1		3	5		11*	12			10			8	9		4	6				2		7						23
1			5	3	11*	12			10			8	9		4	6				2		7						24
		5†		3	11*	12	14		10			8	9		4	6			1	2		7						25
		3	5		11*	12	14		10			8†	9		4	6			1	2		7						26
			5		11	3		9	10*			8	12		4	6			1	2		7						27
		3	5		11	7			10			12	9		4*	6			1	2		8						28
		3	5		11	7			10			4	9			6			1	2		8						29
		3			12	7*	14					4	9	5		6			1	2		8		10	11†			30
		3		2	11	7		9*	10			4		5		6			1			8		12				31
		3			11†	7	12	9	10			4		5*		6			1	2		8		14				32
1		3	5		11	7		9	10			4				6				2		8						33
1		3	5		12	7		9				4				6		10		2		8		11*				34
		3	6		11	7		9	10			4							1	2		8				5		35
		3	6			7		9	10			4			12				1	2		8		11		5*		36
		3	6			7	14		10			4	9†		12				1	2		8		11		5*		37
		3	5			7			10			4	9		8	6			1	2		11		12				38
			5		12	7		9*	10			4			8	6			1	2		11				3		39
			5		10†	7		12				4	9*		8	6		14	1	2		11				3		40
			5		9	7			10			4			8	6			1	2		11				3		41
			5		9	7			10			4			8	6		14	1	2		10		11†		3*		42
23	1	21	22	32	36	34	17	11	36	2	6	36	27	12	21	29		5	19	31		24	1	5		3	4	App
			3	4	4	10	1	1				3	4		3	1		5	1			1	1	2		1	0	Sub
		1	4	1	6	11		5	26			1	12	1		4		2		1		2						Gls

1994-95

#	Month	Date		Opponent	Result		Scorers	Attendance
1	Aug	13	(a)	Darlington	D	0-0		3,800
2		20	(a)	Hereford U	W	2-0	Conroy, Sale	3,039
3		27	(a)	Barnet	L	1-2	Sale	2,441
4		30	(a)	Bury	D	0-0		3,623
5	Sep	3	(h)	Lincoln C	W	4-0	Moyes, Sale 2, Ainsworth	8,337
6		10	(a)	Fulham	W	1-0	Trebble	5,001
7		13	(a)	Gillingham	W	3-2	Sale 2, Fleming	2,555
8		17	(h)	Darlington	L	1-3	Trebble	8,884
9		24	(a)	Doncaster R	L	1-2	Fleming	3,321
10	Oct	1	(h)	Walsall	L	1-2	Whalley	7,852
11		8	(h)	Scunthorpe U	L	0-1		6,895
12		15	(a)	Hartlepool U	L	1-3	Atkinson	2,002
13		22	(a)	Colchester U	L	1-3	Trebble	3,015
14		29	(h)	Exeter C	L	0-1		6,808
15	Nov	5	(a)	Mansfield T	W	2-1	Conroy 2	2,602
16		19	(h)	Northampton T	W	2-0	Moyes, Raynor	7,297
17		26	(a)	Chesterfield	L	0-1		3,191
18	Dec	10	(h)	Hereford U	W	4-2	Magee, Conroy, Bryson 2 (2 pen)	6,581
19		17	(h)	Barnet	W	1-0	Kidd	6,429
20		26	(h)	Rochdale	W	3-0	Smart, Kidd, Conroy	10,491
21		31	(h)	Scarborough	W	1-0	Smart	8,407
22	Jan	2	(a)	Torquay U	L	0-1		3,770
23		10	(h)	Colchester U	W	2-1	Smart, Trebble	6,377
24		17	(a)	Carlisle U	D	0-0		10,684
25		21	(h)	Mansfield T	W	2-1	Bryson, Smart	8,448
26		24	(a)	Wigan A	D	1-1	Cartwright	3,618
27	Feb	4	(h)	Chesterfield	D	0-0		8,544
28		11	(a)	Northampton T	L	1-2	Smart	5,195
29		18	(h)	Carlisle U	W	1-0	Conroy	11,897
30		28	(a)	Walsall	D	2-2	Conroy, Raynor	4,492
31	Mar	4	(h)	Doncaster R	D	2-2	Davey, Beckham	9,624
32		11	(h)	Fulham	W	3-2	Conroy, Raynor, Beckham	8,601
33		18	(h)	Bury	W	5-0	Carmichael 2 Conroy 2, Moyes	9,626
34		21	(a)	Exeter C	W	1-0	Bryson	2,057
35		25	(a)	Lincoln C	D	1-1	Kidd	5,487
36	Apr	1	(h)	Gillingham	D	1-1	Carmichael	9,100
37		8	(a)	Scarborough	D	1-1	Bryson	4,266
38		15	(h)	Wigan A	W	1-0	Smart	10,238
39		17	(a)	Rochdale	W	1-0	Davey	4,012
40		22	(h)	Torquay U	L	0-1		9,173
41		29	(h)	Hartlepool U	W	3-0	Moyes, Holmes, Davey	9,129
42	May	6	(a)	Scunthorpe U	L	1-2	Sale	3,691

FINAL LEAGUE POSITION: 5th in Division Three

Appearances

Sub. Appearances

Goals

Richardson	Fensome	Fleming	Whalley	Hicks	Moyes	Ainsworth	Cartwright	Raynor	Trebble	Bryson	Kidd	Sale	Conroy	Squires	Vaughan	Sharp	Akinson	Holmes	Emerson	Smart	Magee	Rimmer	Lancashire	Davey	Beckham	Carmichael	No.
1	2	3	4	5	6	7	8	9	10	11																	1
1	2	11	4	5	6	7	8	9*			3	10	12														2
1	2	3	4	5		7	8	12	9†	11	6	14	10*														3
1	2	.	4		6	7		11		8	3	10	9	5													4
1	2	14	4		6	7	12	9		8*	3	10	11†	5													5
1	2	11†	4	5	6	7*	12	9	14	8	3	10															6
1	2	11	4*	5	6	7	12	9†	14	8	3	10															7
1	2	11	4		6	7	12	9	14	8	3*	10†		5													8
1	2	9	4		6	7		11	10	8	3			5													9
1	2	14	4		6	7	12	11†	10	8*	3	9		5													10
1	2	10	4	5	6	7		11	12	8	3	9*															11
	2	12	4†	5		7	14		10	8	6	9*			1	3	11										12
	2	14	4	5	6		7†	9		8		12	10*		1	3	11										13
	2	7	4†		6		14	9		8		12	10*		1	3	11	5									14
	2	7	12		6		4	9		8		10	5*		1	3	11										15
1	2	12			6	7	4	9	11*	8†			10			3	5	14									16
1	2				6		4	12	7*	8	11		10			3	5			9							17
1	2	12			6		4	11		8			10			3	5			9†	7*		14				18
1	2				6	7		11		8	5		10			3			4	9*		12					19
1	2				6		4	11		8	5		10			3	12			9†	7*		14				20
1°	2				6		4	11		8	5		10†	15		3*	12			9	7		14				21
	2	3			6	7*	4	12		8	5		14		1	11				9†			10				22
	2	3			6		4	11	12	8	5				1			14		9*	7†		10				23
	2	3			6		4	11	12	8	5				1			14		9*	7†		10				24
	2	3			6		4	11	12	8	5				1			14		9*	7†		10				25
	2	12			6	7	4	11	14	8	5				1	3†				9*			10				26
	2				6		4	11	12	8	5				1	3		14		9*	7†		10				27
	2				6	7*	4	11	12	8	5				1	3		10		9							28
	2				6		4	11		8	5		10		1	3		12		9†	7*		14				29
	2				6		4	11		8	5		10		1	3				9*			12	7			30
	2				6		4	11†		8	5		10		1	3				12			9*	7	14		31
	2				6	12		9		8*	5		10		1	3					11			7	4		32
	2				6					8	5		10		1	3					11			7	4	9	33
	2				6	12				8		10		5	1	3					11*			7	4	9	34
	2				6	12		14		8	5		10		1	3					11*			7	4	9†	35
	2				6	12	4			8	5				1	3†	10			14	11*			7		9	36
	2	3			6	11	4			8	5		10		1								12	7		9*	37
	2	3			6†		4	11		8	5		10		1					9*			12	7	14		38
	2	3			6		4	11		8	5		12	6	1					9†			14	7		10*	39
	2	3			6		4	11		8	5†		10*	6	1					9			12	7	14		40
	2	3			6		4			8					1		5			11			9	7		10	41
	2*	3			6	12	4			8	5		10†		1					11			9	7		14	42
17	42	20	14		38	16	25	34	8	41	32	10	22	11	25	21	8	5	1	17	14		9	13	4	7	
		7	1		11	4	11				3	3	1			7				1	2	2	8		1	3	
		2	1		4	1	1	3	4	5	3	7	10			1	1			6	1			3	2	3	

131

1995-96

#							Scorers	Att.
1	Aug	12	(h)	Lincoln C	L	1-2	Saville	7,813
2		19	(a)	Plymouth Argyle	W	2-0	Hammond (og), Bryson	6,862
3		26	(h)	Wigan A	D	1-1	Atkinson	6,837
4		29	(a)	Bury	D	0-0		4,682
5	Sep	2	(h)	Cambridge U	D	3-3	Saville, Wilkinson, Lancashire	7,034
6		9	(a)	Hereford U	W	1-0	Saville	3,124
7		12	(a)	Colchester U	D	2-2	Cartwright, Bryson	2,869
8		16	(h)	Scunthorpe U	D	2-2	Atkinson, Bryson	7,397
9		23	(a)	Fulham	D	2-2	Bryson (pen), Davey	5,209
10		30	(h)	Chester C	W	2-0	Wilkinson, Saville	8,544
11	Oct	7	(h)	Scarborough	W	3-2	Saville, Wilkinson, Davey	7,702
12		14	(a)	Torquay U	W	4-0	Bryson 2, Saville 2	4,058
13		21	(h)	Mansfield T	W	6-0	Wilkinson 3, Saville 3	8,981
14		28	(a)	Doncaster U	D	2-2	Davey 2	4,413
15		31	(a)	Northampton T	W	2-1	Wilcox, Saville	4,695
16	Nov	4	(h)	Leyton Orient	W	4-0	Saville 3, Davey	9,823
17		18	(a)	Exeter C	D	1-1	Moyes	3,550
18		25	(h)	Hartlepool	W	3-0	Moyes, Atkinson, Saville	9,449
19	Dec	9	(h)	Fulham	D	1-1	Bryson	8,422
20		16	(a)	Chester C	D	1-1	Wilkinson	5,004
21		23	(h)	Gillingham	D	0-0		10,669
22	Jan	1	(h)	Cardiff C	W	5-0	Davey, Brown, Saville 2, Atkinson	8,354
23		6	(a)	Barnet	L	0-1		2,737
24		13	(h)	Plymouth Argyle	W	3-2	Bryson, Davey, Cartwright	11,126
25		20	(a)	Lincoln C	D	0-0		5,185
26		30	(a)	Darlington	W	2-1	Cartwright, Saville	2,599
27	Feb	3	(a)	Wigan A	W	1-0	Kilbane	5,567
28		10	(h)	Barnet	L	0-1		9,974
29		17	(h)	Colchester U	W	2-0	Saville 2	9,335
30		24	(a)	Scunthorpe U	W	2-1	Saville, Lancaster	3,638
31		27	(h)	Hereford U	D	2-2	Atkinson, Saville	9,761
32	Mar	2	(h)	Rochdale	L	1-2	Saville	9,697
33		9	(a)	Gillingham	D	1-1	Davey	10,602
34		12	(a)	Rochdale	W	3-0	Birch, Wilkinson, Moyes	4,597
35		16	(h)	Darlington	D	1-1	Bryson	12,070
36		23	(a)	Cardiff C	W	1-0	Saville	3,511
37		26	(h)	Bury	D	0-0		12,260
38		30	(a)	Scarborough	W	2-1	Davey, Bennett	3,771
39	Apr	2	(h)	Torquay U	W	1-0	Wilkinson	11,965
40		6	(h)	Doncaster R	W	1-0	Birch	12,773
41		8	(a)	Mansfield T	D	0-0		4,661
42		13	(h)	Northampton T	L	0-3		11,774
43		16	(a)	Cambridge U	L	1-2	Saville	2,831
44		20	(a)	Leyton Orient	W	2-0	Saville	5,170
45		27	(a)	Hartlepool U	W	2-0	Davey, Saville	5,076
46	May	4	(h)	Exeter C	W	2-0	Saville, Wilkinson	18,700

FINAL lEAGUE POSITION: 1st in Division Three

Appearances

Sub. Appearances

Goals

Vaughan	Fensome	Fleming	Davey	Kidd	Moyes	Raynor	Bryson	Saville	Wilkinson	Atkinson	Lancashire	Sharp	Magee	Ainsworth	Squires	Holmes	Cartwright	Brown	Richardson	Johnson	Barrick	Smart	Wilcox	Kilbane	McDonald	Bishop	Moilanen	Sparrow	Birch	Grant	Bennet	Gage	Lucas
1	2*	3	4	5	6	7	8	9	10	11	12																						
1	2*		7	5	6		8	9	10	4°		3	11	12	13																		
1		2	3		6		8	9	10	4			11*	12		5	7																
1		2	3		6		8	9	10	4			11			5	7																
1		2	3		6*	13	8	9	10	4	12		11†			5	7°	14															
	2		3			11	8	9	10	4					5		7		1	6													
	2*		3				8	9	10†	4				12	5		7	11†	1	6	13	14											
	2	12	6				8	9	10	1					5		7°	11*	1		3	13											
1	2		7		6		8*	9	10	4							12	11			3		5										
1	2		7		6		8	9	10	4							12	11*			3		5										
1	2		7	12	6		8	9	10	4							13	11°			3		5*										
1	2		7	12	6		8	9	10	4°							11				3		5*	13									
1	2		7*		6		8	9	10	4							11				3		5	12									
1	2		7	12	6		8	9	10	4							11				3		5*										
1	2		7		6		8	9	10	4							11*				3		5	12									
1	2		7		6		8	9	10	4							11				3		5										
1	2		7	12	6		8	9	10	4							11°				3		5*		13								
1	2		7		6		8	9		4								12			3		5		10								
1	2*		7°		6		8	9		4							12	13			3		5		10								
1			7		6		8	9		4								11			3		5		10	2							
			7		6		8*	9	12	4								11			3		5		10	2	1						
			7	12	6			9	13	4								11			3		5	8*	10°	2	1						
1			7	5*	6		8°	9	10	4					12			11			3			13		2							
1			7		6			9	12	4*					2			11			3		5	8	10								
1			7	5	6		8	9	10	4					2			11			3												
1			7	5	6		8	9	10	4	12				2			11*			3												
1			7	5	6*		8	9	10°	4†	11			12	2			13			3												14
1			7		6		8	9	12		10*			14	2°			11†			3					4							
1					6		8	9	10	4											3		5						2	11			
1					6		8	9	10	4											3		5	7					2	11			
1					6		8	9	10	4											3		5	7*					2	11	12		
1			7	12	6		8	9	10	4											3		5*						2	11			
1			7	5	6		8	9	10	4											3								2	11			
1			7	5	6		8		10	4											3								2	11	9		
1			7	5	6		8		10	4											3								2*	11		9	12
1			7	5	6		8	9		4											3								2	11		10	
1			7	5	6		8	9	12	4											3								2°	11*		10	13
1			7	5	6		8	9	12	4°											3								2	11*		10	13
1			7	12	6		8	9	10	4*											3		5							11†		13	2
1			7		6		8	9	10												3		5	4*					2			12	11
			7		6		8	9	10												3		5	4					2			11	1
1			7		6		8	9	10	12											3		5	4°					2			13	11*
40	20	5	37	23	41	2	44	44	36	42	2	1	4		3	8	22	6	3	2	39		27	7	8	4	2	13	11		5	4	1
			1	7		1			6	2	4		1	2	4		4	4			1	2			4	3					1	3	3
			10		3		9	29	10	5							3	1								2							

1996-97

1	Aug	17	(a)	Notts Co	L	1-2	Bryson	6,879
2		24	(h)	Bristol R	D	0-0		9,752
3		27	(h)	Crewe Alex	W	2-1	Wilkinson 2	9,498
4		30	(a)	Plymouth Arg	L	1-2	Wilkinson	9,209
5	Sep	7	(a)	Bristol C	L	1-2	Kilbane	8,016
6		10	(h)	York C	W	1-0	Ashcroft	7,608
7		14	(h)	Bournemouth	L	0-1		8,268
8		21	(a)	Wrexham	L	0-1		5,299
9		28	(h)	Millwall	W	2-1	Holt, Saville	9,400
10	Oct	1	(a)	Watford	L	0-1		6,436
11		5	(h)	Peterborough U	L	3-4	Ashcroft 2, Holt	8,874
12		12	(a)	Stockport Co	L	0-1		8,405
13		15	(a)	Walsall	L	0-1		3,224
14		19	(h)	Shrewsbury T	W	2-1	Seabury (og), Reeves	8,333
15		26	(a)	Gillingham	D	1-1	Kilbane	6,256
16		29	(h)	Burnley	D	1-1	Reeves	12,652
17	Nov	2	(h)	Rotherham U	D	0-0		8,997
18		9	(a)	Chesterfield	L	1-2	Reeves	4,759
19		19	(h)	Luton T	W	3-2	Moyes 2, Ashcroft	7,004
20		23	(a)	Wycombe W	W	1-0	Ashcroft (pen)	4,920
21		30	(h)	Gillingham	W	1-0	Davey	9,616
22	Dec	3	(a)	Bury	L	0-3		5,447
23		13	(h)	Blackpool	W	3-0	Bennett 2, Reeves	14,626
24		21	(a)	Brentford	D	0-0		5,365
25		28	(h)	Bristol C	L	0-2		10,905
26	Jan	11	(a)	Millwall	L	2-3	Davey 2 (1 pen)	7,096
27		18	(h)	Watford	D	1-1	Bennett	8,735
28		25	(a)	Burnley	W	2-1	Ashcroft 2	16,186
29	Feb	1	(h)	Chesterfield	L	0-1		8,681
30		8	(a)	Rotherham U	W	1-0	Reeves	3,556
31		11	(a)	Bournemouth	L	0-2		4,769
32		15	(h)	Wycombe W	W	2-1	McKenna, Davey	7,923
33		22	(a)	Luton T	L	1-5	Reeves	6,454
34		25	(a)	York C	L	1-3	Cartwright	2,515
35	Mar	1	(h)	Bury	W	3-1	Moyes, Reeves, Stallard	8,749
36		8	(h)	Brentford	W	1-0	Bryson	9,489
37		15	(a)	Blackpool	L	1-2	Davey	8,017
38		18	(h)	Wrexham	W	2-1	Reeves, Ashcroft	8,271
39		23	(a)	Bristol R	L	0-1		6,405
40		29	(h)	Notts Co	W	2-0	Reeves, Moyes	9,472
41		31	(a)	Crewe Alex	L	0-1		4,407
42	Apr	5	(h)	Plymouth Arg	D	1-1	Reeves	8,503
43		12	(a)	Peterborough U	L	0-2		5,040
44		19	(h)	Stockport Co	W	1-0	Bryson	10,298
45		26	(a)	Shrewsbury T	W	2-0	Gregan, Davey	5,341
46	May	3	(h)	Walsall	W	2-0	Holt, Reeves	10,800

FINAL LEAGUE POSITION: 15th in Division Two

Appearances

Sub. Appearances

Goals

Moilanen	Gage	Barrick	Atkinson	Wilcox	Kidd	Davey	Bryson	Saville	Wilkinson	Kilbane	Squires	Holt	Kay	Moyes	Brown	McDonald	Mimms	Ashcroft	Rankine	Bennett	Paterson	Reeves	Sparrow	Gregan	Beckford	McKenna	O'Hanlon	Cartwright	Teale	Stallard	Nogan	Jackson	Lucas	
1	2*	3	4	5	6	7	8	9	10	11†	12	13																						1
1		3	4†	5		7	8	9	10	11*			2	6	12	13																		2
1		3	4*	5		7	8	9	10	11			2	6		12																		3
1		3	4*	5		7	8	9	10	11			2	6		12																		4
		3	12	5†	13	7	14	9	10	11°			2	6		4*	1	8																5
		3	10	5		7	12	9		11			2	6		4*	1	8																6
		3	10*	5		7	12	9		11		13	2	6		4†	1	8																7
		3	12	5	6	7		9		11		10	2				1	8	4*															8
		3	12	5	6	7	8	9		11	2	10*					1	4																9
		3	12	5	6	7	8	9		11*	2	10†					1	4	13															10
		3	12	5	6	7	8	9			2†	13					1	11*	10	4														11
	2	3		5	6*	7	12	9		11†							1	4	13	8		10												12
	2	3		5	6		8			11					7		1	4	10			9												13
	2	3		5	6	12	8			11		13			7*		1	4	10†			9												14
	2	3		5	6		8			11		12			7		1	4	10*			9												15
	2	3		5	6		8*			11		13			7	12	1	4	10†			9												16
	2	3*		5	6		8			11	12	13			7°	14	1	4	10†			9												17
				5	3†	12	8		13	11		10		6		7	1	4*				9	2											18
				5	3				10*	11		12		6		8	1	7	4			9	2											19
				5*	3	12	13		10†	11				6		8	1	7	4			9	2											20
				5	3†	12	13		10°	11		14		6		8	1	7	4*			9	2											21
	12			5	3*	13	14			11		10°		6		8	1	7	4†			9	2											22
	2	3	10*	5	4					11						8	1	7	12			9		6										23
		3		5	4	12				11		2				8	1	7*	13	10†		9		6										24
	2*	3†		5	4					11		13				8	1	7	12	10		9		6										25
		3†	7	5	4	12				11*	2	10°				13	1	8	14			9		6										26
	2	3	7	5	4		8			11†				6			1	10*				9			12	13								27
		3		5	7	4	8			11				6				10	9*							12	1	2						28
		3†		5		4	8*			11				7		12		10	9					6	13		1	2						29
	12		7†	5		4	8									13		10°	11	14		9		6				1	2*	3				30
		3*	10†			7	8			12				5				11	13			9	2	6				1		4				31
	12					7	8			11†				5		13			2			9		6		3*	1			4	10			32
	12					7	8			13				5*		3†			2			9		6			11	1		4	10			33
	2	3	4			7	8			12							1					9		6			11			5	10*			34
	2	3		5	11		8							4			1					9		6						7	10			35
	2	3		5	10		8			11				4			1					9		6						7				36
	2	3		5*	12	11†	8							4			1	13				9		6						7	10			37
	2			5	3		11							4				8*	12			9		6				1		7	10			38
	2*			5	3		8			12				4				7				9		6			11	1			10			39
		3	2											5				8	7†			9		6			11*	1			10	4		40
		3	2			12	10		13					5				8	7†			9		6			11*	1				4		41
				5	3	12	11			7								8				9		6				1	2		10*	4		42
	12			5*	3	10	11†			7°								8	13			9		6				1	2		14	4		43
				5	3	10	11	7*				12		6		13		8†				9						1	2	7†		4		44
	12			5	3	10	11					13		2								9		6			7†				12	4	1	45
				5	3	7		11				10*	2				8					9		6							12	4	1	46
	16	30	12	35	33	30	32	12	8	32	6	8	7	26	5	12	27	26	19	10	2	33	6	21	4	13	14	5	4	5	7	2		
	6	5		2	7	9		2	4	3	11			1	10			1	4	6		1			2	1					2			
				6	3	1	3	2		3				4				8		3		11				1	1	1		1	1			

135

1997-98

1	Aug	9	(a)	Gillingham	D	0-0		6,562
2		16	(h)	Millwall	W	2-1	Macken, Ashcroft	11,486
3		23	(a)	Chesterfield	L	2-3	Rankine, Barrick	6,288
4		30	(h)	Watford	W	2-0	Nogan 2	11,042
5	Sep	2	(h)	Grimsby T	W	2-0	Reeves, Ashcroft	9,489
6		9	(a)	Oldham Ath	L	0-1		8,732
7		13	(h)	Walsall	D	0-0		9,092
8		20	(a)	Burnley	D	1-1	Nogan	13,809
9		27	(a)	Wycombe W	D	0-0		4,838
10	Oct	4	(h)	Brentford	W	2-1	Ashcroft, Murdock	8,804
11		11	(h)	Bournemouth	L	0-1		8,531
12		17	(a)	Carlisle U	W	2-0	Parkinson, Ashcroft	6,541
13		21	(a)	Bristol C	L	1-2	Dyche (og)	9,039
14		25	(h)	Wrexham	L	0-1		9,098
15	Nov	1	(h)	Plymouth Arg	L	0-1		8,405
16		4	(a)	York C	L	0-1		3,370
17		8	(a)	Luton T	W	3-1	Lormor, Eyres, Ashcroft	5,767
18		18	(h)	Bristol R	L	1-2	Jackson	7,798
19		22	(a)	Wigan Ath	W	4-1	Cartwright 2, Ashcroft, Kidd	5,649
20		29	(h)	Fulham	W	3-1	Ashcroft 3 (1 pen)	9,723
21	Dec	2	(a)	Southend U	L	2-3	Lormor 2	2,307
22		13	(h)	Northampton T	W	1-0	Macken	7,448
23		20	(a)	Blackpool	L	1-2	Holt	8,342
24		26	(h)	Oldham Ath	D	1-1	Holt	13,441
25		28	(a)	Grimsby T	L	1-3	Gregan	6,725
26	Jan	10	(h)	Gillingham	L	1-3	Gregan	7,776
27		17	(a)	Watford	L	1-3	Parkinson	10,182
28		24	(h)	Chesterfield	D	0-0		8,233
29		31	(a)	Walsall	D	1-1	Nogan (pen)	5,377
30	Feb	7	(h)	Burnley	L	2-3	Nogan, Jackson	12,263
31		14	(a)	Brentford	D	0-0		4,952
32		21	(h)	Wycombe W	D	1-1	Macken	7,665
33		24	(h)	Carlisle U	L	0-3		8,985
34		28	(a)	Bournemouth	W	2-0	Davey, Appleton	5,009
35	Mar	3	(h)	Luton T	W	1-0	Kidd	6,992
36		7	(a)	Plymouth Arg	L	0-2		4,201
37		14	(h)	York C	W	3-2	Eyres, Appleton, Parkinson	7,664
38		21	(a)	Bristol R	D	2-2	Davey, Ashcroft	5,278
39		25	(a)	Millwall	W	1-0	Ashcroft	5,888
40		28	(h)	Wigan Ath	D	1-1	Ashcroft	10,171
41	Apr	4	(a)	Fulham	L	1-2	Macken	8,814
42		11	(h)	Southend U	W	1-0	Parkinson	8,096
43		13	(a)	Northampton T	D	2-2	Ashcroft, Macken	5,664
44		18	(h)	Blackpool	D	3-3	Eyres, Parkinson, Macken	13,500
45		25	(a)	Wrexham	D	0-0		7,302
46	May	2	(h)	Bristol C	W	2-1	Ashcroft, Eyres	12,067

FINAL LEAGUE POSITION: 15th in Division Two

Appearances

Sub. Appearances

Goals

Moilanen	Parkinson	Kidd	Murdock	Jackson	Gregan	Cartwright	Ashcroft	Reeves	Macken	Rankine	Nogan	Barrick	Appleton	Darby	Atkinson	Holt	Lucas	Moyes	Eyres	Lormor	Davey	Mullin	Sissoko	McKenna	Sparrow	#
1	2	3	4	5	6	7	8	9	10*	11	12															1
1	2	3	4*	5	6†	7	8	9	10	11		12	13													2
1	2	4		5	6°	7*	8	9	10†	11	12	3	13	14												3
1	2	6		5		7†	8	9	12	11	10*	3	4	13												4
1	2	6*		5	12	7†	8	9		11	10	3	4	13												5
1	2			5	6	7	8	9	12	11	10*	3	4													6
1	2	12		5	6	7	8	9*	13	11	10†	3	4													7
1	2	4		5	6	7	8	9		11	10*	3	12													8
1	2	3	4	5	6†		8	12	9	10		11*	7	13												9
1	2	3*	4	5	6	12	8	9†		10		11	7	13												10
	2	3	4	5*		7	8			10	13	11	6	12†		9	1									11
1	2	3	4			7	8	9		10		11	6					5								12
1	2	3	4			7	8	9		10		11	6					5								13
1	2	3	4			7†	8	9		10			6	13	11*	12		5								14
1	2*	3	4		13	12	8		7†	10	9°		6			14		5	11							15
1	2	3	4*		6	13	8		7°	10	9†		12			14		5	11							16
1	2	4		5	6		8*		12	10		3	7						11	9						17
1	2	3*	4	5	6		8†			10		12	7	13					11	9						18
1	2	4		5	6	11*	8			10		3	7	12						9						19
1	2	4		5	6	11	8*			10		3	7			12				9						20
1	2	4		5	6	11*	8					3	7	10		12				9						21
1	2	4		5	6				10*			3	7	8		12			11	9						22
1	2	4		5	6	12			10			3†	7	8*		14		13	11	9°						23
1	2†		4	12	6	8			10°			3*	7	13		9		5	11	14						24
1	12		4	2	6	8				13		3	7	10†		9°		5*	11	14						25
		3	4	5	6	12		9	8	13		7	2*			10†	1		11							26
	2	6		5		7	12		8	10		3*					1		11	9		4				27
	2	3		5	6	7	12		8	10							1		11	9*		4				28
	2	3		5	6	7	9†		8	10	12						1		11*	13		4				29
	2	3		5	6	7	9		8	10	12						1		11*			4				30
1	2	3*	4	5	6	7	8			10	12	11									9†	13				31
1	2		4	5	6	7	8		12	10*		3							11		9†	13				32
1	2			5	6	7°	8†		12	10		3	4	13		14			11		9*					33
1	2	3	4	5	6		9*						7						11		8	12	10			34
1	2	3	4	5	6		9						7						11		8	12	10*			35
1	2	3*	4	5	6	12	9						7						11		8	13	10†			36
1	2	4		5	6	12	9					3	7						11		8†	10*	13			37
1	2	3	4	5		12	9		10†	6*		13	7						11		8					38
1	2	3*	4	5		13	9°		10†	6	14	12	7						11		8					39
1	2	3	4	5		12	9		10†	6		3	7						11*		8			13		40
1	2		4	5		12			10†	6		3	7*			13			11		8					41
1	2		4	5	6*	12	9		10			3	7†						11		8			13		42
1	2		4	5		12	9		10			3	7	13					11†		8*			6		43
1	2		4		6		9		10		12	3	7						11*		8		5			44
1	2			5	6		9		10		12		7						11*		8		4	3		45
1	2			5	6		9		10			3	7						11		8		4			46
40	44	32	27	39	33	24	37	12	20	34	14	29	31	6	1	4	6	8	26	9	17	4	4	4	1	
1	1		1	2	12		1	9	1	8	4	7	6	2	10		1	2	3	1	3	3	1			
5	2	1	2	2	2	14	1	6	1	5	1	2			2			4	3	2						

1998-99

#	Month	Date		Opponent	Res	Score	Scorers	Att
1	Aug	8	(h)	York C	W	3-0	Appleton, Rankine, Nogan	8,656
2		15	(a)	Luton T	D	1-1	Macken	5,392
3		22	(h)	Stoke C	L	3-4	Nogan 2, Eyres	11,587
4		29	(a)	Lincoln C	W	4-3	Eyres, Macken 2, Nogan	4,130
5		31	(h)	Chesterfield	W	2-0	Harris, Kidd	9,249
6	Sep	5	(a)	Bristol R	D	2-2	Harris, Jackson	6,702
7		8	(a)	Wycombe W	W	1-0	Nogan	3,800
8		12	(h)	Reading	W	4-0	Jackson 2, Eyres 2	9,836
9		19	(a)	Oldham Ath	W	1-0	Appleton	8,205
10		26	(h)	Gillingham	D	1-1	Harris	10,506
11	Oct	3	(a)	Walsall	L	0-1		5,802
12		12	(a)	Manchester C	W	1-0	Parkinson (pen)	28,779
13		17	(h)	Colchester U	W	2-0	Eyres, Nogan	10,483
14		20	(h)	Macclesfield T	D	2-2	Harris, Jackson	10,316
15		24	(a)	Northampton T	D	1-1	Hill (og)	6,085
16	Nov	7	(h)	Burnley	W	4-1	Rankine, Nogan, Eyres, Byfield	15,888
17		10	(h)	Millwall	L	0-1		10,228
18		21	(a)	Blackpool	D	0-0		10,868
19		28	(h)	Wigan Ath	D	2-2	Macken, Rankine	11,562
20	Dec	12	(a)	Notts Co	W	3-2	Gregan, Cartwright, Harris	5,096
21		19	(h)	Fulham	L	0-1		12,321
22		26	(a)	Stoke C	W	1-0	Jackson	23,272
23		28	(h)	Wrexham	W	3-1	Nogan, Cartwright 2	12,106
24	Jan	9	(a)	York C	W	1-0	Nogan	5,744
25		16	(h)	Luton T	W	2-1	Nogan, Harris	11,034
26		23	(a)	Chesterfield	W	1-0	Kidd	6,138
27		26	(a)	Bournemouth	L	1-3	Nogan	6,170
28		30	(a)	Wrexham	W	5-0	Jackson, Nogan, Macken, Eyres, Kidd	6,394
29	Feb	6	(h)	Bristol R	D	2-2	Cartwright, Nogan	12,170
30		13	(h)	Wycombe W	W	2-1	Basham 2	10,686
31		20	(a)	Reading	L	1-2	Basham	10,937
32		23	(h)	Lincoln C	W	5-0	Basham 2, Nogan 2, Macken	9,849
33		27	(h)	Oldham Ath	W	2-1	Nogan, Jackson	12,965
34	Mar	6	(a)	Gillingham	D	1-1	Gregan	9,581
35		14	(a)	Burnley	W	1-0	Nogan	11,561
36		20	(h)	Bournemouth	L	0-1		12,882
37		27	(h)	Northampton T	W	3-0	Basham 2, Macken	10,686
38	Apr	2	(a)	Colchester U	L	0-1		5,644
39		5	(h)	Manchester C	D	1-1	Basham	20,857
40		10	(a)	Macclesfield T	L	2-3	Basham 2	4,325
41		13	(a)	Wigan Ath	D	2-2	Murdock, Eyres	5,396
42		17	(h)	Blackpool	L	1-2	Nogan	15,337
43		20	(h)	Walsall	W	1-0	Gregan	13,337
44		24	(a)	Millwall	D	2-2	Darby, Jackson	6,016
45	May	1	(h)	Notts Co	D	1-1	Macken	11,862
46		8	(a)	Fulham	L	0-3		17,176

FINAL LEAGUE POSITION: 5th in Division Two

Appearances

Sub. Appearances

Goals

Moilanen	Parkinson	Kidd	Murdock	Jackson	Gregan	Appleton	Rankine	Nogan	Macken	Eyres	Holt	McKenna	Ludden	Cartwright	Harris	Darby	Lucas	Byfield	Harrison	Basham	Gray	Wright	Alexander	McGregor	Clement	#
1	2	3	4	5	6*	7†	8	9	10	11°	12	13	14													1
1	2		4	5	6	7	8	9*	10†	11	12		3	13												2
1	2	3		5	6	7	8	9	10*	11	12	4														3
1	2°	3	4	5	6		8	9	10	11*		7†	12	13	14											4
1	2	3	4	5	6		8†	9°	10*	11		7	12	13	14											5
1	2	3		5	6		8	9°	10	11†		7*	4	12	13	14										6
1	2	4		5	6		8	9*	10†	11		7	3	12	13											7
1	2	4	5*	6	12	8†	9	10°	11			7	3	13	14											8
1	2	4*	12	5		6		9†	10°	11		7	3	13	14											9
1	2		4	5	6		8		10†	11		7*	3	12	13											10
1	2		4	5	6	12	8*	9	10	11°		7†	3	13	14											11
1	2		4	5	6	12	8	9*	13	11		7°	3	14	10†											12
1	2	5	4		6		8	9	10	11		7	3													13
1	2*	12	4	5	6†		8	9	10°	11		7	3	13	14											14
1	2	4		5	6	12	8	9*		11		7	3	10												15
	2	4		5		6	8†	9	12	11		7	3	13			1	10*								16
	2	4		5	12	6*	8	9		11°		7†	3	13	14		1	10								17
	2	4		5	6		8	9	10*			11	3	7	12		1									18
	2*	4		5	6		8	9	12			11	3	7	10		1									19
	2	4	12	5	6		8	9†	13				3	7*	10	11°	1	14								20
	2	4		5	6	12	8	9°	13				3*	7	10	11†	1	14								21
	2	3	4	5	6		8	12	9†	11		7	13				1	10*								22
	2	3	4	5	6	12	8	9	10†	11*		14		7	13°		1									23
	2	3*	4	5		6	8	9	10	11		7		12			1									24
	2		4	5	6	12	8	9°	10†	11*		7		13	14		1		3							25
	2°	4	12	5	6		8	9*	10†	11		7		13	14		1		3							26
		4		5	6		8	9	10†	11*		13	12	7	13	2	1		3							27
		4		5	6*		8	9†	10°	11		13	12	7	14	2	1		3							28
		4		5	6		8	9	10†	11*				7	12	2	1		3	13						29
		5	4		6		8	9*		11†		13	12	7	14	2	1		3	10°						30
	2°	4	12	5	6		8	9				11†	3*	7	13	14	1			10						31
		4*	12	5	6		8	9	13				3	7†	14	2	1			10°		11				32
		4	5	6		8	9	12					3	13		2	1			10†	7		11*			33
		4	5	6		8	9	12	11				3			2	1			10*	7		12			34
		4	5	6*	12	8	9	13	11†				3		14	2	1			10°	7					35
		4	5	6†		8	9	12	11			3		13		2	1			10	7*					36
		4	5	6	8*	9	7	3	11					12			1			10†		13	2			37
		4	5	6	11†	8	9	7*	12			13					1			10			2		3	38
		4	5	6	12	8*	9†	13	11			7					1			10			2		3	39
		4	5	6	12		9	13	11	8							1			10	7†		2	3*		40
		4	5	6	12	8*	13	9†	11			7					1			10			2		3	41
		4	5	6	12	8*	13	9†	11	7°		3		14			1			10			2			42
		4	5	6	8		9		11	7		3			12		1			10*			2			43
		4	5	6			9		7	3		11*	8				1			10			2		12	44
		4	5	6	8		9		7	3		11*					1			10			2		12	45
	3	4	5	6	11	8*	9		7					10†	12		1			13			2			46
15	27	27	28	44	40	13	42	39	30	33		31	26	14	9	12	31	3	6	15	5	1	10	1	4	
	1	5		1	12		3	12	1	3	3	5	6	13	25	8		2		2				3		
		1	3	1	8	3	2	3	18	8	8				4	6	1	1		10						

139

1999-2000

#	Month	Date		Opponent	Result	Score	Scorers	Attendance
1	Aug	7	(a)	Oldham Ath	W	1-0	Macken	9,432
2		14	(h)	Stoke C	W	2-1	Nogan, Murdoch	11,465
3		21	(a)	Wycombe W	D	1-1	Nogan	5,091
4		28	(h)	Wigan Ath	L	1-4	Basham	13,885
5	Sep	1	(a)	Reading	D	2-2	Eyres, Basham	7,628
6		4	(h)	Chesterfield	L	0-2		8,506
7		11	(h)	Burnley	D	0-0		13,708
8		18	(a)	Gillingham	W	2-0	Macken, Gregan	6,610
9		25	(a)	Brentford	D	2-2	Macken, McKenna	7,100
10	Oct	2	(h)	Cambridge U	W	2-1	Macken 2	9,522
11		9	(h)	Bristol C	W	1-0	Mathie	10,042
12		16	(a)	Scunthorpe U	D	1-1	Macken	5,336
13		19	(a)	Millwall	W	2-0	Cartwright, Nethercott (og)	6,355
14		23	(h)	Brentford	W	2-1	Alexander (pen), Marshall (og)	10,382
15	Nov	3	(h)	Bournemouth	W	3-0	McKenna, Macken, Alexander (pen)	9,630
16		6	(a)	Colchester U	D	2-2	Mathie, Nogan	3,818
17		12	(h)	Notts Co	W	2-0	Macken 2	14,226
18		23	(a)	Luton T	W	2-0	Eyres 2	5,124
19		27	(a)	Bury	W	3-1	Jackson, Gregan, Macken	6,469
20	Dec	4	(h)	Oldham Ath	W	2-0	Macken 2	10,970
21		18	(h)	Blackpool	W	3-0	Eyres 2, Appleton	16,821
22		26	(a)	Wrexham	D	0-0		7,872
23		28	(h)	Bristol R	W	2-1	Alexander (pen), Macken	16,680
24	Jan	3	(a)	Cardiff C	W	4-0	Edwards, Alexander 2 (1 pen), Nogan	10,142
25		14	(a)	Stoke C	L	1-2	Alexander (pen)	10,285
26		22	(h)	Wycombe W	W	3-2	Murdock, Macken 2	10,969
27	Feb	1	(a)	Oxford U	W	4-0	Macken 2, Eyres, Appleton	5,164
28		5	(h)	Reading	D	2-2	Macken, Jackson	12,618
29		12	(a)	Chesterfield	W	1-0	Gregan	4,726
30		19	(h)	Bury	D	1-1	Macken	13,901
31		26	(h)	Gillingham	L	0-2		13,246
32	Mar	4	(a)	Burnley	W	3-0	Jackson, Macken, Edwards	22,310
33		7	(h)	Colchester U	L	2-3	Angell 2	11,323
34		11	(a)	Bournemouth	W	1-0	Angell	5,317
35		14	(h)	Oxford U	W	3-1	Angell 2, Macken	12,008
36		18	(h)	Luton T	W	1-0	Anderson	13,731
37		21	(a)	Notts Co	L	0-1		6,401
38		25	(h)	Wrexham	W	1-0	Anderson	12,481
39	Apr	1	(a)	Blackpool	D	0-0		9,042
40		4	(a)	Wigan Ath	W	1-0	Jackson	15,593
41		8	(h)	Cardiff C	D	0-0		13,794
42		15	(a)	Bristol R	W	2-0	Macken, Gunnlaugsson	10,111
43		22	(h)	Scunthorpe U	W	1-0	Angell	15,518
44		24	(a)	Cambridge U	L	0-2		6,068
45		29	(h)	Millwall	W	3-2	Eyres, Jackson, Angell	19,407
46	May	6	(a)	Bristol C	W	2-0	Angell, Appleton	11,160

FINAL LEAGUE POSITION: 1st in Division Two

Appearances

Sub. Appearances

Goals

Lucas	Alexander	Ludden	Murdock	Jackson	Gregan	Appleton	Rankine	Nogan	Macken	Eyres	Edwards	Basham	Kidd	McKenna	Cartwright	Moilanen	Mathie	Gunnlaugsson	Diaf	Wright	Darby	Beresford	Angell	Anderson	Beesley	Parkinson	Barry-Murphy	
1	2	3*	4	5	6	7	8	9†	10	11	12	13																1
1	2		4	5	6	7	8	9	10*	11†		12	3	13														2
1	2		4	5	6	7	8	9*	10	11†		12	3	13														3
1	2		4	5	6†	7	8	12	9*	11°			10	3		13	14											4
1	2		4	5	6	7	8	9		11†	12		10	3*		13												5
1	2	6	4	5			8	9	12	11*	3	10			7													6
	2	3	4	5		12†	8	9	14	11°	13	10		6*	7	1												7
	2			5	6		8	9		11	3		4	12	7*	1		10										8
	2			5	6		8	12	9	11	3		4	11	7*	1		10										9
	2	12		5	6		8	9	13		3		4*	11†	7	1		10°	14									10
	2			5	6		8	12	9	13	3		4	11†	7	1		10*										11
	2		4	5	6		8	12	9	13	3			11†	7	1		10*										12
	2		4	5	6		8	9*	10†	12	3			11	7	1		13										13
	2		4	5	6		8	9†	10	12	3			11*	7°	1		13	14									14
	2		4	5	6		8	9†	10°		3			11*	7	1	12	13	14									15
	2		4	5	6		8	9	10		3				7†	1	12	13	11*									16
	2		4	5	6		8	9†	10°	11*	3	12			7	1		13		14								17
	2			5	6		8	10	9	11	3		4		7	1												18
	2			5	6	12	8	9	10†	11°	3		4		7*	1		13	14									19
	2			5		7	8	9*	10	11	3		4			1		12		6								20
	2			5	6	12	8	13	10†	11	3		4			1	14	9°				7*						21
	2			5	6	7	12		10†	11	3	13	4			1	14	9*				8°						22
	2	12		5	6	7	8	9	10	11†	3		4*			1						13						23
	2		4	5	6	7	8	9	10*	11†	3					1		12				13						24
	2		4	5	6	7*	8	9	10	11†	3					1		12				13						25
	2		4	5	6	11	8	10			3			12	7*	1		9										26
	2		4	5	6*	7	8	9°		11	3		10†	12		1				13				14				27
	2		4	5	6	7	8	9		11	3		10*	12		1												28
	2		4	5	6	7		10		11*	3	12			8*	1		9†		13								29
	2		4	5	6	7	8	10		11*	3	12				1		9										30
	2		4	5	6	7*	8	10		12	3	13				1		9°					14	11†				31
	2		4	5	6†		8	10°		12	3	9	7		13	1							14	11*				32
	2†		4	5				10		12	3	9°	6		7	1		13					14	11*				33
	2		4	5		12	8	10		11*	3†	14	6	13	7	1							9°					34
	2		4	5			8	10*		11	13	3	6		7°	1		12					9†	14				35
	2		4	5	6		8	10†		11*	12	13	3	14		1							9	7°				36
	2		4	5		12		10°		13	3		6*	14	7	1							9	11†				37
	2		4	5	6	12	8	10°			3	13		14	7*	1							9	11†				38
	2			5	6			10†		12	3		4	13	7	1							9	11*				39
	2			5	6°		8	10		12	3	14	4	13	7	1		9*						11†				40
	2			5			8	10†		12	3	6*	4	14	7	1		9					13°	11				41
	2			5		7	8	10*		12	3	6	4		13	1		9°					14	11†				42
	2			5		7	8	10°		12	3	6†	4		13	1		9					14	11*				43
	2°	12		5		11†	8	13			3	14	4	6	7*	1		10					9					44
	2	12		5		7	8	13		11	3*		4	6		1		10†					9					45
	2†		4	5		7	8	10		11°	3	12		6		1							9*			13	14	46
6	46	3	29	46	33	21	44	16	40	26	37	11	28	17	22	40	5	12	1	2	1		9	11				
			4		5	6	4	15	4	13	1	7	8	1	7		14	2	2	1	3	6	1	1	1	1		
	6		2		5	3	3	4	22	7	2	2	2	1	2		1	2	1				8	2				

141

2000-2001

#	Month	Date		Opponent		Score	Scorers	Attendance
1	Aug	12	(a)	Grimsby T	W	2-1	Appleton, Macken	5,755
2		19	(h)	Sheffield U	W	3-0	Appleton, Macken 2	13,948
3		26	(a)	Bolton W	L	0-2		19,954
4		28	(h)	Wimbledon	D	1-1	Appleton	13,519
5	Sep	2	(h)	Portsmouth	W	1-0	Basham	13,343
6		9	(a)	QPR	D	0-0		11,092
7		12	(a)	Birmingham C	L	1-3	Rankine	16,464
8		16	(h)	Stockport Co	D	1-1	McKenna	12,735
9		23	(a)	Sheffield W	W	3-1	Alexander, Anderson, Walker (og)	17,379
10		30	(h)	Crystal Palace	W	2-0	Macken, McKenna	13,028
11	Oct	14	(h)	Tranmere R	W	1-0	Basham	14,511
12		17	(h)	Norwich C	W	1-0	Gunnlaugsson	13,002
13		21	(a)	Huddersfield T	D	0-0		13,161
14		24	(a)	Fulham	W	1-0	Appleton	14,354
15		27	(h)	Barnsley	L	1-2	Macken	13,566
16	Nov	4	(a)	Nottingham F	L	1-3	Macken	19,504
17		10	(h)	Crewe Alex	W	2-1	Appleton, Rankine	12,632
18		18	(a)	Watford	W	3-2	Macken, Rankine, Anderson	13,066
19		25	(a)	WBA	L	1-3	Anderson	20,043
20	Dec	2	(h)	Fulham	D	1-1	Jackson	16,047
21		9	(h)	Burnley	W	2-1	Macken, Alexander	17,355
22		16	(a)	Gillingham	L	0-4		8,198
23		23	(h)	Grimsby T	L	1-2	Macken	14,667
24		26	(a)	Wolverhampton W	W	1-0	Anderson	24,306
25		30	(a)	Sheffield U	L	2-3	Healy, Rankine	22,316
26	Jan	1	(h)	Bolton W	L	0-2		15,863
27		10	(a)	Blackburn R	L	2-3	Macken, Healy (pen)	23,983
28		13	(a)	Wimbledon	L	1-3	Robinson	7,242
29	Feb	3	(a)	Portsmouth	W	1-0	Healy	13,331
30		10	(h)	QPR	W	5-0	Macken 2, McBride, Healy, Anderson	14,423
31		13	(a)	Stockport Co	W	1-0	Healy	7,590
32		20	(h)	Birmingham C	L	0-2		14,864
33		24	(h)	Sheffield W	W	2-0	McKenna, Macken	14,379
34	Mar	3	(a)	Crystal Palace	W	2-0	Healy, Alexander (pen)	15,160
35		6	(a)	Tranmere R	D	1-1	Macken	10,335
36		14	(h)	Wolverhampton W	W	2-0	McKenna, Cresswell	15,457
37		17	(a)	Norwich C	W	2-1	Healy, Gregan	16,282
38		31	(h)	Gillingham	D	0-0		13,550
39	Apr	6	(a)	Burnley	L	0-3		16,591
40		10	(h)	Huddersfield T	D	0-0		15,185
41		14	(h)	Nottingham F	D	1-1	Healy	16,842
42		16	(a)	Barnsley	W	4-0	Macken, Anderson, McKenna, Cresswell	16,361
43		22	(h)	Watford	W	3-2	Alexander (pen), Macken 2	14,071
44		28	(a)	Crewe Alex	W	3-1	Healy, Macken 2	9,415
45	May	2	(h)	Blackburn R	L	0-1		16,975
46		6	(h)	WBA	W	2-1	Gregan, Alexander (pen)	16,226

FINAL LEAGUE POSITION: 4th in Division One

Appearances

Sub. Appearances

Goals

Moilanen	Alexander	Edwards	Murdock	Gregan	Appleton	McKenna	Rankine	Macken	Basham	Anderson	Eyres	Robinson	Cartwright	Jackson	Parkinson	Lucas	Gunnlaugsson	O'Hanlon	McBride	Meijer	Kidd	Ludden	Barry-Murphy	Healy	Cresswell	Lonergan	Keane	Eaton	
1	2	3	4	5	6	7	8	9	10*	11†	12	13																	1
1	2	3	4	5	6	7	8	9	10	11																			2
1	2†	3	4		6	7*	8	9	10	11		12	13	5															3
1		3	4	6	11	7	8	9	10	12				5*	2														4
1	2	3		6	4	7*	8	9	10†	11°	12	13	14	5															5
	2	3	4	5	6	7	8	9*	10	11†	12		13			1													6
	2	3	4	5	6°	7	8	9	10†			13	11*	12		1	14												7
	2	3	4	5	6	7†	8		10*		12	13	11			1°		14	9										8
	2	3	4	5	6	7†	8		10°	13	12	14	11			1			9*										9
	2	3		4	6	7*	8		9†	10	12	13	11	5		1													10
	2	3	4	5	6	7	8*		9†	12		10	11			1	13												11
	2	3	4	5	6	7			11*		10	8			1	12			9										12
	2	3	4	5	6	7*	8		12		10	11†			1	13			9										13
	2	3	4	5	6	7	8	10*		12	11			1				9											14
	2	3	4*	5	6	7	8	10	13°			11†	12	1	14			9											15
	2	3	4	5	6	7	8	10*	11†		14		13	1	12			9°											16
	2		4	5	6	7	8	10*	11		13			1	12			9†	3										17
	12			5	6	7	8	10°	11†	14	13	4	3	1			9	2*											18
		3		5	6	7	8*	10	11		13	4	2†	1	12			9											19
		3		5		7	8	10	11*	6°	12	4	2	1	13			9†		14									20
	2	3	4	5		7	8	10		12	11	6		1	9*														21
	2	3	4	5	12	7	8	10		13	11†	6*		1	9														22
1	2	3	12	5	6	7	8°	10		13	11*	4		9†					14										23
	2*	3	12	5	6	7	8	9	11°	10†	13	4	1						14										24
	3†		5	6	7	8	12		11*	4	2	1		9			13		14	10°									25
		4*	5	6	7	12	10°	11†		13		8	2	1		9	3		14										26
		12	5	6	7°	8	9		11	4	2*	1		13	3†		14	10											27
	3	4		6	12	8†	9	7	11*	5		1			2	13	10												28
1		3	4		7	8	10*		6	5	2	12	9			13	11†												29
1		3	4	6°	8	9†	12		7	5	2	13	11*			14	10												30
1		3	4		6	8	9		7	5	2	11	10																31
1		3	4	12	6	8*	11†		7°	5	2	13	9			14	10												32
1	2	3	4	12	6	8	9		7	5		11*				13	10†												33
1	2	3	4	5	7	8	9		11	6						12	10*												34
1	2	3	4	5	7	8	9		11	6							10												35
1	2	3	4	5	7	8	9		11	6							10*	12											36
1	2	3	4*	5	7	8	9†		11	6						12								10	13				37
1	2	3		5	7	8	9		12	11*	6					4								13	10†				38
1†	2	3	4	5	7	11	9*		12	6						13								10	8				39
	2	3	4	5	7	8*	12		13	11°		1				6			14	10†	9								40
	2	3	4	5	7	8	9		11*	12		1				6				10†	13								41
	2	3	4	5	7	8†	9*		11			1	12			6			13	10°	14								42
	2	3	4	5	7	8	9		11†	12						6				10*	13	1							43
	2	3		5	7	8	9		11*	12	4†	1				6			13	10°	14								44
	2	3		5		8°	9		11*	7		1	12			4			6	13	10†			14					45
	2		12	5°			13		7	4		1	11†			6			8	10	9			14	3*				46
17	34	41	33	39	25	43	43	37	11	19		6	29	27	11	28	5		8	9	13	2	19	5	1		1		
	1	4	2	1	1	1	1		12	5		16	9	3		1	14	1	1	2	2	12	3	6		2			
	5		2	5	5	4	19	2	6		1		1		1	1								9	2				

2001-2002

1	Aug	11	(a)	Gillingham	L	0-5		9,412
2		18	(h)	Walsall	D	1-1	Murdock	11,402
3		25	(a)	Grimsby T	D	2-2	Murdock, Healy	5,789
4		27	(h)	Wimbledon	D	1-1	Keane	13,349
5	Sep	8	(h)	Wolverhampton W	L	1-2	Lucketti	14,381
6		15	(h)	Millwall	W	1-0	Anderson	11,371
7		18	(a)	WBA	L	0-2		18,209
8		23	(a)	Birmingham C	W	1-0	Edwards	23,004
9		26	(h)	Norwich C	W	4-0	Alexander (pen), Macken 2, Edwards	12,014
10		30	(a)	Watford	D	1-1	Macken	18,911
11	Oct	13	(a)	Crewe Alex	L	1-2	Rankine	7,746
12		16	(a)	Sheffield W	W	2-1	Rankine, Macken	15,592
13		21	(h)	Manchester C	W	2-1	Healy, Macken	21,014
14		23	(h)	Sheffield U	W	3-0	Macken, Healy, Gallacher	14,027
15		27	(a)	Portsmouth	W	1-0	Cartwright	15,402
16		31	(a)	Coventry C	D	2-2	Cresswell 2	15,755
17	Nov	3	(h)	Stockport Co	W	6-0	Healy 3, Lucketti, Cresswell, McKenna	13,776
18		8	(h)	Barnsley	D	2-2	Rankine, Cresswell	19,042
19		17	(a)	Nottingham F	D	1-1	Cresswell	21,020
20		20	(h)	Bradford C	D	1-1	Alexander (pen)	13,763
21		24	(h)	Crystal Palace	W	2-1	Cresswell, Alexander (pen)	15,264
22	Dec	1	(a)	Sheffield U	D	2-2	Healy, Cresswell	16,270
23		9	(h)	Burnley	L	2-3	McKenna, Alexander (pen)	20,370
24		15	(a)	Rotherham U	L	0-1		6,558
25		22	(h)	Grimsby T	D	0-0		14,667
26		26	(a)	Wolverhampton W	W	3-2	Healy, Anderson, Gregan	24,024
27		29	(a)	Wimbledon	L	0-2		6,501
28	Jan	12	(a)	Walsall	W	2-1	Anderson, Basham	6,314
29		19	(h)	Gillingham	L	0-2		13,289
30		29	(a)	Bradford C	D	1-0	Keane	15,217
31		31	(h)	Watford	D	1-1	Alexander	12,749
32	Feb	5	(h)	Sheffield W	W	4-2	Etuhu, Macken, Reid, Healy	14,038
33		10	(a)	Manchester C	L	2-3	Macken, Anderson	34,220
34		22	(a)	Norwich C	L	0-3		19,506
35		26	(h)	WBA	W	1-0	Etuhu	14,487
36	Mar	2	(h)	Birmingham C	W	1-0	Purse (og)	15,543
37		5	(a)	Millwall	L	1-2	Healy	11,071
38		9	(h)	Rotherham U	W	2-1	Cresswell 2	14,579
39		17	(a)	Burnley	L	1-2	Anderson	18,388
40		20	(h)	Crewe Alex	D	2-2	McKenna, Cresswell	13,396
41		23	(a)	Stockport Co	W	2-0	McKenna, Cresswell	6,139
42		30	(h)	Portsmouth	W	2-0	Wijnhard, Alexander (pen)	16,832
43	Apr	1	(a)	Barnsley	L	1-2	Wijnhard	14,188
44		6	(h)	Coventry C	W	4-0	Wijnhard, Etuhu, Ainsworth, Cresswell	15,665
45		13	(a)	Crystal Palace	L	0-2		21,361
46		21	(h)	Nottingham F	W	2-1	Rankine, Cresswell	17,390

FINAL LEAGUE POSITION: 8th in Division One

Appearances

Sub. Appearances

Goals

	Lucas	Alexander	Edwards	Murdock	Jackson	Gregan	Cartwright	Rankine	Macken	Healy	Cresswell	McKenna	Anderson	Gallacher	Barry-Murphy	Lucketti	Keane	Moilanen	Robinson	Basham	Kidd	Eaton	Skora	Etuhu	Reid	Gudjonsson	Hendry	Wijnhard	Ainsworth	
1	1	2	3	4	5	6	7	8	9	10	11																			1
2	1	2	3	4	5	6	11	8	9°	10*	12	7†	13	14																2
3	1	2		4		6	11	12	9†	10	13		14	7°	3	5	8*													3
4	1°	2		4		6	11	8*		10	9†				3	5	7	14	12	13										4
5	1	2		4		6	12			10°	9	7	11*			5	8†		13	14	3									5
6		2	3	4		6	8		12	10*	9	7	11†		13°	5		1				14								6
7		2	3	4			8	11	10	12	9	7				5		1				6*								7
8		2	3	4		6	11	8	9	10		7				5		1												8
9		2	3	4		6	11	8	9	10*	12	7	11†	13		5		1												9
10		2	3	4		6	11	8	9	10*	12	7				5		1												10
11		2	3	4		6	11	8	9*	10†	12	7	13			5		1												11
12		2	3	4		6	7	8	9	10*	12	13	11†			5		1												12
13		2	3	4		6	11	8	9	10*	12	7				5		1												13
14		2	3*	12	4	6	11	8	9†	10°	13	7		14		5		1												14
15		2		4	3†	6	11	8	9	10*	12	7				5		1				13								15
16		2		4		6	11	8	9	10*	12	7				5		1					3							16
17	14	2		4		6	11	8	9†	10*	12	7	13			5	1°				3									17
18	1	2		4		6	11†	8	9	10*	12	7	13			5					3°	14								18
19	1	2		4		6	11	8	9*	10		7	12			5					3								·	19
20	1	2	3	4		6*	11	8		10	9	7	12			5														20
21	1	2	3	4		6	11	8		10*	9	7				5						12								21
22	1	2	3	4		6	11	8	12	10*	9	7				5														22
23	1	2	3	4		6	11*		10	8	9†	7	12			5				13										23
24	1	2	3	4*		6	11°	8†	9	10		7	12			5	13			14										24
25	1	2	3	4		6		8	9	10		7	11*			5				12										25
26	1	2	3			6	4	8	9*	10		7	11†			5				12	13									26
27	1	2	3	4		6†		8	9*	10	12	7	11°			5				13	14									27
28	1	2	3	4					9	10		7	11			5	8			12			6*							28
29		2	3	4*	12				9	10		7	11			5	8†	1		13			6							29
30		2	3			6	7		12	10	9*		11			5	4	1						8						30
31		2				6	7†		9*	10°	11	12		14		5	4	1		13		3		8						31
32		2			5	6†	7		10	12	9	11*					4	1				3		8	13					32
33		2	3			6	7†		9	10	11*	12				5	4	1						8	13					33
34		2	3			6			10	9	7*	11†				5	4°	1		12			14	8	13					34
35	1		2			6			10*	12	9	7				5	4				3	13	8			11†				35
36	1	2	3			6			10*	12	9°	7	13			5	14						8			11†	4			36
37	1	2	3						10	9	7	12				5	4*			13		14	8			11†	6°			37
38	1	2	3				12		10	9	7	11†				5	13				6		4			8*				38
39	1	2	3			6	7*	8	10†	9		12				5	11			13			4°			14				39
40	1	2	3			6	7	8	10*	9		11				5				12			4							40
41	1	2	3			6	7	8	12	9		11				5							4					10*		41
42		2	3†			6	7°	8	12	9		11				5		1		13			4				14	10*		42
43		2		12		6	7°	8†	13	9	11					5*	4	1					3				14	10		43
44		2	3	5		6			9	12	11						4	1						8			7*	10		44
45		2	3	5		6			12	9	11	13					4†	1						8			7*	10		45
46		2	3	5		6	12		13	9	11	14					4*	1						8°			7	10†		46
	23	45	36	22	12	40	34	24	28	35	27	37	16	1	2	40	17	23			5	6	2	16		4	2	6	3	
	1			1	1	1	2	2	3	9	13	1	15	4	2		3	1	2	16	1	6	2		1	3			2	
		6	2	2		1	1	4	8	10	13	4	5	1			2	2			1			3	1			3	1	

F.A. CUP COMPETITION

1977/78 SEASON

1st Round
Nov 26 vs Lincoln City (h) 3-2
Att: 6,965   Elwiss 2, Bruce

2nd Round
Dec 17 vs Wrexham (h) 0-2
Att: 11,134

1978/79 SEASON

3rd Round
Jan 16 vs Derby County (h) 3-0
Att: 19,884   Bruce 2, Burns

4th Round
Feb 12 vs Southampton (h) 0-1
Att: 20,727

1979/80 SEASON

3rd Round
Jan 5 vs Ipswich Town (h) 0-3
Att: 16,986

1980/81 SEASON

3rd Round
Jan 3 vs Bristol Rovers (h) 3-4
Att: 6,248   Houston, Bruce, McGee

1981/82 SEASON

1st Round
Nov 21 vs Chesterfield (a) 1-4
Att: 5,435   Doyle

1982/83 SEASON

1st Round
Nov 20 vs Shepshed Charterhouse (h) 5-1
Att: 6,200   Elliott 2, Kelly, Coleman, McAteer

2nd Round
Dec 11 vs Blackpool (h) 2-1
Att: 14,008   Coleman, O'Riordan

3rd Round
Jan 8 vs Leeds United (a) 0-3
Att: 16,816

1983/84 SEASON

1st Round
Nov 19 vs Scunthorpe United (a) 0-1
Att: 3,484

1984/85 SEASON

1st Round
Nov 17 vs Bury (h) 4-3
Att: 5,013   Gray, Johnson 2, Naughton

2nd Round
Dec 8 vs Telford United (h) 1-4
Att: 6,134   Hunter

1985/86 SEASON

1st Round
Nov 16 vs Walsall (a) 3-7
Att: 4,035   Thomas, Brazil, Martin

1986/87 SEASON

1st Round
Nov 15 vs Bury (h) 5-1
Att: 7,949   Thomas 3 (1 pen), Jones, Williams

2nd Round (at Blackburn)
Dec 6 vs Chorley (a) 0-0
Att: 15,153

Replay
Dec 9 vs Chorley (h) 5-0
Att: 16,417   Thomas 3 (1 pen), Williams, Brazil

3rd Round
Jan 10 vs Middlesbrough (a) 1-0
Att: 15,458   Hildersley

4th Round
Jan 31 vs Newcastle United (a) 0-2
Att: 30,495

1987/88 SEASON

1st Round
Nov 14 vs Mansfield Town (h) 1-1
Att: 7,415   Atkins

Replay
Nov 17 vs Mansfield Town (a) 2-4
Att: 4,682   Brazil, Jemson

1988/89 SEASON

1st Round
Nov 19 vs Tranmere Rovers (h) 1-1
Att: 7,734   Atkins

Replay
Nov 22 vs Tranmere Rovers (a) 0-3
Att: 7,676

1989/90 SEASON

1st Round
Nov 18 vs Tranmere Rovers (h) 1-0
Att: 7,521   Joyce

2nd Round
Dec 9 vs Whitley Bay (a) 0-2
Att: 4,500

1990/91 SEASON

1st Round
Nov 17 vs Mansfield Town (h) 0-1
Att: 5,230

1991/92 SEASON

1st Round
Nov 16 vs Mansfield Town (a) 1-1
(match abandoned after 32 minutes
due to fog)
Scorer: Shaw

Replay
Nov 27 vs Mansfield Town (a) 1-0
Att: 7,509   Thomas

2nd Round
Dec 7 vs Witton Albion (h) 5-1
*Att: 6,736   Shaw, Swann, Senior,
Flynn, Greenwood*

3rd Round
Jan 4 vs Sheffield Wednesday (h) 0-2
Att: 14,337

1992/93 SEASON

1st Round
Nov 14 vs Bradford City (a) 1-1
Att: 8,553   Fowler

Replay
Nov 25 vs Bradford City (h) 4-5
*Att: 7,905   Graham, Ellis, Davidson,
Callaghan*

1993/94 SEASON

1st Round
Nov 13 vs Mansfield Town (a) 2-1
Att: 4,119   Ellis 2 (1 pen)

2nd Round
Dec 4 vs Shrewsbury Town (a) 1-0
Att: 5,018   Raynor

3rd Round
Jan 8 vs Bournemouth (h) 2-1
Att: 8,457   Moyes, Conroy

4th Round
Jan 29 vs Kidderminster (a) 0-1
Att: 7,000

1994/95 SEASON

1st Round
Nov 14 vs Blackpool (h) 1-0
Att: 14,036   Conroy

2nd Round
Dec 3 vs Walsall (h) 1-1
Att: 9,767   Smart

Replay
Dec 13 vs Walsall (a) 0-4
Att: 6,468

1995/96 SEASON

1st Round
Nov 11 vs Carlisle United (a) 2-1
Att: 7,046   Cartwright, Wilcox

2nd Round
Dec 2 vs Bradford City (a) 1-2
Att: 7,602   Wilkinson

1996/97 SEASON

1st Round
Nov 16 vs Altrincham (h) 4-1
Att: 8,286   Reeves 3, Ashcroft

2nd Round
Dec 7 vs York City (h) 2-3
Att: 7,893   Ashcroft 2 (1 pen)

1997/98 SEASON

1st Round
Nov 15 vs Doncaster Rovers (h) 3-2
Att: 7,953   Gregan 2, Eyres

2nd Round
Dec 6 vs Notts County (h) 2-2
Att: 7,583   Parkinson, Ashcroft

Replay
Dec 16 vs Notts County (a) 2-1 (aet.)
(score after 90 minutes 1-1)
Att: 3,052   Moyes, Eyres

3rd Round
Jan 3 vs Stockport County (h) 1-2
Att: 12,180   Ashcroft (pen)

1998/99 SEASON

1st Round
Nov 14 vs Ford United (h) 3-0
Att: 10,167   Rankine, Harris, Darby

2nd Round
Dec 5 vs Walsall (h) 2-0
Att: 8,488   Nogan, McKenna

3rd Round
Jan 4 vs Arsenal (h) 2-4
Att: 21,099   Nogan 2

1999/2000 SEASON

1st Round
Oct 31 vs Bristol Rovers (a) 1-0
Att: 6,145   McKenna

2nd Round
Nov 20 vs Enfield (h) 0-0
Att: 11,566

Replay
Nov 30 vs Enfield (a) 3-0
Att: 1,808   Eyres, Alexander (pen),
Gunnlaugsson

3rd Round
Dec 11 vs Oldham Athletic (h) 2-1
Att: 9,940   Macken, Alexander (pen)

4th Round
Jan 8 vs Plymouth Argyle (a) 3-0
Att: 10,824   O'Sullivan (og),
Alexander (pen), Beswetherick (og)

5th Round
Jan 29 vs Everton (a) 0-2
Att: 37,486

2000/2001 SEASON

3rd Round
Jan 6 vs Stockport Count (h) 0-1
Att: 9,975

2001/2002 SEASON

3rd Round
Jan 15 vs Brighton & Hove A. (a) 2-0
Att: 6,548   Skora, Macken

4th Round
Jan 26 vs Sheffield United (h) 2-1
Att: 13,068   Cresswell, Alexander (pen)

5th Round
Feb 17 vs Chelsea (a) 1-3
Att: 28,133   Cresswell

LEAGUE CUP COMPETITION

1977/78 SEASON

1st Round (1st leg)
Aug 13 vs Port Vale (a) 1-2
Att: 4,530   Bruce

1st Round (2nd leg)
Aug 16 vs Port Vale (h) 2-1 (agg. 3-3)
Att: 5,816   Elwiss 2

Replay
Aug 23 vs Port Vale (h) 2-1
Att: 2,201   Elwiss, McGifford (og)

2nd Round
Aug 30 vs Walsall (a) 0-0
Att: 5,445

Replay
Sep 6 vs Walsall (h) 0-1
Att: 7,079

1978/79 SEASON

1st Round (1st leg)
Aug 12 vs Huddersfield Town (h) 3-0
Att: 6,841   Baxter, Bruce 2

1st Round (2nd leg)
Aug 15 vs Huddersfield Town (a) 2-2
(aggregate 5-2)
Att: 3,435   Bruce, Thomas

2nd Round
Aug 29 vs Queen's Park Rangs. (h) 1-3
Att: 14,913   Fisher

1979/80 SEASON

2nd Round (1st leg)
Aug 28 vs Birmingham City (a) 1-2
Att: 13,660   Potts

2nd Round (2nd leg)
Sep 4 vs Birmingham City (h) 0-1
(aggregate 1-3)
Att: 11,043

1980/81 SEASON

2nd Round (1st leg)
Aug 26 vs Wigan Athletic (h) 1-0
Att: 8,073   McGee

2nd Round (2nd leg)
Sep 3 vs Wigan Athletic (a) 2-1
(aggregate 3-1)
Att: 9,692   McGee, Coleman

3rd Round
Sep 23 vs Oxford United (h) 1-0
Att: 5,722   Coleman

4th Round
Oct 29 vs West Bromwich A. (a) 0-0
Att: 17,579

Replay
Nov 4 vs West Bromwich A. (h) 1-1
Att: 14,420   Bell

2nd Replay
Nov 12 vs West Bromwich A. (a) 1-2
Att: 15,218   Bruce

1981/82 SEASON

1st Round (1st leg)
Sep 1 vs Halifax Town (a) 2-1
Att: 2,719   Clark, Naughton

1st Round (2nd leg)
Sep 15 vs Halifax Town (h) 0-0
(aggregate 2-1)
Att: 4,090

2nd Round (1st leg)
Oct 6 vs Leicester City (h) 1-0
Att: 5,382   Bruce

2nd Round (2nd leg)
Oct 28 vs Leicester City (a) 0-4
(aggregate 1-4)
Att: 7,685

1982/83 SEASON

1st Round (1st leg)
Aug 31 vs Walsall (a) 1-0
Att: 2,490   Naughton

1st Round (2nd leg)
Sep 14 vs Walsall (h) 1-1
Att: 3,137   Elliott

2nd Round (1st leg)
Oct 6 vs Norwich City (a) 1-2
Att: 7,273   Bruce

2nd Round (2nd leg)
Oct 26 vs Norwich City (h) 1-2
(aggregate 2-4)
Att: 6,082   Elliott

1983/84 SEASON

1st Round (1st leg)
Aug 30 vs Tranmere Rovers (h) 1-0
Att: 3,231   Kelly

1st Round (2nd leg)
Sep 12 vs Tranmere Rovers (a) 0-0
(aggregate 1-0)
Att: 2,986

2nd Round (1st leg)
Oct 4 vs Wolverhampton W. (a) 3-2
Att: 7,790   Hinnigan 2, Naughton

2nd Round (2nd leg)
Oct 25 vs Wolverhampton W. (h) 1-0
(aggregate 4-2)
Att: 8,857   Elliott

3rd Round
Nov 8 vs Sheffield Wednesday (h) 0-2
Att: 11,060

1984/85 SEASON

1st Round (1st leg)
Aug 28 vs Tranmere Rovers (a) 3-2
Att: 2,015   Kelly, Farrelly, Twentyman

1st Round (2nd leg)
Sep 4 vs Tranmere Rovers (h) 2-2 (aet)
(aggregate 5-4)
Att: 2,557   Houghton, Wilkins

2nd Round (1st leg)
Sep 25 vs Norwich City (h) 3-3
*Att: 5,265   Houghton, Wilkins,
Twentyman*

2nd Round (2nd leg)
Oct 10 vs Norwich City (a) 1-6
(aggregate 4-9)
Att: 13,506   Twentyman

1985/86 SEASON

1st Round (1st leg)
Aug 20 vs Blackpool (h) 2-1
Att: 4,704   Keen, Foster

1st Round (2nd leg)
Sep 3 vs Blackpool (a) 3-1 (agg. 5-2)
Att: 5,043   Rudge, Twentyman, Brazil

2nd Round (1st leg)
Sep 30 vs Norwich City (h) 1-1
Att: 4,330   Brazil (pen)

2nd Round (2nd leg)
Oct 7 vs Norwich City (a) 1-2
(aggregate 2-3)
Att: 11,537   Brazil

1986/87 SEASON

1st Round (1st leg)
Aug 29 vs Blackpool (a) 0-0
Att: 3,929

1st Round (2nd leg)
Sep 2 vs Blackpool (h) 2-1 (agg. 2-1)
Att: 5,914   Hildersley, Williams

2nd Round (1st leg)
Sep 23 vs West Ham United (h) 1-1
Att: 13,153   Allardyce

2nd Round (2nd leg)
Oct 7 vs West Ham United (a) 1-4
(aggregate 2-6)
Att: 12,742   Williams

1987/88 SEASON

1st Round (1st leg)
Aug 18 vs Bury (a) 2-2
Att: 2,363   Allardyce, Brazil

1st Round (2nd leg)
Aug 25 vs Bury (h) 2-3
Att: 4,923   Brazil, Hill (og)

1988/89 SEASON

1st Round (1st leg)
Aug 29 vs Wigan Athletic (a) 0-0
Att: 4,035

1st Round (2nd leg)
Sep 5 vs Wigan Athletic (h) 1-0
(aggregate 1-0)
Att: 4,945   Brazil

2nd Round (1st leg)
Sep 28 vs Norwich City (a) 0-2
Att: 7,484

2nd Round (2nd leg)
Oct 11 vs Norwich City (h) 0-3
(aggregate 0-5)
Att: 7,002

1989/90 SEASON

1st Round (1st leg)
Aug 22 vs Tranmere Rovers (h) 3-4
Att: 4,632   Shaw 3 (1 pen)

1st Round (2nd leg)
Aug 29 vs Tranmere Rovers (a) 1-3
(aggregate 4-7)
Att: 5,275   Shaw

1990/91 SEASON

1st Round (1st leg)
Aug 28 vs Chester City (h) 2-0
Att: 3,503   Shaw, Swann

1st Round (2nd leg)
Sep 4 vs Chester City (a) 1-5 (aet.)
(aggregate 3-5)
Att: 1,009   Swann

1991/92 SEASON

1st Round (1st leg)
Aug 20 vs Scarborough (h) 5-4
*Att: 2,683   Wrightson, Swann 2, Shaw,
Joyce (pen)*

1st Round (2nd leg)
Aug 28 vs Scarborough (a) 1-3
(aggregate 6-7)
Att: 2,035   Joyce

1992/93 SEASON

1st Round (1st leg)
Aug 18 vs Stoke City (h) 2-1
Att: 5,581   Tinkler, Ellis

1st Round (2nd leg)
Aug 26 vs Stoke City (a) 0-4 (agg. 2-5)
Att: 9,745

1993/94 SEASON

1st Round (1st leg)
Aug 17 vs Burnley (h) 1-2
Att: 6,283   Ellis

1st Round (2nd leg)
Aug 25 vs Burnley (a) 1-4 (agg. 2-6)
Att: 9,346   Cartwright

1994/95 SEASON

1st Round (1st leg)
Aug 17 vs Stockport County (h) 1-1
Att: 2,385   Fensome (pen)

1st Round (2nd leg)
Aug 23 vs Stockport County (a) 1-4
(aggregate 2-5)
Att: 5,450   Moyes

1995/96 SEASON

1st Round (1st leg)
Aug 14 vs Sunderland (h) 1-1
Att: 6,323   Kidd

1st Round (2nd leg)
Aug 23 vs Sunderland (a) 2-3
(aggregate 3-4)
Att: 7,407   Cartwright, Bryson

1996/97 SEASON

1st Round (1st leg)
Aug 20 vs Wigan Athletic (a) 3-2
Att: 3,713   Wilkinson 3

1st Round (2nd leg)
Sep 3 vs Wigan Athletic (h) 4-4
(aggregate 7-6)
*Att: 5,767   Davey, Wilkinson, Atkinson,
McDonald*

2nd Round (1st leg)
Sep 17 vs Tottenham Hotspur (h) 1-1
Att: 16,258   Holt

2nd Round (2nd leg)
Sep 25 vs Tottenham Hotspur (a) 0-3
(aggregate 1-4)
Att: 20,080

1997/98 SEASON

1st Round (1st leg)
Aug 12 vs Rotherham United (a) 3-1
Att: 2,901   Makin, Reeves 2

1st Round (2nd leg)
Aug 26 vs Rotherham United (h) 2-0
(aggregate 5-1)
Att: 9,441   Reeves, Makin

2nd Round (1st leg)
Sep 17 vs Blackburn Rovers (a) 0-6
Att: 22,564

2nd Round (2nd leg)
Sep 30 vs Blackburn Rovers (h) 1-0
(aggregate 1-6)
Att: 11,472   Barrick

1998/99 SEASON

1st Round (1st leg)
Aug 12 vs Grimsby Town (a) 0-0
Att: 3,008

1st Round (2nd leg)
Aug 18 vs Grimsby Town (h) 0-0 (aet)
Att: 5,650
Grimsby Town won 7-6 on penalties

1999/2000 SEASON

1st Round (1st leg)
Aug 10 vs Wrexham (h) 1-0
Att: 4,930   Appleton

1st Round (2nd leg)
Aug 24 vs Wrexham (a) 2-0 (agg. 3-0)
Att: 2,911   Basham, Macken

2nd Round (1st leg)
Sep 14 vs Sheffield United (a) 0-2
Att: 5,350

2nd Round (2nd leg)
Sep 21 vs Sheffield United (h) 3-0
(aggregate 3-2)
Att: 5,658   Alexander, Mathie 2

3rd Round
Oct 12 vs Arsenal (a) 1-2
Att: 15,239   Macken

2000/2001 SEASON

1st Round (1st leg)
Aug 22 vs Shrewsbury Town (a) 0-1
Att: 2,445

1st Round (2nd leg)
Sep 5 vs Shrewsbury Town (h) 4-1
(aggregate 4-2)
Att: 5,451   Macken 3, Alexander

2nd Round (1st leg)
Sep 19 vs Coventry City (h) 1-3
Att: 10,770   Alexander (pen)

2nd Round (2nd leg)
Sep 27 vs Coventry City (a) 1-4
(aggregate 2-7)
Att: 7,425   Rankine

2001/2002 SEASON

1st Round
Aug 21 vs Kidderminster Harr. (a) 3-2
Att: 2,227   Macken, Gallacher, Jackson

2nd Round
Sep 11 vs Tranmere Rovers (a) 1-4
Att: 5,143   Cresswell

Season 1977/78

DIVISION THREE

Wrexham	46	23	15	8	78	45	61
Cambridge United	46	23	12	11	72	51	58
Preston North End	46	20	16	10	63	38	56
Peterborough United	46	20	16	10	47	33	56
Chester	46	16	22	8	59	56	54
Walsall	46	18	17	11	61	50	53
Gillingham	46	15	20	11	67	60	50
Colchester United	46	15	18	13	55	44	48
Chesterfield	46	17	14	15	58	49	48
Swindon Town	46	16	16	14	67	60	48
Shrewsbury Town	46	16	15	15	63	57	47
Tranmere Rovers	46	16	15	15	57	52	47
Carlisle United	46	14	19	13	59	59	47
Sheffield Wednesday	46	15	16	15	50	52	46
Bury	46	13	19	14	62	56	45
Lincoln City	46	15	15	16	53	61	45
Exeter City	46	15	14	17	49	59	44
Oxford United	46	13	14	19	64	67	40
Plymouth Argyle	46	11	17	18	61	68	39
Rotherham United	46	13	13	20	51	68	39
Port Vale	46	8	20	18	46	67	36
Bradford City	46	12	10	24	56	86	34
Hereford United	46	9	14	23	34	60	32
Portsmouth	46	7	17	22	41	75	31

Season 1979/80

DIVISION TWO

Leicester City	42	21	13	8	58	38	55
Sunderland	42	21	12	9	69	42	54
Birmingham City	42	21	11	10	58	38	53
Chelsea	42	23	7	12	66	52	53
Queen's Park Rangers	42	18	13	11	75	53	49
Luton Town	42	16	17	9	66	45	49
West Ham United	42	20	7	15	54	43	47
Cambridge United	42	14	16	12	61	53	44
Newcastle United	42	15	14	13	53	49	44
Preston North End	42	12	19	11	56	52	43
Oldham Athletic	42	16	11	15	49	53	43
Swansea City	42	17	9	16	48	53	43
Shrewsbury Town	42	18	5	19	60	53	41
Orient	42	12	17	13	48	54	41
Cardiff City	42	16	8	18	41	48	40
Wrexham	42	16	6	20	40	49	38
Notts County	42	11	15	16	51	52	37
Watford	42	12	13	17	39	46	37
Bristol Rovers	42	11	13	18	50	64	35
Fulham	42	11	7	24	42	74	29
Burnley	42	6	15	21	39	73	27
Charlton Athletic	42	6	10	26	39	78	22

Season 1978/79

DIVISION TWO

Crystal Palace	42	19	19	4	51	24	57
Brighton & Hove Albion	42	23	10	9	72	39	56
Stoke City	42	20	16	6	58	31	56
Sunderland	42	22	11	9	70	44	55
West Ham United	42	18	14	10	70	39	50
Notts County	42	14	16	12	48	60	44
Preston North End	42	12	18	12	59	57	42
Newcastle United	42	17	8	17	51	55	42
Cardiff City	42	16	10	16	56	70	42
Fulham	42	13	15	14	50	47	41
Orient	42	15	10	17	51	51	40
Cambridge United	42	12	16	14	44	52	40
Burnley	42	14	12	16	51	62	40
Oldham Athletic	42	13	13	16	52	61	39
Wrexham	42	12	14	16	45	42	38
Bristol Rovers	42	14	10	18	48	60	38
Leicester City	42	10	17	15	43	52	37
Luton Town	42	13	10	19	60	57	36
Charlton Athletic	42	11	13	18	60	69	35
Sheffield United	42	11	12	19	52	69	34
Millwall	42	11	10	21	42	61	32
Blackburn Rovers	42	10	10	22	41	72	30

Season 1980/81

DIVISION TWO

West Ham United	42	28	10	4	79	29	66
Notts County	42	18	17	7	49	38	53
Swansea City	42	18	14	10	64	44	50
Blackburn Rovers	42	16	18	8	42	29	50
Luton Town	42	18	12	12	61	46	48
Derby County	42	15	15	12	57	52	45
Grimsby Town	42	15	15	12	44	42	45
Queen's Park Rangers	42	15	13	14	56	46	43
Watford	42	16	11	15	50	45	43
Sheffield Wednesday	42	17	8	17	53	51	42
Newcastle United	42	14	14	14	30	45	42
Chelsea	42	14	12	16	46	41	40
Cambridge United	42	17	6	19	53	65	40
Shrewsbury Town	42	11	17	14	46	47	39
Oldham Athletic	42	12	15	15	39	48	39
Wrexham	42	12	14	16	43	45	38
Orient	42	13	12	17	52	56	38
Bolton Wanderers	42	14	10	18	61	66	38
Cardiff City	42	12	12	18	44	60	36
Preston North End	42	11	14	17	41	62	36
Bristol City	42	7	16	19	29	51	30
Bristol Rovers	42	5	13	24	34	65	23

Season 1981/82

DIVISION THREE

Burnley	46	21	17	8	66	45	80
Carlisle United	46	23	11	12	65	50	80
Fulham	46	21	15	10	77	51	78
Lincoln City	46	21	14	11	66	40	77
Oxford United	46	19	14	13	63	49	71
Gillingham	46	20	11	15	64	56	71
Southend United	46	18	15	13	63	51	69
Brentford	46	19	11	16	56	47	68
Millwall	46	18	13	15	62	62	67
Plymouth Argyle	46	18	11	17	64	56	65
Chesterfield	46	18	10	18	57	58	64
Reading	46	17	11	18	67	75	62
Portsmouth	46	14	19	13	56	51	61
Preston North End	**46**	**16**	**13**	**17**	**50**	**56**	**61**
Bristol Rovers	46	18	9	19	58	65	61
Newport County	46	14	16	16	54	54	58
Huddersfield Town	46	15	12	19	64	59	57
Exeter City	46	16	9	21	71	84	57
Doncaster Rovers	46	13	17	16	55	68	56
Walsall	46	13	14	19	51	55	53
Wimbledon	46	14	11	21	61	75	53
Swindon Town	46	13	13	20	55	71	52
Bristol City	46	11	13	22	40	65	46
Chester	46	7	11	28	36	78	32

Bristol Rovers had two points deducted

Season 1982/83

DIVISION THREE

Portsmouth	46	27	10	9	74	41	91
Cardiff City	46	25	11	10	76	50	86
Huddersfield Town	46	23	13	10	84	49	82
Newport County	46	23	9	14	76	54	78
Oxford United	46	22	12	12	74	53	78
Lincoln City	46	23	7	16	77	51	76
Bristol Rovers	46	22	9	15	84	57	75
Plymouth Argyle	46	19	8	19	61	66	65
Brentford	46	18	10	18	88	77	64
Walsall	46	17	13	16	64	63	64
Sheffield United	46	19	7	20	62	64	64
Bradford City	46	16	13	17	68	69	61
Gillingham	46	16	13	17	58	59	61
Bournemouth	46	16	13	17	59	68	61
Southend United	46	15	14	17	66	65	59
Preston North End	**46**	**15**	**13**	**18**	**60**	**69**	**58**
Millwall	46	14	13	19	64	78	55
Wigan Athletic	46	15	9	22	60	72	54
Exeter City	46	14	12	20	81	104	54
Orient	46	15	9	22	64	88	54
Reading	46	12	17	17	63	80	53
Wrexham	46	12	15	19	57	76	51
Doncaster Rovers	46	9	11	26	57	97	38
Chesterfield	46	8	13	25	44	68	37

Season 1983/84

DIVISION THREE

Oxford United	46	28	11	7	91	50	95
Wimbledon	46	26	9	11	97	76	87
Sheffield United	46	24	11	11	86	53	83
Hull City	46	23	14	9	71	38	83
Bristol Rovers	46	22	13	11	68	54	79
Walsall	46	22	9	15	68	61	75
Bradford City	46	20	11	15	73	65	71
Gillingham	46	20	10	16	74	69	70
Millwall	46	18	13	15	71	65	67
Bolton Wanderers	46	18	10	18	56	60	64
Orient	46	18	9	19	71	81	63
Burnley	46	16	14	16	76	61	62
Newport County	46	16	14	16	58	75	62
Lincoln City	46	17	10	19	59	62	61
Wigan Athletic	46	16	13	17	46	56	61
Preston North End	**46**	**15**	**11**	**20**	**66**	**66**	**56**
Bournemouth	46	16	7	23	63	73	55
Rotherham United	46	15	9	22	57	64	54
Plymouth Argyle	46	13	12	21	56	62	51
Brentford	46	11	16	19	69	79	49
Scunthorpe United	46	9	19	18	54	73	46
Southend United	46	10	14	22	55	76	44
Port Vale	46	11	10	25	51	83	43
Exeter City	46	6	15	25	50	84	33

Season 1984/85

DIVISION THREE

Bradford City	46	28	10	8	77	45	94
Millwall	46	26	12	8	73	42	90
Hull City	46	25	12	9	78	49	87
Gillingham	46	25	8	13	80	62	83
Bristol City	46	24	9	13	74	47	81
Bristol Rovers	46	21	12	13	66	48	75
Derby County	46	19	13	14	65	54	70
York City	46	20	9	17	70	57	69
Reading	46	19	12	15	68	62	69
Bournemouth	46	19	11	16	57	46	68
Walsall	46	18	13	15	58	52	67
Rotherham United	46	18	11	17	55	55	65
Brentford	46	16	14	16	62	64	62
Doncaster Rovers	46	17	8	21	72	74	59
Plymouth Argyle	46	15	14	17	62	65	59
Wigan Athletic	46	15	14	17	60	64	59
Bolton Wanderers	46	16	6	24	69	75	54
Newport County	46	13	13	20	55	67	52
Lincoln City	46	11	18	17	50	51	51
Swansea City	46	12	11	23	53	80	47
Burnley	46	11	13	22	60	73	46
Orient	46	11	13	22	51	76	46
Preston North End	**46**	**13**	**7**	**26**	**51**	**100**	**46**
Cambridge United	46	4	9	33	37	95	21

Season 1985/86

DIVISION FOUR

Swindon Town	46	32	6	8	82	43	102
Chester City	46	23	15	8	83	50	84
Mansfield Town	46	23	12	11	74	47	81
Port Vale	46	21	16	9	67	37	79
Orient	46	20	12	14	79	64	72
Colchester United	46	19	13	14	88	63	70
Hartlepool United	46	20	10	16	68	67	70
Northampton Town	46	18	10	18	79	58	64
Southend United	46	18	10	18	69	67	64
Hereford United	46	18	10	18	74	73	64
Stockport County	46	17	13	16	63	71	64
Crewe Alexandra	46	18	9	19	54	61	63
Wrexham	46	17	9	20	68	80	60
Burnley	46	16	11	19	60	65	59
Scunthorpe United	46	15	14	17	50	55	59
Aldershot	46	17	7	22	66	74	58
Peterborough United	46	13	17	16	52	64	56
Rochdale	46	14	13	19	57	77	55
Tranmere Rovers	46	15	9	22	74	73	54
Halifax Town	46	14	12	20	60	71	54
Exeter City	46	13	15	18	47	59	54
Cambridge United	46	15	9	22	65	80	54
Preston North End	**46**	**11**	**10**	**25**	**54**	**89**	**43**
Torquay United	46	9	10	27	43	88	37

Season 1986/87

DIVISION FOUR

Northampton Town	46	30	9	7	103	53	99
Preston North End	**46**	**26**	**12**	**8**	**72**	**47**	**90**
Southend United	46	25	5	16	68	55	80
Wolverhampton Wands.	46	24	7	15	69	50	79
Colchester United	46	21	7	18	64	56	70
Aldershot	46	20	10	16	64	57	70
Orient	46	20	9	17	64	61	69
Scunthorpe United	46	18	12	16	73	57	66
Wrexham	46	15	20	11	70	51	65
Peterborough United	46	17	14	15	57	50	65
Cambridge United	46	17	11	18	60	62	62
Swansea City	46	17	11	18	56	61	62
Cardiff City	46	15	16	15	48	50	61
Exeter City	46	11	23	12	53	49	56
Halifax Town	46	15	10	21	59	74	55
Hereford United	46	14	11	21	60	61	53
Crewe Alexandra	46	13	14	19	70	72	53
Hartlepool United	46	11	18	17	44	65	51
Stockport County	46	13	12	21	40	69	51
Tranmere Rovers	46	11	17	18	54	72	50
Rochdale	46	11	17	18	54	73	50
Burnley	46	12	13	21	53	74	49
Torquay United	46	10	18	18	56	72	48
Lincoln City	46	12	12	22	45	65	48

Season 1987/88

DIVISION THREE

Sunderland	46	27	12	7	92	48	93
Brighton & Hove Albion	46	23	15	8	69	47	84
Walsall	46	23	13	10	68	50	82
Notts County	46	23	12	11	82	49	81
Bristol City	46	21	12	13	77	62	75
Northampton Town	46	18	19	9	70	51	73
Wigan Athletic	46	20	12	14	70	61	72
Bristol Rovers	46	18	12	16	68	56	66
Fulham	46	19	9	18	69	60	66
Blackpool	46	17	14	15	71	62	65
Port Vale	46	18	11	17	58	56	65
Brentford	46	16	14	16	53	59	62
Gillingham	46	14	17	15	77	61	59
Bury	46	15	14	17	58	57	59
Chester City	46	14	16	16	51	62	58
Preston North End	**46**	**15**	**13**	**18**	**48**	**59**	**58**
Southend United	46	14	13	19	65	83	55
Chesterfield	46	15	10	21	41	70	55
Mansfield Town	46	14	12	20	48	59	54
Aldershot	46	15	8	23	64	74	53
Rotherham United	46	12	16	18	50	66	52
Grimsby Town	46	12	14	20	48	58	50
York City	46	8	9	29	48	91	33
Doncaster Rovers	46	8	9	29	40	84	33

Season 1988/89

DIVISION THREE

Wolverhampton Wands.	46	26	14	6	96	49	92
Sheffield United	46	25	9	12	93	54	84
Port Vale	46	24	12	10	78	48	84
Fulham	46	22	9	15	69	67	75
Bristol Rovers	46	19	17	10	67	51	74
Preston North End	**46**	**19**	**15**	**12**	**79**	**60**	**72**
Brentford	46	18	14	14	66	61	68
Chester City	46	19	11	16	64	61	68
Notts County	46	18	13	15	64	54	67
Bolton Wanderers	46	16	16	14	58	54	64
Bristol City	46	18	9	19	53	55	63
Swansea City	46	15	16	15	51	53	61
Bury	46	16	13	17	55	67	61
Huddersfield Town	46	17	9	20	63	73	60
Mansfield Town	46	14	17	15	48	52	59
Cardiff City	46	14	15	17	44	56	57
Wigan Athletic	46	14	14	18	55	53	56
Reading	46	15	11	20	68	72	56
Blackpool	46	14	13	19	56	59	55
Northampton Town	46	16	6	24	66	76	54
Southend United	46	13	15	18	56	75	54
Chesterfield	46	14	7	25	51	86	49
Gillingham	46	12	4	30	47	81	40
Aldershot	46	8	13	25	48	78	37

Season 1989/90

DIVISION THREE

Bristol Rovers	46	26	15	5	71	35	93
Bristol City	46	27	10	9	76	40	91
Notts County	46	25	12	9	73	53	87
Tranmere Rovers	46	23	11	12	86	49	80
Bury	46	21	11	14	70	49	74
Bolton Wanderers	46	18	15	13	59	48	69
Birmingham City	46	18	12	16	60	59	66
Huddersfield Town	46	17	14	15	61	62	65
Rotherham United	46	17	13	16	71	62	64
Reading	46	15	19	12	57	53	64
Shrewsbury Town	46	16	15	15	59	54	63
Crewe Alexandra	46	15	17	14	56	53	62
Brentford	46	18	7	21	66	66	61
Leyton Orient	46	16	10	20	52	56	58
Mansfield Town	46	16	7	23	50	65	55
Chester City	46	13	15	18	43	55	54
Swansea City	46	14	12	20	45	63	54
Wigan Athletic	46	13	14	19	48	64	53
Preston North End	**46**	**14**	**10**	**22**	**65**	**79**	**52**
Fulham	46	12	15	19	55	66	51
Cardiff City	46	12	14	20	51	70	50
Northampton Town	46	11	14	21	51	68	47
Blackpool	46	10	16	20	49	73	46
Walsall	46	9	14	23	40	72	41

Season 1991/92

DIVISION THREE

Brentford	46	25	7	14	81	55	82
Birmingham City	46	23	12	11	69	52	81
Huddersfield Town	46	22	12	12	59	38	78
Stoke City	46	21	14	11	69	49	77
Stockport County	46	22	10	14	75	51	76
Peterborough United	46	20	14	12	65	58	74
West Bromwich Albion	46	19	14	13	64	49	71
Bournemouth	46	20	11	15	52	48	71
Fulham	46	19	13	14	57	53	70
Leyton Orient	46	18	11	17	62	52	65
Hartlepool United	46	18	11	17	57	57	65
Reading	46	16	13	17	59	62	61
Bolton Wanderers	46	14	17	15	57	56	59
Hull City	46	16	11	19	54	54	59
Wigan Athletic	46	15	14	17	58	64	59
Bradford City	46	13	19	14	62	61	58
Preston North End	**46**	**15**	**12**	**19**	**61**	**72**	**57**
Chester City	46	14	14	18	56	59	56
Swansea City	46	14	14	18	55	65	56
Exeter City	46	14	11	21	57	80	53
Bury	46	13	12	21	55	74	51
Shrewsbury Town	46	12	11	23	53	68	47
Torquay United	46	13	8	25	42	68	47
Darlington	46	10	7	29	56	90	37

Season 1990/91

DIVISION THREE

Cambridge United	46	25	11	10	75	45	86
Southend United	46	26	7	13	67	51	85
Grimsby Town	46	24	11	11	66	34	83
Bolton Wanderers	46	24	11	11	64	50	83
Tranmere Rovers	46	23	9	14	64	46	78
Brentford	46	21	13	12	59	47	76
Bury	46	20	13	13	67	56	73
Bradford City	46	20	10	16	62	54	70
Bournemouth	46	19	13	14	58	58	70
Wigan Athletic	46	20	9	17	71	54	69
Huddersfield Town	46	18	13	15	57	51	67
Birmingham City	46	16	17	13	45	49	65
Leyton Orient	46	18	10	18	55	58	64
Stoke City	46	16	12	18	55	59	60
Reading	46	17	8	21	53	66	59
Exeter City	46	16	9	21	58	52	57
Preston North End	**46**	**15**	**11**	**20**	**54**	**67**	**56**
Shrewsbury Town	46	14	10	22	61	68	52
Chester City	46	14	9	23	46	58	51
Swansea City	46	13	9	24	49	72	48
Fulham	46	10	16	20	41	56	46
Crewe Alexandra	46	11	11	24	62	80	44
Rotherham United	46	10	12	24	50	87	42
Mansfield Town	46	8	14	24	42	63	38

Season 1992/93

DIVISION TWO

Stoke City	46	27	12	7	73	34	93
Bolton Wanderers	46	27	9	10	80	41	90
Port Vale	46	26	11	9	79	44	89
West Bromwich Albion	46	25	10	11	88	54	85
Swansea City	46	20	13	13	65	47	73
Stockport County	46	19	15	12	81	57	72
Leyton Orient	46	21	9	16	69	53	72
Reading	46	18	15	13	66	51	69
Brighton & Hove Albion	46	20	9	17	63	59	69
Bradford City	46	18	14	14	69	67	68
Rotherham United	46	17	14	15	60	60	65
Fulham	46	16	17	13	57	55	65
Burnley	46	15	16	15	57	59	61
Plymouth Argyle	46	16	12	18	59	64	60
Huddersfield Town	46	17	9	20	54	61	60
Hartlepool United	46	14	12	20	42	60	54
Bournemouth	46	12	17	17	45	52	53
Blackpool	46	12	15	19	63	75	51
Exeter City	46	11	17	18	54	69	50
Hull City	46	13	11	22	46	69	50
Preston North End	**46**	**13**	**8**	**25**	**65**	**94**	**47**
Mansfield Town	46	11	11	24	52	80	44
Wigan Athletic	46	10	11	25	43	72	41
Chester City	46	8	5	33	49	102	29

Season 1993/94

DIVISION THREE

Shrewsbury Town	42	22	13	7	63	39	79
Chester City	42	21	11	10	69	46	74
Crewe Alexandra	42	21	10	11	80	61	73
Wycombe Wanderers	42	19	13	10	67	53	70
Preston North End	42	18	13	11	79	60	67
Torquay United	42	17	16	9	64	56	67
Carlisle United	42	18	10	14	57	42	64
Chesterfield	42	16	14	12	55	48	62
Rochdale	42	16	12	14	63	51	60
Walsall	42	17	9	16	48	53	60
Scunthorpe United	42	15	14	13	64	56	59
Mansfield Town	42	15	10	17	53	62	55
Bury	42	14	11	17	55	56	53
Scarborough	42	15	8	19	55	61	53
Doncaster Rovers	42	14	10	18	44	57	52
Gillingham	42	12	15	15	44	51	51
Colchester United	42	13	10	19	56	71	49
Lincoln City	42	12	11	19	52	63	47
Wigan Athletic	42	11	12	19	51	70	45
Hereford United	42	12	6	24	60	79	42
Darlington	42	10	11	21	42	64	41
Northampton Town	42	9	11	22	44	66	38

Season 1994/95

DIVISION THREE

Carlisle United	42	27	10	5	67	31	91
Walsall	42	24	11	7	75	40	83
Chesterfield	42	23	12	7	62	37	81
Bury	42	23	11	8	73	36	80
Preston North End	42	19	10	13	58	41	67
Mansfield Town	42	18	11	13	84	59	65
Scunthorpe United	42	18	8	16	68	63	62
Fulham	42	16	14	12	60	54	62
Doncaster Rovers	42	17	10	15	58	43	61
Colchester United	42	16	10	16	56	64	58
Barnet	42	15	11	16	56	63	56
Lincoln City	42	15	11	16	54	55	56
Torquay United	42	14	13	15	54	57	55
Wigan Athletic	42	14	10	18	53	60	52
Rochdale	42	12	14	16	44	67	50
Hereford United	42	12	13	17	45	62	49
Northampton Town	42	10	14	18	45	67	44
Hartlepool United	42	11	10	21	43	69	43
Gillingham	42	10	11	21	46	64	41
Darlington	42	11	8	23	43	57	41
Scarborough	42	8	10	24	49	70	34
Exeter City	42	8	10	24	36	70	34

Season 1995/96

DIVISION THREE

Preston North End	46	23	17	6	78	38	86
Gillingham	46	22	17	7	49	20	83
Bury	46	22	13	11	66	48	79
Plymouth Argyle	46	22	12	12	68	49	78
Darlington	46	20	18	8	60	42	78
Hereford United	46	20	14	12	65	47	74
Colchester United	46	18	18	10	61	51	72
Chester City	46	18	16	12	72	53	70
Barnet	46	18	16	12	65	45	70
Wigan Athletic	46	20	10	16	62	56	70
Northampton Town	46	18	13	15	51	44	67
Scunthorpe United	46	15	15	16	67	61	60
Doncaster Rovers	46	16	11	19	49	60	59
Exeter City	46	13	18	15	46	53	57
Rochdale	46	14	13	19	57	61	55
Cambridge United	46	14	12	20	61	71	54
Fulham	46	12	17	17	57	63	53
Lincoln City	46	13	14	19	57	73	53
Mansfield Town	46	11	20	15	54	64	53
Hartlepool United	46	12	13	21	47	67	49
Leyton Orient	46	12	11	23	44	63	47
Cardiff City	46	11	12	23	41	64	45
Scarborough	46	8	16	22	39	69	40
Torquay United	46	5	14	27	30	84	29

Season 1996/97

DIVISION TWO

Bury	46	24	12	10	62	38	84
Stockport County	46	23	13	10	59	41	82
Luton Town	46	21	15	10	71	45	78
Brentford	46	20	14	12	56	43	74
Bristol City	46	21	10	15	69	51	73
Crewe Alexandra	46	22	7	17	56	47	73
Blackpool	46	18	15	13	60	47	69
Wrexham	46	17	18	11	54	50	69
Burnley	46	19	11	16	71	55	68
Chesterfield	46	18	14	14	42	39	68
Gillingham	46	19	10	17	60	59	67
Walsall	46	19	10	17	54	53	67
Watford	46	16	19	11	45	38	67
Millwall	46	16	13	17	50	55	61
Preston North End	46	18	7	21	49	55	61
Bournemouth	46	15	15	16	43	45	60
Bristol Rovers	46	15	11	20	47	50	56
Wycombe Wanderers	46	15	10	21	51	56	55
Plymouth Argyle	46	12	18	16	47	58	54
York City	46	13	13	20	47	68	52
Peterborough United	46	11	14	21	55	73	47
Shrewsbury Town	46	11	13	22	49	74	46
Rotherham United	46	7	14	25	39	70	35
Notts County	46	7	14	25	33	59	35

Season 1997/98

DIVISION TWO

Watford	46	24	16	6	67	41	88
Bristol City	46	25	10	11	69	39	85
Grimsby Town	46	19	15	12	55	37	72
Northampton Town	46	18	17	11	52	37	71
Bristol Rovers	46	20	10	16	70	64	70
Fulham	46	20	10	16	60	43	70
Wrexham	46	18	16	12	55	51	70
Gillingham	46	19	13	14	52	47	70
Bournemouth	46	18	12	16	57	52	66
Chesterfield	46	16	17	13	46	44	65
Wigan Athletic	46	17	11	18	64	66	62
Blackpool	46	17	11	18	59	67	62
Oldham Athletic	46	15	16	15	62	54	61
Wycombe Wanderers	46	14	18	14	51	53	60
Preston North End	**46**	**15**	**14**	**17**	**56**	**56**	**59**
York City	46	14	17	15	52	58	59
Luton Town	46	14	15	17	60	64	57
Millwall	46	14	13	19	43	54	55
Walsall	46	14	12	20	43	52	54
Burnley	46	13	13	20	55	65	52
Brentford	46	11	17	18	50	71	50
Plymouth Argyle	46	12	13	21	55	70	49
Carlisle United	46	12	8	26	57	73	44
Southend United	46	11	10	25	47	79	43

Season 1998/99

DIVISION TWO

Fulham	46	31	8	7	79	32	101
Walsall	46	26	9	11	63	47	87
Manchester City	46	22	16	8	69	33	82
Gillingham	46	22	14	10	75	44	80
Preston North End	**46**	**22**	**13**	**11**	**78**	**50**	**79**
Wigan Athletic	46	22	10	14	75	48	76
Bournemouth	46	21	13	12	63	41	76
Stoke City	46	21	6	19	59	63	69
Chesterfield	46	17	13	16	46	44	64
Millwall	46	17	11	18	52	59	62
Reading	46	16	13	17	54	63	61
Luton Town	46	16	10	20	51	60	58
Bristol Rovers	46	13	17	16	65	56	56
Blackpool	46	14	14	18	44	54	56
Burnley	46	13	16	17	54	73	55
Notts County	46	14	12	20	52	61	54
Wrexham	46	13	14	19	43	62	53
Colchester United	46	12	16	18	52	70	52
Wycombe Wanderers	46	13	12	21	52	58	51
Oldham Athletic	46	14	9	23	48	66	51
York City	46	13	11	22	56	80	50
Northampton Town	46	10	18	18	43	57	48
Lincoln City	46	13	7	26	42	74	46
Macclesfield Town	46	11	10	25	43	63	43

Season 1999/2000

DIVISION TWO

Preston North End	**46**	**28**	**11**	**7**	**74**	**37**	**95**
Burnley	46	25	13	8	69	47	88
Gillingham	46	25	10	11	79	48	85
Wigan Athletic	46	22	17	7	72	38	83
Millwall	46	23	13	10	76	50	82
Stoke City	46	23	13	10	68	42	82
Bristol Rovers	46	23	11	12	69	45	80
Notts County	46	18	11	17	61	55	65
Bristol City	46	15	19	12	59	57	64
Reading	46	16	14	16	57	63	62
Wrexham	46	17	11	18	52	61	62
Wycombe Wanderers	46	16	13	17	56	53	61
Luton Town	46	17	10	19	61	65	61
Oldham Athletic	46	16	12	18	50	55	60
Bury	46	13	18	15	61	64	57
Bournemouth	46	16	9	21	59	62	57
Brentford	46	13	13	20	47	61	52
Colchester United	46	14	10	22	59	82	52
Cambridge United	46	12	12	22	64	65	48
Oxford United	46	12	9	25	43	73	45
Cardiff City	46	9	17	20	45	67	44
Blackpool	46	8	17	21	49	77	41
Scunthorpe United	46	9	12	25	40	74	39
Chesterfield	46	7	15	24	34	63	36

Season 2000/2001

DIVISION ONE

Fulham	46	30	11	5	90	32	101
Blackburn Rovers	46	26	13	7	76	39	91
Bolton Wanderers	46	24	15	7	76	45	87
Preston North End	**46**	**23**	**9**	**14**	**64**	**52**	**78**
Birmingham City	46	23	9	14	59	48	78
West Bromwich Albion	46	21	11	14	60	52	74
Burnley	46	21	9	16	50	54	72
Wimbledon	46	17	18	11	71	50	69
Watford	46	20	9	17	76	67	69
Sheffield United	46	19	11	16	52	49	68
Nottingham Forest	46	20	8	18	55	53	68
Wolverhampton Wands.	46	14	13	19	45	48	55
Gillingham	46	13	16	17	61	66	55
Crewe Alexandra	46	15	10	21	47	62	55
Norwich City	46	14	12	20	46	58	54
Barnsley	46	15	9	22	49	62	54
Sheffield Wednesday	46	15	8	23	52	71	53
Grimsby Town	46	14	10	22	43	62	52
Stockport County	46	11	18	17	58	65	51
Portsmouth	46	10	19	17	47	59	49
Crystal Palace	46	12	13	21	57	70	49
Huddersfield Town	46	11	15	20	48	57	48
Queen's Park Rangers	46	7	19	20	45	75	40
Tranmere Rovers	46	9	11	26	46	77	38

Season 2001/2002

DIVISION ONE

Manchester City	46	31	6	9	108	52	99
West Bromwich Albion	46	27	8	11	61	29	89
Wolverhampton Wands.	46	25	11	10	76	43	86
Millwall	46	22	11	13	69	48	77
Birmingham City	46	21	13	12	70	49	76
Norwich City	46	22	9	15	60	51	75
Burnley	46	21	12	13	70	62	75
Preston North End	**46**	**20**	**12**	**14**	**71**	**59**	**72**
Wimbledon	46	18	13	15	63	57	67
Crystal Palace	46	20	6	20	70	62	66
Coventry City	46	20	6	20	59	53	66
Gillingham	46	18	10	18	64	67	64
Sheffield United	46	15	15	16	53	54	60
Watford	46	16	11	19	62	56	59
Bradford City	46	15	10	21	69	76	55
Nottingham Forest	46	12	18	16	50	51	54
Portsmouth	46	13	14	19	60	72	53
Walsall	46	13	12	21	51	71	51
Grimsby Town	46	12	14	20	50	72	50
Sheffield Wednesday	46	12	14	20	49	71	50
Rotherham United	46	10	19	17	52	66	49
Crewe Alexandra	46	12	13	21	47	76	49
Barnsley	46	11	15	20	59	86	48
Stockport County	46	6	8	32	42	102	26

SOCCER BOOKS LIMITED

72 ST. PETERS AVENUE (Dept. SBL)
CLEETHORPES
N.E. LINCOLNSHIRE
DN35 8HU
ENGLAND

Tel. 01472 696226   Fax 01472 698546

Web site http://www.soccer-books.co.uk
e-mail info@soccer-books.co.uk

Established in 1982, Soccer Books Limited has the biggest range of English-Language soccer books and videos available. We are now expanding our stocks even further to include many more titles including German, French, Spanish and Italian-language books.

With over 100,000 satisfied customers already, we supply books to virtually every country in the world but have maintained the friendliness and accessibility associated with a small family-run business. The range of titles we sell includes:

YEARBOOKS – All major yearbooks including Rothmans (many editions), Calcios (many editions), Supporters' Guides, Playfair Annuals, North & Latin American Guides (all editions), African Guides, Non-League Directories.

CLUB HISTORIES – Complete Records, Official Histories, 25 Year Records, Definitive Histories plus many more.

WORLD FOOTBALL – World Cup books, International Line-up & Statistics Series, European Championships History, International Statistical Histories (many titles) and much more.

BIOGRAPHIES & WHO'S WHOS – on Managers and Players plus Who's Whos etc.

ENCYCLOPEDIAS & GENERAL TITLES – Books on Stadia, Hooligan studies, Histories and dozens of others.

VIDEOS – Season's highlights, histories, big games, World Cup, European Championships, player profiles, F.A. Cup Finals – including many back items.

For a current listing of our titles, please contact us using the information at the top of the page.